FIRESIDE

Kathy
Burns

INDEPENDENT PHOTOGRAPHY

A
Biased Guide to 35mm Technique
and Equipment
for the Beginner, the Student,
and the Artist

by Robert Foothorap
with
Vickie Golden

Illustrations by Gretchen Schields

A FIRESIDE BOOK PUBLISHED BY
SIMON AND SCHUSTER • NEW YORK

A Fireside Book
Published by Simon and Schuster
A Division of Gulf & Western Corporation
Simon & Schuster Building
Rockefeller Center
1230 Avenue of the Americas
New York, New York 10020

ISBN 0-671-21976-6
Library of Congress Catalog Card Number 77-72319
Design direction by Tony Lane
Book design by Catherine Flanders
Manufactured in the United States of America
      2   3   4   5   6   7   8   9   10

To My Father

CONTENTS

1

In the Beginning 2

2

The 35mm Camera 25

3

Buying Equipment 45

4

The Language of Camera Controls 68

5

Camera Technique 81

6

Film 94

7

Light 109

8

Exposure 127

9

The Darkroom 144

10

Developing 170

11

Printing 184

12

Professional Considerations 216

Bibliography 225

Index 227

ACKNOWLEDGMENTS

Two years ago the publishers of this book reminded me that the manuscript was a year behind schedule. Perhaps I could use some help, they suggested. Good working partners are hard to find, so I was reluctant.

I was reluctant, that is, until I met Vickie Golden—a Phi Beta Kappa, magna cum laude graduate of UCLA who has worked on books dealing with psychology, geology, nutrition, literature, James Dean, underground comics, Hunter Thompson, and municipal bicycle paths. Ideally, she knew nothing about photography.

The two years of working with Vickie were exceptional. Beyond her extraordinary competency and capacity for work, she proved to be a most gentle and consistent friend. I am eternally grateful for her help. Without her, the book would have been crumpled paper in a wastebasket.

What can I say about Gretchen—my partner, my wife, and the illustrator of this book—except that I love her dearly. Her drawings are nice too. Both she and I were very happy to work with designer Cathy Flanders, whose sensitivity to the photographs and illustrations put me completely at ease—a joy to work with.

Many thanks to Linda Gunnarson and Richard Reynolds at Straight Arrow for their patience, perseverance, and attention to every detail; to Dick Palmer for his obvious expertise in production matters, which made me feel confident about the quality of reproduction; to Kingsport Press for their fine printing; to Arne Norberg at Straight Arrow for his work on the halftones; to Phil Cohen of Brooks Institute for his technical review; and to David Chesnick and Larry Miller for their careful readings of the manuscript and perceptive suggestions. And thanks to Judy Lawrence, one of the few people from the original *Rolling Stone* crew who was still working there when the book was finished and whose warm southern style artfully masks the chaos that goes on behind the scenes.

Thanks to the following people, who have helped in a number of ways: Robert Altman, Barbara Burgower, David Calloway, Alan Copeland, Mike Edwards, David Fein, Joshua Freiwald, Ruth Goldhammer, Jon Goodchild, Marilyn Holmes, Bob Kingsbury, Tony Lane, Stephanie Lipney, Jim Marshall, Rosemary Nightingale, Linda Osborne, Chet Roaman, Ted and Meg Santos, Robert Scheu, Michael Snowdon, Christopher Springmann, Barry Stolmack, and Douglas Symes. And special thanks to Alan Rinzler, who said, "Sign here and the fun begins . . . ."

1
IN THE BEGINNING

When I first picked up a camera fourteen years ago, I became an instant photo-addict. I subscribed to every camera magazine and read every page. I bought every photo book I could and read every word. It took me three years of utter confusion to weed out a cogent body of knowledge from this morass of myth and equipment-hawking. When I finally discovered Ansel Adams, an author who knew how photography worked, it took me another couple of years to decipher his books. Today, the same situation exists: Adams' books remain the bibles of photography and they're just as difficult to read now as they were when they were first published in 1950. Also, Adams' books are oriented toward contemplative photo studies taken with a large-format camera. Presently, most photographers are using the small, versatile 35mm camera, which has the mobility to record active people and fast-moving events. A photographer working in this more spontaneous, journalistic style might shoot three or four rolls of film in the time it takes another photographer to set up a large camera, carefully compose the picture, wait for the correct lighting, and shoot a beautiful photograph of a relatively static subject. Nevertheless, both the journalistic and large-camera styles depend on the same basic principles of photography—

those governing the interaction of light and film. It is in the choice of equipment and technique that they differ.

This book, then, is about what I know best—photojournalistic technique carried out with a 35mm single-lens-reflex camera. Approximately sixty percent of my work is done with black and white film; so, although color work is discussed here, you'll find that black and white photography is emphasized.

Recent advances in photo equipment have made for a high level of mediocrity when it comes to photographic technique. Almost anyone can pick up a modern 35mm camera with a built-in exposure meter, follow the instructions, ship the film to a lab, and expect consistent results that photo types even five years ago were struggling to achieve. But there's more to it than that, of course. Photography is a lot more than capturing a sharp, well-exposed image; it is an exquisitely alive and plastic blend of art and science. Rendering even the simplest scene on black and white photo paper calls into play a vast number of variables which can be controlled to a certain extent by you, the photographer. But you don't need a head full of formulas, chemistry, rules, graphs, and numbers to achieve satisfying results. What you do need is clear conceptual knowledge of how it all works, and I have tried to get that down here as simply as possible. When you're out there with the world swirling around you, you won't be able to refer to a handbook—you'll just have to do it.

Photography is expensive, and the high costs can inhibit you from taking pictures. But it does not have to be as costly as the photo equipment industry would have you believe. By carefully selecting equipment, whether new or used, and by passing up all that useless gadgetry pictured in photo magazines and pushed by camera stores, you can avoid crippling yourself financially. Throughout this book you'll find ideas for keeping your photo costs to a minimum.

Equipment and technique are basic to photography, but the aim here is to help you get beyond these to the most important thing—the picture. Although this book is not an art lesson—what you photograph and how you compose it are your choices—we should talk a bit here about visual language.

A photograph communicates to you on a primal, nonverbal level and triggers all sorts of conscious and unconscious responses in your mind. You might say that a photograph is a sentence in the visual language while technique is its grammar. Like a sentence, a photograph has form as well as content. That is to say, it's not only the subject that matters in a photograph. The way in which the subject is presented is integral to the picture's content: the form supports content. You may look at a picture of a person and say, "That's a beautiful photo." That doesn't necessarily mean that the person is beautiful; it doesn't even mean it's a good likeness of him or her. It means that you've seen the picture as an entity in its own right—that you've reacted to form and content as if they were one.

The implication is that there's an essential difference between the subject on one hand and the photographic print on the other. To begin to understand this difference and some of the many interconnected relationships between the two—psychological, philosophical, aesthetic, optical, chemical, and technical—is to begin to understand the nature of photography.

In Western culture, photographs have often been taken as duplications of reality. Because of their ability to record precise detail and capture an instant, they are seen as "truth." But this is not the case. You cannot say that the camera never lies; in fact, you might say that it always lies, or rather, produces a reality all its own. With the help of a person, it produces a photograph, a thing in its own right, a piece of paper with silver on it. This photograph has qualities and merits that have nothing to do with the original subject; the fact that we see it as "truth" is our own cultural bias. There's a story about a film crew which visited and filmed a Stone-Age culture that had been isolated from modern civilization. The movie people returned a few months later with the footage, a projector, a generator, and a screen, and showed the film. The natives had absolutely no idea what they were looking at. Even though the pictures were of them and their neighbors, the film images were meaningless—they were just flashing colors on a screen. While our cultural orientation allows us to look at the pictures and see ourselves, we should remember that the photographic image is a representation of reality, not a duplication of it.

A central theme of this book is that the print's the thing. Whether we're discussing camera controls, technique, choice of equipment, or selection of exposure, the ultimate concern is how the resulting print will look. Sometimes the equipment itself is so seductive or the process of taking the picture so all-consuming that it's easy to lose sight of your goal. The long lapse between taking the photograph and holding the actual print in your hand also tends to increase your loss of perspective. But over and over again you'll find me emphasizing the importance and beauty of that final print. I'm completely taken with images expressed in silver on paper, with their potential for beauty and excitement.

I don't want to belabor the connection between this book and Adams' books, but I'd like to point out that one of his favorite terms is *previsualization*, the act of visualizing in advance exactly how the scene will appear in the photographic print. While this is a helpful concept, it's important to remember that photography is not totally predictable. This is one of its joys. You don't always know exactly how a scene will translate into silver, and it can be a real thrill to find a totally unexpected, truly alive print.

The surprise element in photography arises because you are working with a phenomenon that exists independently of you: the interaction of camera, light, and silver. The camera is blind; it can perform its image-making task completely indifferent to you and your intentions. You'll find that the camera sees the world much differently than you do. Your mind is very selective; it filters out or edits unwanted information. It makes presumptions, fills in spaces, smooths wrinkles, and generally melts your perceptions into your preconceptions. The camera is not so discriminating; it has no preconceptions, it just records. It picks up all the wrinkles, ash cans, and candy wrappers—all the disorder your eye chooses to gloss over. As technique becomes second nature, you become aware of things like this and the camera becomes an extension of your eye, a smooth-working means to your aesthetic end.

In reading this book, you may find that I treat casually certain aspects of photography which you consider quite important. This is not intended to be the only book you read concerning photography, and I've offered a few suggestions for further reading in the Bibliography. Also, I've assumed a certain ignorance on the part of the reader, so you'll find that some explanations are very basic. On the other hand, you'll see that I've handled various aspects of photography with a less-than-traditional approach, based on my own experience as a working photographer.

Before you read the rest of the book, let's define a few basic terms. The following is a very brief and extremely simple explanation of the whole photographic process.

The *camera* is a light-tight box. The *film*, a light-sensitive material, is held flat at one end of the box. At the other end is a *lens* which gathers the light rays bouncing off the subject and projects them onto the film as an upside-down and backwards image. Between the lens and film is a *shutter* which keeps the film shielded from light until the right moment. When the *shutter release* is pressed, the shutter opens for a brief instant, allowing the light rays projected by the lens to strike the film.

Film needs a fairly specific amount of light, or *exposure*, to perform correctly. The length of time which the shutter remains open is adjustable and partially controls the amount of light that strikes the film. The longer the shutter is open, the more light is allowed in.

Built into the lens is another controller of light, the *diaphragm*. It is an adjustable hole similar to the pupil of your eye, and the light rays must pass through the diaphragm, then the shutter, to strike the film. The smaller the hole, the less light passes through. The term *f*/stop refers to the diameter of the hole.

Most cameras have a system for aiming the camera and composing the image. The *viewfinder* is the opening in the camera through which you aim. In addition, cameras have a mechanism for replacing the exposed film inside the box. Usually this mechanism also cocks the shutter so it can be released again for the next picture.

Only objects at a certain distance from the lens will be projected sharply onto the film. This distance can be varied by moving the lens closer to or farther from the film. This is called *focusing,* and most cameras have some sort of focusing device.

Those objects which are nearer to or farther away from the camera than the object focused upon will be projected onto the film less sharply. The human eye is not as good an optical instrument as the lens for judging detail and will accept some objects nearer to or farther from the focused object as sharp. The zone in front of and behind the focused object within which other objects can lie and still be seen as sharp by the human eye is called *depth of field.* Depth of field varies according to the type of lens on the camera, the distance to the focused object, and the size of the *f*/stop. It is the total distance from near to far which will be seen as sharp.

The light-sensitive part of the film, called the *emulsion,* is composed of *silver halides* suspended in gelatin and is adhered to a transparent backing. After the film has been struck by the image-producing light rays from the lens, or is *exposed,* it must be kept from any additional light until after it is developed. When the film is exposed, the light rays change the chemical composition of the silver halides, rendering them unstable. During the interval between exposure and development, the film is said to contain a *latent image.*

The film is developed by soaking it in a chemical solution called *developer.* This solution completes the transition begun when the light rays struck the film; it reduces the unstable silver halide compound to a stable, pure element—black metallic silver. After a water rinse, or *stop bath,* the film is then soaked in another solution called *hypo,* or *fixer.* The hypo removes from the emulsion any silver halides which were not exposed by the light and which are thus still light-sensitive. When this step is completed, the image is stable and can be exposed to light without any further change in the image. Next the film is washed to remove the hypo from the emulsion, and then it is dried.

The processed film is called a *negative.* In terms of light and dark areas, the black and white negative is the opposite of the original subject. Areas of the negative which were struck by relatively few light rays coming from the shadows of the subject are transparent. That is, they have very little black metallic silver. Those areas of the negative which were exposed by many light rays traveling from highlights on the subject are so thick with silver that they are almost opaque. Areas of the negative which represent parts of the subject that were in between very light and very dark are proportionately translucent.

This process of developing the negative and the next step, printing the negative, are carried out in a *darkroom*, a special light-tight room where the light-sensitive materials can be handled without any unwanted exposure.

The process of printing the negative involves an *enlarger*, which projects light rays from a bulb through the negative, then through a lens which enlarges the image onto *photographic paper*. Photo paper is similar to film in that it has an emulsion filled with light-sensitive silver halides; a developer reduces the halides in the paper into deposits of metallic silver. Unlike film, whose emulsion is bonded to a transparent base, photo paper's emulsion is bonded to a white paper base. Printing paper is not sensitive to orange light; this means that in the darkroom it can be handled under *safelights*, orange lights which provide enough illumination for you to see what you are doing without giving the paper unwanted exposure.

A piece of photo paper is placed under the enlarger and then exposed to the projected image of the negative. Again, the amount of light which provides exposure is crucial. It is controlled by an *enlarging timer*, which turns on the light bulb in the enlarger for a specific amount of time. Like the camera lens, the enlarging lens has a diaphragm which further controls the amount of light striking the photo paper. During printing exposure, those light rays from the enlarger bulb which pass through the highlight areas of the negative are partially blocked by the opaque silver deposits and make a correspondingly weak exposure on the print. Thus fewer of the silver halides in the paper emulsion are converted to metal, and you see the white paper backing through the emulsion. The shadow areas of the negative are relatively transparent, thus allowing more light rays to travel through and make a denser deposit of silver on the paper. The denser the silver on paper, the darker the shadow area appears.

After the photo paper is exposed, it is submerged in a tray full of developer which, like negative developer, converts the latent image into visible silver. The paper is then transferred to a tray full of hypo, which removes unexposed silver halides from the paper and stabilizes the visible image. After the hypo bath, the room lights are turned on, the print is washed to remove the hypo, and then it is dried. Fini.

As you read on, you'll find that all of these terms and processes are discussed in detail. I'd like to suggest that you read the following chapters in progression because they are interrelated and each chapter builds on the chapter before it.

Chapter 2 defines basic terms and provides a perspective on the 35mm camera. Chapter 3 emphasizes building a working photo system at the lowest possible price. In Chapter 4 you'll find an explanation of the language of camera controls: f/stops and shutter speeds. The next chapter, Camera Technique, is a guide to holding the camera in your hands, moving with it, and seeing the tricks that a viewfinder can play. Chapter 6 deals with film in two ways: it provides a listing of the products that are available and a brief description of how film works. Chapter 7 is devoted to light appreciation and hopefully imparts an awareness of the *quality* of light. This chapter contrasts with the following one, which deals with measuring the *quantity* of light and relating that measure to the picture you want to take. The next three chapters cover darkroom procedure. Chapter 9 offers suggestions for making your darkroom a comfortable working environment, and Chapter 10 explains the mechanical process of developing negatives. Chapter 11 covers a part of the photo process very important to me—expressive printing. In the final chapter we deal briefly with the many ways in which photography can pay for a portion of itself.

A friend once said to me, about learning the body of knowledge behind photography, "Do it—it will free your mind."

The man on the preceding page was photographed
in Watts, California with a 105mm lens; he patiently allowed me
one frame. There's a description of how the picture
on the left was printed in Chapter 11; it was taken with a 105mm lens
and a tripod. The head of the porcelain doll pictured
above is actually less than ¾″ high; I used a 105mm lens with a
bellows extension, tripod, and window light.

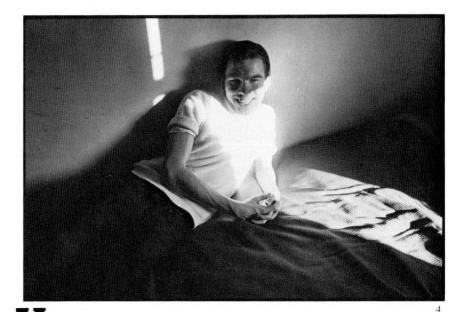

4

Kevin, above, was sitting in his dark attic room with a shaft of sunlight falling across his bed—an extreme mixed-light situation taken with a 24mm lens. The girl at the right was standing in dark shade, while the people behind her were originally blasted white with bright sunlight in this heavily manipulated print described in Chapter 11.

6

Both of these pictures were taken on assignment for
Rolling Stone: Jesse Colin Young and his son Cheyenne on the
ridgetop behind his home; Joan Baez, taken with
a 105mm lens in a San Francisco café shortly after she returned from
Hanoi, following the 1972 Christmas bombing.

7

The boy on the slide was caught with a 105mm lens—an effortless print. In the picture above, the strong flare from the window made the print difficult to keep light, airy, and even. Taken with a 35mm lens.

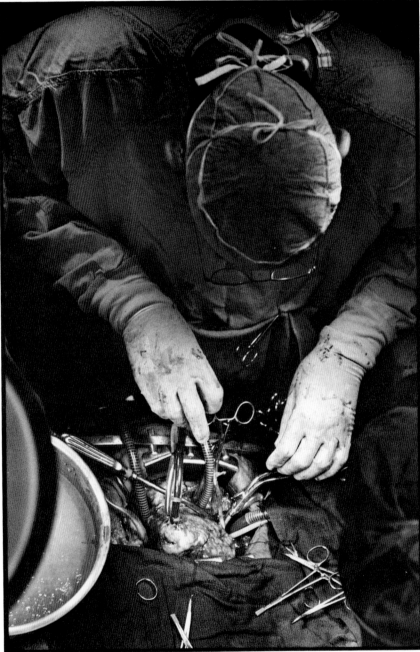

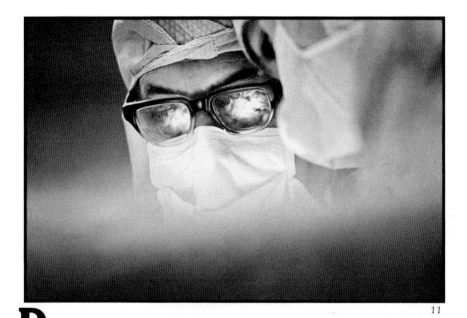

11

B oth pictures were taken during open heart surgery, the one at left from an amphitheater above, using a 180mm lens, and the other from inside the operating room, with a 105mm lens.

A straight print of fun and games in San Francisco. Taken with a 35mm lens. The man at the right was perusing the <u>TV Guide</u> for entertainment in Los Angeles. Taken with a 105mm lens.

13

T

he pictures on these pages are from an essay on a Los Angeles stripper. While all the other pictures in this section were shot with Tri-X at ASA 400, the three stripper pictures were shot with Recording Film at ASA 3000. The two pictures below were taken with a 24mm lens, the one at right with a 50mm.

This dog was in a truck parked in the Haight-Ashbury district of San Francisco. The dog was barking at me, so I barked back until he got it right. Taken with a 35mm lens.

2
THE 35MM CAMERA

Matthew Brady documented the Civil War with his camera, shooting photographs that have become some of America's most poignant historical records. To capture these scenes, Brady had to carry his chemicals and equipment onto the battlefield in a horse-drawn buggy, set up a tent as a makeshift darkroom, and rig up his huge camera with its bulky tripod and black cloth cover.

Today, in a canvas bag the size of Brady's camera, you can carry a couple of cameras, a multitude of lenses and accessories, and enough film to cover several skirmishes. While Brady was pretty much limited to recording static scenes by the size and bulk of his equipment, the much smaller, mobile 35mm camera has enabled modern photographers to flow with the rhythm of the passing scene. No longer is it necessary for the photographer to be burdened by equipment; the 35 allows him to peer into the obscure corners of the world. The remarkable mobility of this camera enables the photographer to capture the instant—a gesture, an elusive mood, an unfolding event. The introduction of the 35mm camera changed the way the world saw itself, spreading a vision that is candid and journalistic in its approach.

Early photographers could choose from only a few lenses to produce varied perspectives and moods: usually a "normal" lens and a "portrait" lens. These were big, clumsy pieces of equipment. Because the lens of a 35mm camera only has to project the image onto a relatively small frame of film, manufacturers of this camera are able to produce an extensive range of optically efficient, lightweight lenses, from extreme telephoto to extreme wide-angle, substantially augmenting the aesthetic tools available to the photographer. Using a telephoto lens, a photographer can pick a single figure in a crowd of people and isolate him. With a wide-angle he can photograph an entire chamber orchestra in a small room and include his own feet in the picture. With special optical equipment he can even take a picture of a fly's eye, an impossible task for Matthew Brady.

The original 35mm camera was designed in 1912 by Oscar Barnack, an employee of the Leitz Microscope firm in Germany. He and his co-worker, Max Berek, spent more than a decade refining it. Their new camera, the Leica, went on the market in 1924 and used the same type of film produced by Eastman Kodak for Hollywood motion pictures. Measuring 35mm in width—each frame is approximately 1"x1½"—the film could be rolled up into a light-tight cassette and inserted in the much smaller camera body. A single roll 5½ feet long held 36 exposures, thus making it possible to take a large number of photographs without frequent reloading, while reducing the price per picture considerably.

Cameras are classified according to *format,* or film size. During the early days of 35mm photography, most serious photographers were using either the large 4x5 or, later, the smaller 2¼ cameras. They considered the newcomer a sub-miniature and didn't take it seriously. The 4x5 camera used individual sheets of cut film measuring 4"x5" which were held in a film holder. The camera itself was quite heavy and the photographer had the additional burden of carrying around dozens of these film holders, each containing only two sheets of film. Every time he wanted to take a picture, the photographer would have to go through an elaborate fast shuffle to insert and pull film and film holders.

The 2¼ camera (e.g., the classic Rolleiflex) was easier to use than the 4x5, for it held a 12-exposure roll of film and was much smaller in size. (The roll of 120-size film is attached with tape to a separate paper backing and is rolled up on 2½"-long spools. Most roll-film cameras produce an image 2¼" square). But the roll-film camera did not have the advantage of interchangeable lenses as the 35mm camera did. At one time there were three different Rolleiflex cameras available, one with a wide-angle lens, another with a telephoto lens, and a third with a normal lens. If the Rollei-user wanted the aesthetic control of interchangeable lenses, he faced the problem of buying all three cameras. Today, many roll-film cameras are used in photography, especially in commercial work. The famous Hasselblad, for instance, has interchangeable lenses. While the Hasselblad is certainly a fine camera, it is very expensive and rather clumsy for the journalist. Other 2¼ cameras include Bronica and Mamiya. Pentax has recently come out with a camera called the 6x7 which uses roll film and produces 6cm x 7cm negatives. It is less clumsy than the Hasselblad but still rather large.

During the Second World War the compact design and high film-load capacity of the 35mm camera began to win acceptance among professional photographers. The great mobility, speed, and unobtrusiveness of the small camera recommended it to photojournalists such as Robert Cappa, Henri Cartier-Bresson, and W. Eugene Smith. The new camera allowed a spontaneity of vision which enabled them to document passing action in a way that had never before been possible. However, commercial picture buyers on the home front—the advertising industry, the magazine business, and others—were unhappy with the poorer quality of image produced by the smaller film size and often chose to forego the new spontaneity of vision.

To make a long story short, technical advances over the years have improved the image quality of 35mm photographs to an astounding degree. Gradual improvements in lens design have been an important factor. Research and development by Eastman Kodak, the "Great Yellow Father," has been another. Year after year, Kodak has improved the quality of its film, making it possible to achieve extraordinarily sharp images with subtle gradations.

Tastes have also changed in the last decades. Through the influence of magazines such as *Life, Look,* and *National Geographic,* we have become accustomed to the spontaneity of vision which the 35mm camera made possible. In the course of their daily lives Americans see countless photographs in newspapers and magazines, on book and record jackets, and on billboards. Most of these pictures are taken with the 35mm camera.

THE SLR VERSUS THE RANGEFINDER

There are probably hundreds of models of cameras that use 35mm film, but if you are interested in a camera as an artist's tool, there are certain essential features you should look for that will narrow the field considerably. You want an adjustable camera that allows complete control of exposure. Also, you want to be able to build a high-quality camera system—to gather a set of interchangeable lenses, accessories, and camera bodies that are compatible with one another and long-lasting. These requirements narrow the field of acceptable cameras to about half a dozen.

For the 35mm camera, there are two basic viewing and focusing systems available: the *rangefinder* and the *SLR (single-lens-reflex)*. Leica is the only serious rangefinder camera generally available today. Although a number of other cameras use the same viewing and focusing system as the Leica, most do not have interchangeable lenses. At present, Leitz is producing the CL, a compact, relatively inexpensive model made in conjunction with a Japanese firm, and the large, rather awkwardly designed M-5. The old classic rangefinders—the M-2, M-3, and M-4—are getting more difficult to find because they are becoming collectors' items. Leitz also makes an SLR called the Leicaflex.

When you look into the viewfinder of an SLR camera, you see exactly the same image that your camera lens sees. A small mirror in the body deflects the image onto a piece of *ground glass* in the body of the camera. (The ground glass is a piece of etched glass with a matte surface; it has this type of surface so that the image is projected onto the glass, not through it.) When you look into the viewfinder you see the image on ground glass. To focus, you turn the focusing ring around the lens until the image on the ground glass is sharp. During the brief instant when the

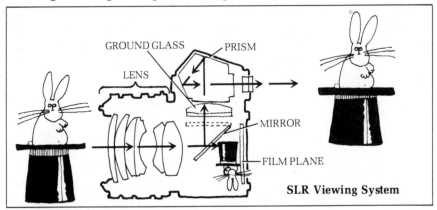

GROUND GLASS   PRISM   LENS   MIRROR   FILM PLANE

SLR Viewing System

film is exposed, the mirror flips up out of the way while the shutter admits light to the film.

With the rangefinder, you do not see exactly what the lens sees. The viewfinder, generally set on the top of the camera and slightly to the left of the lens, is more like a window; you look directly through it to view your subject. The focusing apparatus includes a second window on the right side of the camera. A delicate system of prisms and cams projects the image seen by the second window over the image seen in the actual viewfinder. If your subject is out of focus, you see a double image in a small rectangle in the center of the viewfinder. To focus, you adjust the focusing ring until the double image becomes a single, sharp image. This method of focusing might be called mechanical, as opposed to the SLR's optical mode.

Rangefinder fans—and there are millions—say that the directness of vision, the hairline precision of coincidental focusing, and the quiet afforded by eliminating the sound of the SLR's moving mirror make the

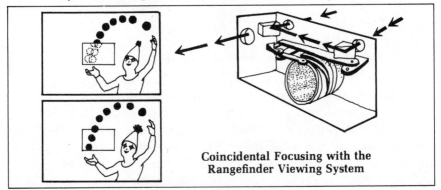

Coincidental Focusing with the Rangefinder Viewing System

rangefinder the very embodiment of speed, mobility, and unobtrusiveness. If you think your photography might lean toward slice-of-life realism, if you are intrigued by the deftness or mystique of the invisible observer, if you regard capturing the instant—the decisive moment—as being of the utmost importance, then you should look into rangefinders. And if you are at all into machines, you'll find the older Leicas such as the M-2 and M-3 a delight to hold and use.

But there is a fallacy in believing that a quiet, efficient camera will help you achieve total invisibility. Photojournalists have come to realize that the mere fact of their presence alters the scene. In some situations it is possible to achieve a measure of invisibility, and some photographers do have a knack for melting into the scenery.

The SLR may be a bit noisier than the rangefinder, but there is nothing slow or clumsy about it. It was developed more recently than the rangefinder and has far outdistanced its predecessor in sales. One important factor is that the design of the SLR continues to evolve at a more rapid rate. The built-in, through-the-lens meter advances in the SLR, for instance, have never been equaled in the rangefinder. Also, the SLR is a more versatile camera and works well with a wider variety of lenses. The rangefinder performs effectively with a wide-angle lens—actually, when using a wide-angle lens in low-light situations, a rangefinder is easier to focus than an SLR—but it becomes less effective when a telephoto lens is needed. In fact, with lenses longer than 135mm, you have to use a special

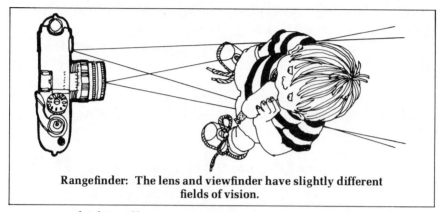

Rangefinder: The lens and viewfinder have slightly different fields of vision.

apparatus which in effect converts the camera into an SLR.

Another problem with the rangefinder lies in the fact that you frame your picture through a window an inch or so from the lens. Thus, the photographer's line of vision through the viewfinder is slightly different from that of the lens. When you focus on distant objects the difference is negligible, but as you approach your subject the difference in view increases. Most rangefinders are equipped with *parallax correction,* a mechanical means of compensating for this difference in view. However, once you move to within a couple of feet of your subject, parallax correction becomes less accurate. Thus, a big advantage of the SLR over the rangefinder is the former's ability to take extreme close-ups without a parallax problem.

The single greatest advantage of the SLR is that the image you see on the ground glass is identical to the one the lens will project on your film. And ground-glass viewing and focusing leads to a different psychology of camera use than that inspired by the rangefinder. With a rangefinder, the viewfinder is primarily an aiming device. When you view your subject through the viewfinder everything appears in focus, as it does when you look through a pane of glass. With an SLR you see the image as the lens sees it—you see how the lens is projecting the image of your

WIDE-ANGLE   NORMAL   TELEPHOTO

SLR: You see the image as the lens sees it.

subject. On the ground glass you can see exactly which areas are in focus and which are blurred. If you are using a wide-angle or telephoto lens, you witness the optical effects produced by the lens. You can adjust the *f*/stop and focus and watch how the image on the ground glass is altered. With experience you can learn the effects of using different lenses and settings on your rangefinder, but you won't see the precise results of a particular experiment until you've developed the film. With an SLR you can see the results right there on the ground glass before you have even released the shutter.

If you are concerned with achieving precision in composition, if you desire a studied, contemplative vision, it's likely that you'll prefer the SLR camera. It offers most of the speed and mobility of the rangefinder plus the tremendous advantages of ground-glass viewing. There is a visual thrill to viewing an image on ground glass—to using a telephoto,

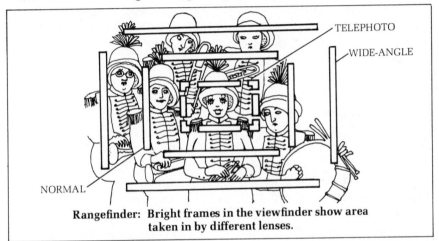

TELEPHOTO

WIDE-ANGLE

NORMAL

Rangefinder: Bright frames in the viewfinder show area taken in by different lenses.

for example, and isolating that figure in the distance and watching it loom up at you, filling the viewfinder. That kind of visual excitement is the soul of photography.

BASIC CAMERA STRUCTURE

Besides offering us picture-recording ability, cameras tempt and seduce us as beautifully complicated instruments. Their size and weight make them satisfying to hold; they are responsive to touch; they have numbers, dials, buttons, levers, and gauges; and it has been claimed that they are similar to guns in their psychological attraction. You might say that cameras are as much a part of the American Dream as cars or stereos.

Early in your photography career it is easy to get hooked on the camera as an object unto itself, but the important thing is to get beyond the camera—to create pictures. Before you can get beyond the camera, however, you've got to understand the basics of its structure and operation and become familiar with them so that your equipment becomes an extension of your eye.

Serious 35mm camera systems are modular. The manufacturer makes various interchangeable parts which can be assembled to make it possible for you to create a wide range of images under many special circumstances.

Central to this system is the camera *body,* a beautiful piece of machinery constructed for superior mechanical endurance and able to perform its intricate maneuvers over and over again with great speed and accuracy. Within the body, the film is held flat across the back of the camera; the film advance mechanism, the shutter and its parts, and most of the viewing and focusing apparatus are also found inside the body.

The body, however, can't take pictures without a *lens.* Each camera manufacturer makes an assortment of interchangeable lenses to fit only his particular body. In other words, each manufacturer makes a closed system: lenses and accessories for one brand are not designed to fit other brands. (Although some firms do make lenses which can fit a number of different cameras through the use of special adaptors, their quality makes them a lesser alternative.)

The Lens

Light rays travel in a straight line. When they strike an object, they bounce off and scatter in almost all directions from all points on that object. If we look at just two of the millions of rays which hit, let's say, the tip of someone's nose, we can begin to see how a lens works.

These two rays reflect off the nose and into the lens. One ray enters through the top of the lens, the other at the bottom. One of the properties of light is that it bends when it travels through one transparent material into another, for instance from air to glass. This bending is called *refraction.* In order for refraction to take place, the ray must enter the material at an angle. When light rays strike a curved surface, each ray enters at a slightly different angle because of the curve. With a convex curved surface, like a simple camera lens, the rays are bent inward. So our two nose rays strike different parts of the curved lens surface, are refracted toward each other, and converge at a point on the other side of the lens. This point of convergence is called the *focal point,* and in order for the nose to be sharp in the picture, this point must fall on the film. There are millions of focal points on one frame of film corresponding to the infinite number of points all over the subject which bounce light rays through the lens. These millions of points comprise the *focal plane*. Thus the film is held flat at the focal plane.

The degree to which light is refracted depends on the type of glass, its thickness, and its curvature. Thick, curvy, dense glass bends light rays more acutely, so the focal point falls closer to the lens. Thinner, flatter, less dense glass bends the rays less acutely, so they converge at a point further from the lens.

When the lens is focused at infinity, the distance between the focal point and the optical center, or *nodal point*, of the lens is called *focal*

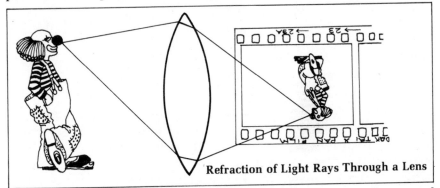

Refraction of Light Rays Through a Lens

length. A simple camera lens made with one piece of glass has an optical center in the middle of the glass. With more sophisticated lenses containing several pieces of glass, the optical center is determined with the use of optical formulas. All you really need to know about focal length is that it is described in millimeters and engraved on the lens housing, and that lenses range in focal length from a few millimeters to more than a thousand. Some of the more common lenses for 35mm cameras have focal lengths of 24mm, 50mm, 85mm, and 200mm. Lenses can be divided into three categories according to focal length. Lenses with a focal length shorter than 50mm are *wide-angle*; those with a focal length of approximately 50mm are called *normal*; and those with a focal length longer than 50mm are *telephoto*.

When photographing an object at a given distance, the longer the focal length lens you use, the bigger the image of that object on the film. In fact, if focal length is doubled, the image size of an object pictured on the film is doubled. If you were to stand ten feet from the man with the nose and photograph him with a long focal length lens, his nose would take up nearly the entire frame, surrounded by some face. Thus telephotos enlarge a small area. If you photographed the man from the same distance using a short focal length lens, his nose would take up a small portion of the frame, surrounded by the face and body and much of the scene around

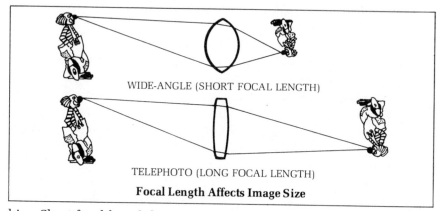

WIDE-ANGLE (SHORT FOCAL LENGTH)

TELEPHOTO (LONG FOCAL LENGTH)

Focal Length Affects Image Size

him. Short focal length lenses, then, have a wide-angle view and show objects as relatively small on the film.

PERSPECTIVE

Perspective is the apparent size relationship between objects near and far. If you were to approach the man, he would appear larger and larger relative to the background, until he filled your field of vision. Hold your hand up about a foot from your face and note the size of the background area it covers. Now keep your hand there and move your face closer. Note that your hand covers a larger background area. You could say that the hand grew larger or, relative to the hand, the background got smaller. Now move your head back and stretch out your arm, and see that your hand now blocks a smaller area of the background. You could say that the hand got smaller or, relative to the hand, the background grew larger. The distance between the camera (or your face) and the subject (your hand) controls the perspective, or relative size of objects near and far.

Suppose you want to take a picture of the man so that he fills the frame, with the top of his head at the top of the frame and his feet at the bottom edge. If you use a wide-angle lens, you have to get very close to him, because the lens creates a small image. The act of moving closer to him alters the perspective, shrinking the background relative to the man. If you use a telephoto lens, you have to back away from the man until his image is small enough to just fill the frame. As you move away, the background relative to the man looms larger.

So you see that you can alter the perspective of a scene by moving in close with a wide-angle or stepping back with a telephoto. For this reason, it's said (somewhat incorrectly) that focal length determines perspective. Actually, the focal length influences the distance you position yourself from the subject, and it is this distance which determines the perspective. If you were to stand at a certain distance from the subject and just change focal length, the perspective would remain constant, and the telephoto shot would just be a detail of the wide-angle.

A half-hour spent looking through different lenses will make this clearer to you than rereading this section. You'll see that, in use, the wide-angle has the effect of exaggerating your sense of space, making objects seem farther apart, while the telephoto compresses space, making objects seem closer together than usual. With the "normal" lens, spatial relationships appear as you usually see them.

DEPTH OF FIELD

The lens you choose and the way you use it determine the amount of depth of field. Depth of field, as said in Chapter 1, is the zone from near to far in the scene which will be seen as sharp in the photograph. When a lens is focused on an object—for example, the man with the nose—only that man and anything else in that *plane of focus* will be recorded as absolutely sharp on the film. Objects which are in front of or behind the man will be recorded less sharply. The farther an object is from the man, the less sharp it will be. Those objects which are behind or in front of the man and are still seen as sharp fall within the depth of field.

Because the human eye is not as precise an optical instrument as a camera lens, the eye has a greater tolerance for unsharpness. The lens can converge light rays to a point 1/2000″ in diameter on the negative. When the negative is enlarged, so is the tiny point. Thus if you enlarge the negative to eight times its original size (about 8″x10″), the point will be enlarged to 1/250″ on the resulting print. However, the human eye can just differentiate between two points 1/100″ in diameter and 1/100″ apart in an 8″x10″ photo when it views the photo at a normal distance for an 8x10 (about ten inches). Even though the lens can create smaller points on the print, the eye cannot tell the difference between a point 1/100″ in diameter and any points smaller; the eye accepts them all as sharp. When the points are larger than 1/100″, we begin to see them as unsharp.

These points in the negative or the print, whether they are 1/2000″ or ½″ in diameter, are appropriately called *circles of confusion*. To recap, any circles of confusion 1/100″ or smaller on the print are considered sharp by the human eye. The larger circles are seen as unsharp.

Let's see how the camera lens projects circles of varying size onto the film. Remember the two light rays bouncing off the man's nose into the lens and how they converged as a point on the film? If you imagine this three-dimensionally and consider all the light rays bouncing off the nose, you'll see that many of the light rays leaving the nose strike the lens all over its front surface. These rays which strike the lens are converged in

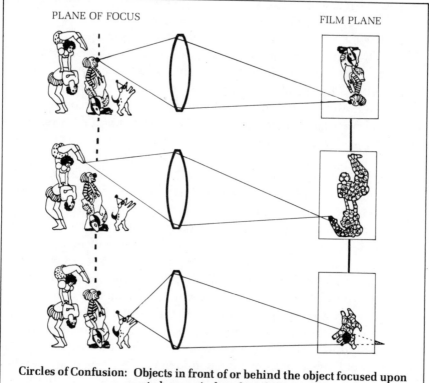

PLANE OF FOCUS

FILM PLANE

Circles of Confusion: Objects in front of or behind the object focused upon create larger circles of confusion.

the form of a cone. If the man's nose is focused, the tip of the "nose" cone will fall on the film, creating the smallest possible circle of confusion. Any light rays coming from an object between the nose and camera will converge at a point behind the film. When this happens, a broader cross section of the cone from that object will be recorded as a larger circle on the film. Light rays coming from an object behind the man converge in front of the film, then cross and begin to spread out into another cone which passes through the film and also records a circle. The nearer an object is to the man, the closer to the film its bounced light rays converge, and the smaller the circles it records on the film. If the circles are small enough so that they are 1/100″ or smaller when enlarged, then the object will be accepted as sharp—the object will fall within the depth of field.

Now we can explore how the focal length of a lens affects depth of field. Wide-angle lenses have more depth of field than telephotos. Because the curvy glass elements in wide-angles refract light rays more acutely, the diameter of cones diminishes more abruptly. The cone of light rays from an object in front of the man, for instance the dog, reduces to an appropriately small circle of confusion by the time it intersects the film plane. If you photograph the same scene using a telephoto, the diameter of the cone of light rays diminishes much less abruptly and records a larger circle of confusion as it passes through the film plane. Thus the dog will not be considered sharp.

The diameter of the *f*/stop, or *aperture*, also influences the depth of field. The smaller the hole, the more the depth of field. This is because the small hole blocks those light rays from an object which strike the outer edges of the lens. If they were allowed to pass through, these rays would form a cone with a diameter as big as the largest diameter of the lens, thus recording a large circle of confusion. As the diameter of the hole decreases, so does the diameter of the various cones projected from different objects in the scene, and the result is smaller circles recorded on the film.

The focal length of a lens further influences depth of field, in that wide-angle lenses need smaller holes to deliver the same amount of light as telephotos. This is because of the Inverse Square Law, which is discussed in Chapter 7—the longer the distance light has to travel to get from lens to film, the weaker the light when it strikes the film. Light rays travel a long distance in telephoto lenses, so these lenses need larger holes to deliver a given amount of light. Light travels a shorter distance in wide-angle lenses, so they use smaller holes to deliver the same amount of light to the film. These smaller holes in wide-angles result in smaller circles recorded on the film and thus a greater depth of field.

This is a good place to point out that the *f*/stop numerals marked on

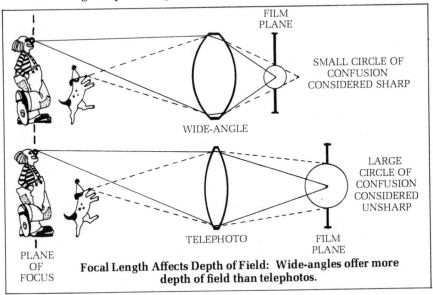

Focal Length Affects Depth of Field: Wide-angles offer more depth of field than telephotos.

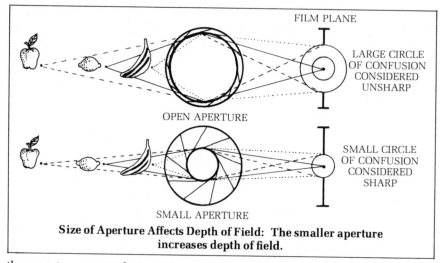

FILM PLANE

LARGE CIRCLE
OF CONFUSION
CONSIDERED
UNSHARP

OPEN APERTURE

SMALL CIRCLE
OF CONFUSION
CONSIDERED
SHARP

SMALL APERTURE

**Size of Aperture Affects Depth of Field: The smaller aperture
increases depth of field.**

the aperture control ring of a lens refer to ability to deliver a specific amount of light. The numbers do not indicate the actual diameter of the hole. So $f/5.6$ on a long lens is a much larger hole than $f/5.6$ on a short lens. Each numeral refers to a fraction; the larger the numeral, the smaller the corresponding hole.

Another factor determining depth of field is the distance from camera to subject. The longer the distance, the more depth of field. When the lens is focused on a distant subject, the rays from that distant object and other objects nearby form cones of approximately the same diameter. If the lens is focused on a nearby subject, the cones from other objects near the subject (in front of or behind it) will have widely varying diameters.

Still another factor is the size of the print relative to viewing distance. Remember, the more a negative is enlarged, the more each circle of

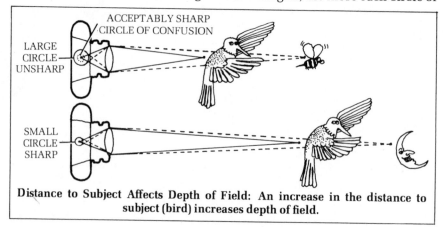

ACCEPTABLY SHARP
CIRCLE OF CONFUSION

LARGE
CIRCLE
UNSHARP

SMALL
CIRCLE
SHARP

**Distance to Subject Affects Depth of Field: An increase in the distance to
subject (bird) increases depth of field.**

confusion is enlarged, so larger prints have less depth of field. But the ability of your eye to differentiate between circles of confusion is dependent on your viewing distance. The closer you are to a print, the more precisely you can discriminate between what is sharp and what isn't. Thus if you are close to a large print, it will appear to have less depth of field. In practice, though, this is a self-canceling factor, because we tend to view larger prints from a longer distance.

To sum up: depth of field diminishes the closer you are to your subject, the longer the lens, the bigger the print or the closer you are when viewing it, and the wider the aperture. And vice versa.

Going through all of this theory to explain what kind of image a lens will produce is as effective as listing ingredients to describe what pudding tastes like. We all know the proof is in the eating. And so it is with lenses—the proof is in the looking.

In practice, you'll find that with wide-angles the transition from sharp to not-so-sharp is gradual and it is hard to make any part of the image really unsharp. With telephotos, the transition is quite abrupt and those objects which are out of focus are very out of focus. In a close-up portrait taken with a long lens and with the aperture wide open, if the eyes are sharp, the nose and ears will be blurred. A picture taken with a wide-angle lens from a relatively long distance with a small aperture might record as sharp everything from a few feet in front of the camera all the way to infinity.

Remember that those parts of an image which are out of focus are comprised of overlapping circles of confusion. In order to gain a visual understanding of these circles, I suggest that you go to a nearby body of water on a day when the sun is glinting off the water. Take a telephoto and focus on the sparkling highlights, then throw the image in and out of focus and notice how the points of light blur into overlapping discs. These discs are circles of confusion.

PARTS OF THE LENS

The modern 35mm lens is much more complex than the single piece of convex glass used here to describe how lenses function. The fact is, a single piece of glass by itself can't form a very sharp image. This is because of *aberrations*, or inherent faults, in the way glass bends light. The most prominent of these faults is *chromatic aberration*, or the inability of a lens to bend light rays of different colors at the same angle. Blue light, for instance, bends more than red light. We've all seen this effect in prisms which bend a beam of white light into a spectrum of its component colors; rainbows are also a result of this phenomenon. Compound lenses correct this fault by employing another piece of glass, or *element*,

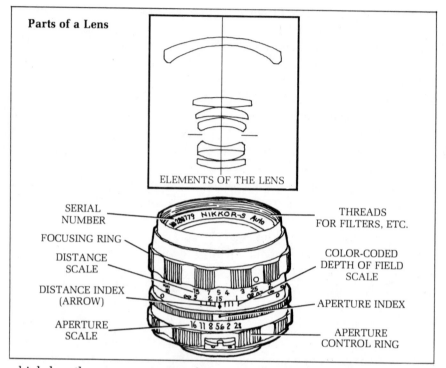

Parts of a Lens

ELEMENTS OF THE LENS

SERIAL NUMBER

FOCUSING RING

DISTANCE SCALE

DISTANCE INDEX (ARROW)

APERTURE SCALE

THREADS FOR FILTERS, ETC.

COLOR-CODED DEPTH OF FIELD SCALE

APERTURE INDEX

APERTURE CONTROL RING

which has the exact opposite aberration; the different colored rays are bent back together.

Other faults inherent in simple lenses include spherical aberrations, astigmatisms, coma, and curvature of field. These are all problems which the lens manufacturer remedies by using several elements designed to correct each other's mistakes.

Each element surface which meets a space of air in the lens is covered with a special *anti-reflection* coating. Without this coating, some light rays would scatter around inside the lens, eventually reaching the film and creating a haze rather than a precisely focused image.

Lens elements are precisely mounted in the metal barrel which also holds the diaphragm mechanism. The diaphragm is comprised of a number of thin metal blades which close down to produce the correct size aperture. Selection of aperture is controlled by the *aperture control ring* on the outside of the lens. The ring is marked with a range of *f*/stop numbers (for instance, 1.4, 2, 2.8, 4, 5.6, 8, 11, 16, 22) which indicate the amount of light allowed to pass through the hole. With lenses on rangefinder cameras, the *f*/stop mechanism is fairly simple: as you move the control ring, the diaphragm *stops down*, or decreases the size of the aperture. With lenses on the SLR cameras, the mechanism is more complex. The diaphragm remains wide open for viewing and focusing until the instant of exposure. When the shutter release is pressed, the diaphragm automatically stops down to the *f*/stop indicated on the control ring. The exposure is made, then the diaphragm instantly returns to wide open.

In the back of the lens is the *lens mount*, a term sometimes used to describe the barrel which holds the elements; actually it is a flat flange which serves as the interface between lens and body. It is rigidly constructed so that the lens is held firmly in place and will project its image to the film accurately. The lens mount also functions to lock the lens to the camera, and its locking mechanism varies with different cameras. Most cameras have some sort of *bayonet mount* as a locking device. On other cameras the lens is screwed into the body using a *screw mount*. With a bayonet mount, lenses can be attached to the camera much more quickly than with a screw mount.

The *focusing control ring* moves the lens barrel in or out to focus the image. This is accomplished with a *helical mount* which surrounds the lens barrel and screws the lens in or out without actually rotating it.

In the front of the lens are female threads which enable you to attach various accessories such as filters or lens hoods.

The Body

The camera body performs a number of functions. The primary one is to hold the film flat at the focal plane. The focal plane must be perpendicular to the axis of the lens and an exact distance from the lens. To insure this, the body is designed so that the film plane is actually the back end of a rigidly constructed box set within the body. A rectangle (1"x1½" in the 35mm camera) is cut into the back of the box to allow the light to strike the film; at the box's front end is the lens mount. The inside of the box is painted matte black to stifle any unwanted reflections.

The camera back, which you open or remove to load the camera, plays an important role in keeping the film flat at the focal plane. A *pressure plate* presses the film tightly against the rectangular hole at the rear of the rigid inner box. In order for the pressure plate to work properly, the camera back must be rigid and unsusceptible to warping. It's difficult for camera manufacturers to design a back which is both strong and easy to open for loading.

Within the body, the distance between lens and focal plane has a very slight tolerance for error. This tolerance is called *depth of focus*, not to be confused with depth of field.

Inside the black box, parallel to the focal plane and right in front of it, is the *shutter*. Because of its location near the film, it is called a *focal plane shutter*. (In some cameras, primarily the 2¼ and 4x5, the shutter is a diaphragm-type mechanism built into the lens; it is called a *leaf shutter* or sometimes a *Compur shutter*, after a particular brand name.)

The focal plane shutter is a moving curtain composed of two vertical panels. At speeds up to a 60th of a second, one panel travels across the frame of film and then is followed by the second panel. The point at

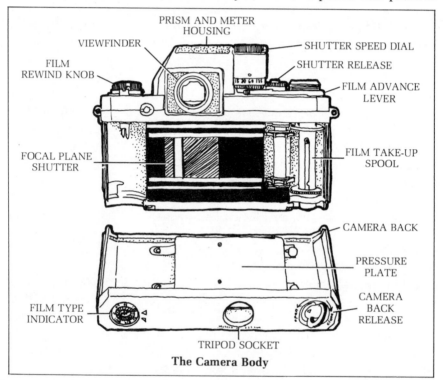

The Camera Body

which the first panel completes its movement across the frame and the second is about to begin, the film frame is totally uncovered for an instant. At shutter speeds greater than a 60th, the second panel begins to move almost immediately after the first has begun; thus, the panels produce a narrow vertical slit, which travels across the frame exposing the film as it passes. These shutter movements will take on special significance later, in the discussion of strobes in Chapter 7.

The speed of the shutter is controlled by the *shutter speed dial*, usually on the top of the camera. The dial is marked with numbers like 1, 2, 4, 8, 15, 30, 60, 125, 250, and 500, which, like *f*/stop numbers, actually represent fractions. Thus, 1 is one second, 2 is half a second, 4 is a fourth of a second, and so on. The higher the number on the dial, the shorter the exposure. Also included on the dial are the letters "B" and "T". "B" stands for "bulb" and will hold the shutter open as long as your finger is pressing the release button. This setting is used for exposures longer than one second. If the dial is set on "T" (for "time"), the shutter will remain open even though you take your finger off the release button. This setting is used for especially long exposures. The shutter is usually unlocked from the "T" setting by rotating the shutter speed dial.

The shutter is driven by spring mechanisms concealed in a dust-proof section of the body (under the shutter speed dial). Actually, there are two different spring mechanisms, one to propel the shutter at speeds of a 60th or slower and one for the high speeds.

Electronically connected to the shutter, the *synchronizing mechanism* triggers a flash bulb or strobe at the correct instant. The timing of the mechanism is adjustable according to the kind of flash you are using. The flash is connected to the synch in one of two places: the *hot shoe* for flash units which are attached to the camera and a terminal *PC outlet* for units used separate from the camera. The control for adjusting synch timing is usually incorporated into the shutter speed dial.

Also built into the body is the viewing and focusing system. With the rangefinder, this is a system of windows and prisms which focus the lens mechanically. With the SLR, the image projected from the lens is deflected to a ground glass placed at a right angle to the focal plane. The ground glass is exactly the same total distance from the lens as the focal plane, so what's sharp on the ground glass will be sharp on the film. The image is deflected to the ground glass by a fine mirror. As mentioned earlier, the mirror must move out of the way at the instant of exposure so the image from the lens reaches the film and not the ground glass. The mechanism which flips the mirror out of the way also activates the automatic diaphragm in the lens.

On top of the ground glass is a prism which allows you to look down at the image while holding the camera at eye level. The prism also corrects the upside-down, backwards image projected by the lens. On some SLRs, this unit is removable so that you can change the ground glass.

Also incorporated in the body is the *film advance mechanism*, which is operated by a lever on the camera. This lever also cocks the shutter and advances the frame counter so that you know how many exposures you have used. A battery-operated *motor drive* is available for many cameras; it is an attachment which fires the shutter, then advances the film and cocks the shutter for you.

After the film is exposed, it is rewound into the cassette using the *rewind knob.* This knob usually has a folding crank to make the job easier. To rewind the film, you must release a ratchet which prevents accidental rewind. Incidentally, you can tell whether there's film in the camera by checking the rewind knob. If it turns freely, the camera is empty.

Some odds and ends found on camera bodies include eyelets for the camera strap, a ¼" tripod socket on the bottom, and a film indicator in case you forget what type of film is inside. Most cameras also have a *self-timer* which trips the shutter after approximately ten seconds, so that you can jump into the picture if you are so inclined. SLRs have a depth-of-field preview button which manually stops down the diaphragm and enables you to see changes in depth of field on the ground glass. Many SLRs also have a provision for locking the mirror up to minimize camera vibration during long exposures.

Many cameras have miniature exposure meters built into their bodies. Various parts of the meter, including battery, photoelectric cells, on/off switch, and voltage meter, are cleverly concealed within the camera. Most of these meters read the exposure after the light has passed through the lens, often when the light reaches the ground glass, and are called TTL (through-the-lens). The built-in meter is basically an on/off instrument: when exposure is correct, the meter says "yes," and when the exposure isn't right, the meter indicates whether there is too much or too little light, but not exactly how much. The meter is cross-coupled with the *f*/stop and shutter speed controls, and most cameras have an especially sophisticated version of this coupling which allows the photographer to take a reading with the lens wide open. The needle in the meter is visible in the viewfinder, and most cameras also have shutter speed and/or *f*/stop indicated in the viewfinder. Exposure is correct when the needle is either centered or matched up with a second needle in the viewfinder—a system called *match-needle.*

Now that you have a basic idea of what a 35mm camera is and the advantages of using one, the numbers and dials on the lens and body should seem less mysterious. As we ease into lengthier explanations, their functions will become clearer.

3
BUYING EQUIPMENT

The care with which you select your equipment will influence the kind of pictures you take. For example, the decision to use an SLR or rangefinder camera, a preference for a wide-angle or telephoto lens or both—choices like these will contribute to your photographic style. Cameras are very expensive tools for the beginner or even the working photographer. Fortunately, though, their high resale value, versatility, and endurance make for a strong used market. Armed with that knowledge and some cash, you can buy a perfectly operative 35mm camera for a fraction of the cost of a new one. If used equipment isn't your style, you still don't have to pay list price for a brand new camera system.

Success in avoiding unneeded photo gadgets is a significant point in equipment buying. Money spent on unneeded gadgets means less money available for important equipment. Almost every photographer I know has a pack-rat box somewhere filled with useless photo gadgets. Half of these gadgets work perfectly well to fill some nonexistent need dreamed up by the photographer or the salesman; the other half must have been designed by draftsmen who never left the drawing board to try them out. I once bought a tripod whose structural integrity was so neat and complete that Buckminster Fuller himself would have been thrilled. Trying to get a camera attached to it, however, was a joke. I went through a crisis with a pair of Vise-Grips every time I wanted to get the camera off the thing. If you select equipment wisely, you'll avoid frustration which can impair your picture-taking.

The lenses and accessories you buy will influence your approach to photography, and it's common for a photographer to feel that the lack of certain equipment will inhibit creativity. But it's important to remember that if the subject isn't there or the lighting is wrong, there isn't really a picture, and no lens or piece of equipment is going to create one. A certain economy of means can be an asset in photography, for it encourages you to get the most from your own ingenuity and skill. Too much equipment, on the other hand, tends to weigh heavily on your mind as well as your body.

CONSIDERATIONS IN BUYING A CAMERA

What equipment do you need to start a well-balanced, efficient system? For starters, I'd recommend a body with a built-in meter and two lenses with lens hoods. Add to that a neck strap and you've got the beginnings of a good system.

What brand of camera should you look for? As mentioned in Chapter 2, there are more than half a dozen good 35mm camera systems: Canon,

Nikon FTN

Honeywell-Pentax, Leica, Mamiya, Minolta, Miranda, Olympus, and Nikon, to name a few. However, almost every working photographer I've ever talked to owns Nikons or Leicas, or plans to. These machines display unfaltering quality of construction, are accompanied by extensive and innovative systems, and have earned their incredible reputation. Before you Pentax- or Canon-lovers slam the book down in disgust, let me make

Pentax Spotmatic

it clear that the brand of camera you use has very little to do with the quality of your photographs. The photographer takes the picture, not the camera. It is highly improbable that anyone looking at a photograph could tell you what kind of 35mm camera was used to take it. Although one manufacturer's lenses may prove sharper in tests than those of another manufacturer, the differences are virtually indistinguishable in practice. Furthermore, most of the time uneven camera technique will result in photos of a quality far below the camera's potential.

So why, then, does it matter which brand of camera you use? Differences show up in performance over a period of time, specifically in a camera's ability to perform efficiently and without frequent breakdown. Remember, when you buy a camera you buy the whole system. And as time passes you build quite an inventory of that particular brand of equipment. A friend of mine, a professional photographer, invested his money in a non-Nikon system. After giving them three or four years of professional use, he found that his two camera bodies were always in the repair shop and that his telephoto lens was taking yellow pictures. He gave up, sold his equipment at a loss, and started all over building a Nikon system. Making a switch like that costs a fortune, so if you are just starting out and feel your interest will be long-lasting, I think it would be wise to make a greater initial investment and buy a Nikon. If you decide later that you'd rather write poems, sell to the next person.

Nikon has been a leader in the field of 35mm cameras for several decades, offering an extensive and beautifully engineered system. No other manufacturer makes as many lenses, motors, meters, and other accessories as Nikon. Furthermore, Nikon provides a constant flow of innovations, for the most part without the onus of planned obsolescence.

The Nikon system dates back to the end of World War II when a few photographers discovered a brand of lens from Japan that was at least as sharp as Leitz' German glass and less expensive. Sensing that they had found a rising market, the firm, Nippon Kogaku, asked working photographers to help convert fledgling 35mm SLR design into the "perfect" camera to suit their lenses. Several models later, in 1959, the company announced the Nikon F, an SLR camera that was at that time a quantum leap forward in design. In addition to using interchangeable lenses, the new F had interchangeable ground glass and prism parts in its viewing system, which meant that it could accommodate technological advances like the built-in meter. Other manufacturers had to redesign their cameras and produce new models in order to use the built-in meter. The intelligent, flexible design of the entire Nikon system meant that it was adaptable to a wide range of special purposes, including medical, astronomic, microscopic, and architectural photography.

The Nikkormat, a Nikon camera with a more moderate price tag, was introduced in 1965. This model accepts all Nikkor lenses and some system accessories and has a built-in exposure meter.

The most recent model is the Nikon F2, which was put on the market in 1971 and offers a number of new features. For instance, the body shape

Nikon F2 with Motor Drive

was modified to fit your hand more comfortably, the back was hinged to the body for easier loading, and the accessory motor drive was designed to be more compact and easily transferable from one body to another. Also, the shutter speed controls were altered so that at higher speeds the photographer can set the dial at intermediate increments.

From my abundant enthusiasm it may sound as though I'm in the employ of Nikon. I'm not, not in any way. I know there are those of you who don't, or for some reason won't, own Nikons and you can rest assured that your camera will work very well and take pictures as well as

Canon F-1

other brands, that you can buy a substantial range of accessories, and that your camera will last if used judiciously. But you should realize that the dollar value of your system will depreciate rapidly, that used equipment will be rare, and that it will be hard to rent or borrow exotic accessories. You should also consider the possibility that your system could be rendered obsolete because it isn't designed to accommodate technological advances. And, again, should you decide later that you want Nikon, changing systems could be very expensive. In my opinion, if you have a limited budget, it would be wise to buy a used Nikon rather than a new model of one of the other top brands.

For those of you who don't like Nikons, Canons are very well made, have excellent optics, and probably give Nikons their closest competition. They are often the first SLR camera choice of Leica-users, because

Olympus OM

their focusing rings turn in the same direction (opposite from the Nikon). Photographers who think Nikons are too big often try Pentax. The new Olympus OM has received very good reviews from those who have tried it. Of course, the Leicaflex is extremely well made, but is very expensive and doesn't have as wide a range of accessories as the other brands.

It should be mentioned that the Pentax is of lesser quality than

Leicaflex SL2

Canon, and that the high-quality Canon and Leica will probably not depreciate in value as fast as cameras of lesser quality. All of these non-Nikon brands have changed their system designs frequently in the past, requiring the purchase of new lenses and accessories to fit the new models.

When looking for used equipment, you'll find there are thousands of used Nikons floating around. Primarily, this is because they are the most popular serious 35mm camera. Since they are so well constructed and so long-lasting, they can easily be converted into cash by an owner in need. One steady source of used Nikons is people who dabble in photography and then decide to sell their camera and move on to other interests. A real advantage of using Nikon is that you have a better chance of buying, renting, borrowing, or sharing the equipment of numerous fellow Nikon-owners. On a given day in most major cities there are perfectly good working Nikons for sale from about $100 up. You probably won't stumble onto that $100 deal unless you travel with a very fast group of friends; on the other hand, there's no need to spend $1000. But considering the current rate of inflation in the United States and Japan, prices are sure to rise appreciably in the next couple of years. Other factors which influence camera prices include fluctuating currency exchange rates and the changing availability of various cameras.

As this book goes to press, the most recent innovation in 35mm camera design is the automatic exposure system, which takes a light reading and sets either the shutter speed or the f/stop for you. In the future we can expect more sophisticated automatic exposure systems and the incorporation of solid-state electronics.

Shopping for a Camera
If you are buying new equipment, keep in mind that most brands are not

Fair Trade items (their prices are not fixed), and you shouldn't have to pay list price for them. If you live in a large city, you should be able to take advantage of competition among stores. Many camera shops offer their steady customers a standard 20 percent "student/professional" discount on both materials and equipment. The accessibility of this discount seems to vary. Some stores ask for proof—such as a student I.D. or resale permit—while others offer the discount to just about anyone. Large cities usually have one or more stores that cater especially to professional photographers. They're easily identified in the Yellow Pages by the list of equipment they are franchised to sell. Such brand names as Leica, Hasselblad, Omega, Ascor, Linhoff, Sinar, or mention of an industrial department are clues. Needless to say, you should check them out.

Probably the best way to buy new cameras is to shop in the Orient. If you happen to be traveling in Japan or Hong Kong, or have a friend who plans to, you can buy a camera there for approximately 25 percent less than what you would pay in the States (even after taxes). You'll be asked to pay 12½ percent of the cost to U.S. Customs and you should have the receipt to show them. Many working photographers have cherished connections with camera dealers in the Orient, and if you know of one who will divulge the name of his dealer, you can purchase a camera through the mail. The better dealers take two to three weeks to send the camera by air mail, while others have been known to take six months—so some investigation is required on your part. Don't order blind. Again, you'll have to pay 12½ percent duty. Manufacturers usually have established trademark restrictions which require you to remove any identifying marks on the camera once it has entered this country—a law observed more in the breach.

If you are traveling abroad with a camera, register your equipment with Customs before you leave the United States. This way, there's no chance of your being asked to pay duty on it when you re-enter the States.

If you are looking for a used camera, the first place to check is the classified ads in your local newspaper. There are also good listings in the neighborhood throw-away papers of most large cities. Sometimes pawn shops are surprising for good buys. With Nikons, because of their wide use, there's usually a photographers' "grapevine" about used paraphernalia floating around.

When you check camera stores for used equipment, be sure to know what you want before you go in. Remember that retailers are middlemen and they take a profit. Don't be swayed by a sales pitch; you could walk out of the shop looking like a Christmas tree, loaded down with all sorts of accessories you don't need. Camera salesmen are often very nice and some are quite knowledgeable, but remember that they make their livings selling these things, not using them. The best policy is not to buy anything until you've actually experienced a need for it.

If you find a used camera you'd like to buy, it's a good idea to locate a professional camera repairman and ask him to run a check on it. You might talk to one or two professional photographers and ask them where they take their equipment. If you live in a small town, contact the local newspaper and ask their staff photographer. Since a camera repairman usually has a large backlog of work, it's wise to make arrangements in advance. He's a good source of used equipment too. There are a few things in particular which your repairman should check: all of the camera's critical measurements and tolerances which could be inaccurate if the body has been dropped; both the high and low shutter speeds; the accuracy of the built-in meter, if there is one; and the advance mechanism.

When you are looking over a used camera, don't be put off by signs of wear. The fact that a camera has some dents in it and shows some signs of normal use does not mean that it will not perform well. My cameras have been knocked, dinged, and banged—and they almost always work.

You might want to use signs of camera wear, however, as a bargaining point to haggle down the price. Pawnshop owners or private parties will not necessarily know that a worn camera can work just as well as a new one. You can determine the exact age of a Nikon by referring to the serial number on the top of the body—the first two digits are the year the camera was made (on cameras made since 1965). One place to look for wear is the eyebolt where the camera straps hook on to the body. Also, you might check to see if the camera has been used with a motor drive, which puts a lot of strain on the camera. A motor drive trips the camera shutter and advances the film as quickly as four times a second. This is a real bread-and-butter tool for working photographers who can't miss a shot and to whom film is cheap. Listen for the whirr/click/whirr/click from the cameras of photographers hunting for telling gestures at television press conferences. You can tell if a Nikon F has been used with a motor drive by removing the back and looking to see whether two holes have been drilled in the base of the body.

A word about black bodies: generally, 35mm cameras have chrome trim, but the photographers who used them during the Second World War found that the sun would glint off the chrome, giving enemy riflemen a good target. So they went to the manufacturers, who at the time had only a small, select market to serve, and asked them to make bodies that would not reflect the sun. Today, when you pay the extra cost of having an all-black exterior, you are paying for the mystique. Personally, though, I like the black cameras—they have a professional look to them.

Most working photographers have more than one camera body, and this is especially true of the photojournalist. He uses different focal length lenses attached to different bodies so that he can cover moving events without taking the time to change lenses. In addition, this gives him a greater amount of film already loaded. Sometimes photographers put black and white film in one body and color in another. Also, working photographers need back-up equipment to cover the possibility of camera failure.

CONSIDERATIONS IN BUYING LENSES

Having a variety of lenses with which to work is invaluable to a photographer, since focal length is a major control over the appearance of a photograph. Unless you're a lens purist or never advance beyond the snapshot stage, you'll eventually own more than one lens. If photography becomes important to you, you won't level off and take stock until you've got four or five lenses. If you're a commercial photographer, prospective clients won't even take your business card until you've got a whole closetful of equipment.

As we've said before, much of the excitement of 35mm photography results from the possibilities opened up by interchangeable lenses. Limiting yourself to the 50mm lens, the one most often sold with the camera, is a very sparse economy of means. Wide-angle and telephoto lenses do more than cover a wide area or bring subjects closer—they add their own expressive flavorings to photographs. In normal use, the telephoto lens flattens perspective, isolating or simplifying subjects. It's characteristic perspective and selective focus produce pictures that have a distant, dreamlike quality. The wide-angle lens, on the other hand, stretches perspective; its pictures are more immediate, real, open, and honest. The wide-angle is inclusive while the telephoto is selective.

The degree of apparent distortion a lens produces (remember that distance determines perspective) increases the farther away its focal length is from 50mm: the distortion from a 20mm lens is greater than that of a 35mm lens; a 200mm flattens more than a 105mm.

The problem with lens distortion is that it may be so striking it becomes the subject itself. You end up producing pictures of 20mm distortions instead of your subject. The extremely distorted lens speaks loudly, but it's so much fun to work with that it's hard to resist.

By comparison, the normal lens is so quiet it's rather dull. You might say the 50mm lens is normal in the extreme. A number of photographers never use it, but then there are some who use it exclusively. Remember, when you buy your camera you do not necessarily have to buy a 50mm lens with the body. In fact, you can buy the body alone. If you are buying a camera from a private party or pawn shop, they may be reluctant to break up a set. But if you are dealing with a camera store, they should be agreeable to selling you any lens you want with the body.

Perhaps the best idea is to give yourself a chance with different types of lenses. After you have been taking pictures long enough, you will develop your own style. And you will find that how you think in focal length is one of the more distinctive marks of your style. In a sense, some photographers have telephoto vision and some, wide-angle.

If you buy lenses at the camera store, be sure to avoid a very common occurrence. The salesman shows you a camera with its 50mm lens. Then, at his suggestion, you look through a 135mm lens, and the image is so startling and exciting that you buy it as your second lens. The 50mm and off-brand 135mm combination is a standard camera-store package. So seduced are you by the relatively extreme telephoto image and by the way the long lens looks hanging on your camera that the 50mm ends up merely as filler for your camera bag. A year later you have a portfolio of close-up character studies and back-lit flowers that would put even your grandmother to sleep. Meanwhile, you've effectively blocked yourself off from a whole area of wide-angle excitement and all that lies in between.

I like to use various lenses to flavor my pictures, but I don't want the choice of lenses to be obvious. If I had one lens only, it would be a 35mm; two lenses, a 35mm and 85mm; three lenses, a 24mm, 35mm, and 85mm; four lenses, a 24mm, 35mm, 50mm, and 85mm. You might prefer the 105mm over the 85mm, since the former is the classic portrait lens. If I had a camera body with a 50mm, my second lens would be a 24mm. You can see I lean toward wide-angle.

One camera body and two lenses, 35mm and 85mm, make a flexible and well-balanced system. When you've got the money to add a third, a 24mm or 50mm lens might be good. Keep in mind that the use for a lens longer than 105mm is limited. On a job, I usually carry three or four bodies (one with a built-in meter), a motor drive, and 24mm, 28mm, 35mm, 50mm, 85mm, 105mm, and 180mm lenses.

Most of the lenses I've recommended are grouped closely around the normal. But there is a world of lenses beyond the average range which serve a variety of special functions—for example, the *fish-eye* or extreme wide-angle lenses, which were originally designed to photograph the insides of huge storage vats. They run from 6mm to 16mm, project a circular image on the film, and create extreme *barrel distortion* (straight lines bow outward). Not all extreme wide-angles are fish-eyes, but it's a very complicated task to produce an extreme wide-angle that has a rectilinear, or nonbarrel-distorted, image. For instance, Nikon makes a rectilinear 15mm lens that costs $1200. Special perspective lenses, such as the Nikkor 35mm PC (Perspective Control), are used by architectural photographers to counteract distortion. Mirror telephotos, or *catadioptic lenses*, are a physically shorter alternative to the extreme length of the Big Bertha long lenses, and because they have less glass are lighter weight. The mirror telephotos work like telescopes and come in 500mm and 1000mm. *Zoom* lenses offer a continuum of focal lengths (mostly telephoto) in the same lens, but they have the reputation of being less sharp than other lenses. They are also slow in terms of lens speed and tend to be clumsy. The 43–86mm zooms are the most useful, while the 50–300mm ones are the most spectacular.

Variations in Lens Speed

Sometimes manufacturers make more than one model of a particular focal length lens. For example, Nikon ' as four different "normal" lenses (50mm $f/2$, 50mm $f/1.4$, 55mm $f/1.2$, and 55mm $f/3.5$ macro). For the most part, these lenses vary in *speed*, or their widest possible aperture. Look for an f/number on the lens; it indicates speed. The faster the lens, the more light it allows to enter the camera with the aperture wide open. If there is only a small amount of available light, you can use a fast lens to allow more light into the camera and thus achieve proper exposure. The smaller the f/number of a lens, the larger its maximum diaphragm opening and the faster the lens. For example, an $f/1.4$ lens is faster than an $f/2.8$.

In practice, though, a lens is rarely used at its fastest setting. So it would be a good idea to consider carefully whether the extra dollars spent in acquiring a superfast lens are actually worth it. One additional factor you should consider, though, is that in SLR cameras the speed of a lens also reflects ease of focusing. The faster the lens, the shallower the depth of field and, consequently, the easier it is to focus. Wide-angles, because of their relatively great depth of field, are hard to focus. Thus extra speed is particularly helpful with the wide-angles.

I would recommend an $f/1.4$ normal lens and an $f/2$ 35mm. The 85mm lens comes in $f/1.8$ only, and the 105 in $f/2.5$.

The greater the lens speed, the greater the complexity of lens design and the higher the price of the lens. Also, the normal is the easiest lens to design and produce, and as focal length increases or decreases from 50mm and lens design becomes more sophisticated, the lens becomes more expensive. Extreme telephotos and wide-angles with great speed are very expensive.

Shopping for a Lens

Lenses do not deteriorate with time, so you might consider buying a used one. As with camera bodies, it's a good idea to have a camera repairman check over a used lens before you buy it. The diaphragm blades may malfunction and the focusing mount may be loose, but these are problems that can be repaired at a reasonable cost. Within the past year or so, however, many camera companies began producing lenses with a super-coating that greatly reduces lens flare. The new coating is so good that it warrants your consideration, and you might want to locate a used lens that is still pretty new so that you will have the benefit of this special coating.

As mentioned in Chapter 2, you can buy lenses specially designed to fit a number of different camera brands. These *universal mount lenses* may be attractive because of their low price, but they are not nearly as well constructed as other lenses, often have lens mount problems, and are just not as sharp as the closed-system lenses.

Apart from the case of universal mount lenses, there's really little reason to worry about differences in lens sharpness among various

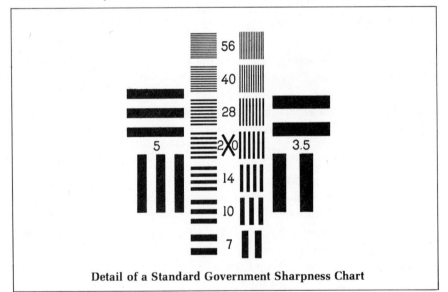

Detail of a Standard Government Sharpness Chart

brands of lenses. The camera magazines, though, make a big issue of it. Every year or so they run a series of tests to determine the sharpness of various lenses. The tests are conducted with standard government charts that consist of groupings of parallel lines. Each grouping is spaced differently; for instance, one section has 50 lines/millimeter, another 80 lines/millimeter. In the test, a lens is used to photograph various sections of the chart; at a certain frequency of lines/millimeter the lens will no longer be able to distinguish among the lines and the resulting portion of the photograph will be a blur. Thus the sharpness of a lens is stated in terms of its ability to resolve lines/millimeter. For example, a particular lens may be able to resolve at 80 lines/millimeter but not at 85 lines/ millimeter. Today a modified standard for testing lenses called M-T Curves (Modulation-Transfer) combines resolving power with its sister, contrast.

In spite of what the photo magazines indicate, slight differences in resolving ability among brands of lenses are relatively inconsequential in terms of the final picture. In fact, most lenses resolve detail more precisely than most films. Only the really cheap lenses have noticeably poorer resolving ability. This whole question of sharpness will come up later, and you'll see that the quality of the lens is only one aspect of sharpness. In the final print, what's important is the *impression* of sharpness created by the type of light and subject matter.

METERS

I strongly recommend buying a camera with a *built-in exposure meter*. The built-in, through-the-lens meter is one of the major advances which have helped to make the 35mm SLR camera so popular. These meters do have some disadvantages: they are delicate and have a somewhat limited range. But these problems are far outweighed by their speed and ease of use in the field.

One difficulty with the separate, *hand-held meters* is uncertainty in knowing what area of the scene is included in the exposure reading. With the built-ins, you can see in the viewfinder exactly what area is being read without taking the camera from your eye. The meter needle and the shutter speeds, and sometimes *f*/stops, are visible in the viewfinder, so you can make all adjustments with the camera held in "taking" position. Furthermore, using the built-in meter, you can immediately detect any changes in light level resulting from subtle camera or subject movement.

As a back-up meter and for low-light situations, you'll want a hand-held meter, and these run from $100 up. Their calculator dials provide a great deal of information at a glance, and this can be important at times, as explained later in the chapter on exposure.

All of the technique in this book is based upon use of *reflected light meters*, which are used at camera position and pointed at the subject. They read the light that is bounced off the subject—in other words, the light that is received by the lens and then recorded on your film. Built-in meters are reflected light meters, and so are many hand-helds. This type of meter is good for uncontrolled, available light situations: those that a journalist is most likely to encounter.

The other type of meter is the *incident light meter,* which is held at the subject position and aimed back at the camera. The incident light meter's photoelectric cell is usually covered by a plastic dome which resembles half of a ping pong ball. This type of meter measures the light which falls on the subject and does not take into account what happens to the light once it hits the subject and bounces off. Incident light meters are most commonly found on movie sets and in photo studios, or other situations where the light is tightly controlled. The Spectra is an expen-

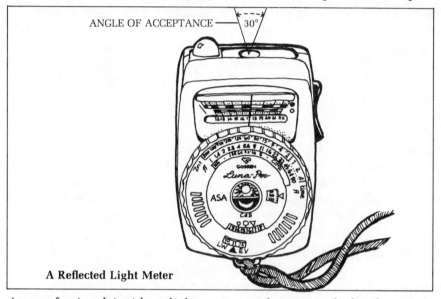

ANGLE OF ACCEPTANCE — 30°

A Reflected Light Meter

sive professional incident light meter used extensively by the movie industry; the Sekonic is a reliable and popular brand.

Either meter system, when used intelligently and with a certain amount of experience, can yield proper exposures most of the time. However, they require different ways of thinking, and making a choice between them is like making a choice between the rangefinder and SLR.

Most light meters today employ a *cadmium-sulfide,* or *CdS, cell* which regulates power flow from the battery. The *selenium cell,* which generates electricity when light strikes it, is now almost obsolete. CdS cells are much more accurate in low-light situations than the selenium cells and are also much smaller; their small size made possible the development of built-in meters. However, the CdS cells have a minor drawback in the form of "memory"; that is, if you take a reading of a bright-light situation and then immediately take a reading for a dimly lit

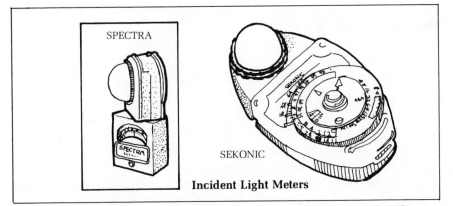

SPECTRA

SEKONIC

Incident Light Meters

scene, the latter reading will be influenced by the bright-light reading.

Angle of acceptance refers to the area of a scene which is read by the meter, and the angle differs with the particular meter. In the case of built-in meters, the angle of acceptance varies with the particular lens attached to the camera and with the design of the meter. A 135mm lens, for instance, has a 9-degree angle of acceptance, and a 180mm lens has a smaller one. As far as built-in design goes, some meters take center-

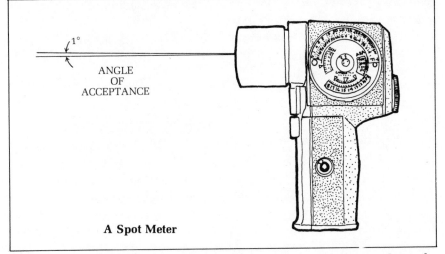

1°

ANGLE
OF
ACCEPTANCE

A Spot Meter

weighted readings, others take averaged readings, and some only read a spot in the center of the viewfinder. When a meter is *center-weighted*, 60 percent of its sensitivity is concentrated in the center area of the viewing screen. *Averaging meters* take even readings from the entire viewing screen.

Spot meters are hand-held meters which read only a spot in the center of a viewing screen incorporated in the meter body. They can take light readings for as little as a half-degree arc. Sitting in the audience of a large hall, you can aim a spot meter at a performer on the stage and get an accurate reading of the light on his or her face. Honeywell-Pentax and Minolta both make excellent spot meters.

The Gossen Luna-Pro is probably the best universal hand-held meter. It provides both reflected and incident light readings, is well built, and remains accurate at extremely low light levels. Its angle of acceptance is 30 degrees, about the same as that of an 85mm lens, but it has a number of attachments which can be used to change the angle.

Meters vary in the way information is transferred from the meter face to the calculator dial. Some meters use a series of lines to relate the light level indicated by the needle to the calculator dial, with its *f*/stops and shutter speed markings. You line up the arrow on the calculator dial with the line indicated by the meter needle. Other meters use integers; a meter needle might point to the number 18, and you have to rotate the calculator dial until its arrow points to 18. Each meter on the market has its own system of integers, so that a reading of 18 on the Gossen Luna-Pro might be equivalent to 15 on the Weston, or to A, B, C, or D on another brand.

If you decide to use the Zone System, which is described later in the book, there are two meters on the market whose calculator dials are well suited to using zones: the Pentax 1-degree Spotmeter and the Weston line. The dials on these meters allow you to see all the integers at once, so that you can determine at a glance their relationship to Zone 5. In addition, there are special plastic overlays marked with zones which can be placed on the dial of the Weston or Pentax.

All meters are prone to inaccuracy, and this is especially true of the delicate built-ins. I know some photographers who simply won't trust the built-ins, but I must say that in fourteen years of photography I've never owned two meters of any sort which read exactly alike over their entire range from light to dark. It's this kind of problem which supports the statement that photography is not an exact science.

ACCESSORIES
Tripods and Other Stabilizers

There are some situations where a shaking camera destroys the image. If you find you've got a propensity for using long lenses, taking close-ups or still lifes, or shooting in low-light situations, then a *tripod* will be essential.

A good tripod costs seventy or eighty dollars or more. It should be heavy and sturdy, but also portable. With a good tripod, you can place the camera at floor level or extend it about 70 inches above the ground. This extension is accomplished with telescoping legs and a rising center column.

Some tripod legs are round tubes; others are rectangular. The round legs are locked in place with threaded rings that create friction; the rectangular legs are locked with set screws which also create friction. It

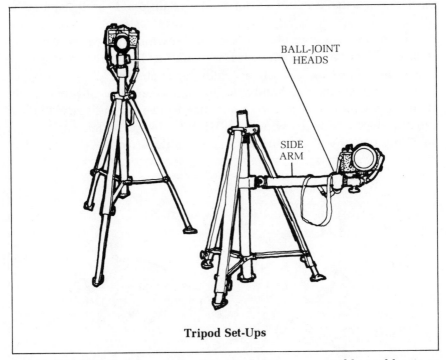

BALL-JOINT
HEADS

SIDE
ARM

Tripod Set-Ups

seems that threaded screws tend to wear out more quickly and begin to stick after a period of time, but if you buy a well-made tripod this shouldn't be a problem.

The simplest, cheapest tripods have rubber feet; the better models have spikes along with the rubber so that the tripod can be stabilized into the earth or a rug.

There are two different type tripod heads. One is called a *tilt/pan head*; the tilt and pan movements are controlled by separate levers. The other is a *ball joint* which can move in an infinite number of directions using one locking control; I feel it's the better alternative because it is more flexible. Some tripods take an accessory called the *side arm*, which extends out from the center post and increases the tripod's flexibility considerably.

The Tilt-All and Quickset Husky are the two most popular tripods. They're very sturdy, but because they don't have a ball-joint head or provision for a side arm, I feel they aren't very flexible. Gitzo sells a very good tripod in a modular package that can be assembled with a ball-joint head and takes a side arm.

I had my tripod modified by a camera repairman. He filled the center column with molten lead to increase its weight and sliced off the top of the column so that it could accommodate a ball-joint head instead of the tilt/pan.

There are a number of other accessories which can serve as camera stabilizers. The table-top tripod is less than a foot high and can be used to brace the camera on table tops, walls, or even your chest. Ordinary beanbags are sometimes handy for holding a long lens steady. For instance, a photographer covering a parade from a second-story window can put a beanbag on the window sill, rest his telephoto lens on top, and smoothly pan along with the movement on the street. With a modified

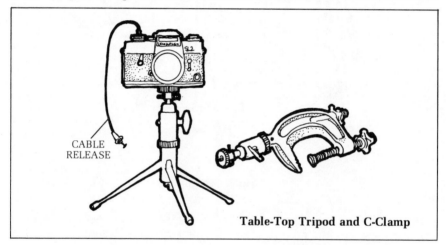

CABLE
RELEASE

Table-Top Tripod and C-Clamp

C-clamp you can attach the camera to shelves, doors, or any other available surface. These devices were popularized by *National Geographic* and *Life* photographers who used long lenses for special situations such as moon shots and nature studies.

Filters

Filters are colored pieces of optical glass that screw onto the front of the lens. They alter the color characteristics of the light entering the camera and thus change the way in which different colors are recorded on film. While they are quite useful in color work, it's my feeling that they are not essential to black and white photography (though there are black and white photographers who employ filters almost all of the time). They lighten objects of their own color and darken objects of complementary colors, so orange and yellow filters make blues darker and thus heighten the contrast between blue sky and white clouds in a black and white photograph. Orange and yellow filters are used mostly by architectural and landscape photographers.

The *skylight* or *1A filter* is good for protecting your lens; better *it* should get shattered by a flying pebble than the much more expensive front element in your lens. The skylight filter is designed to cut down ultraviolet light, which is invisible to the human eye but records blue on color film.

You can also buy a variety of special effect filters; for example, there are filters that diffuse or soften the image and filters that put stars in all of the highlights. (If you want to diffuse the image, a nylon stocking over the lens will also do the job.) Polarizing filters are used to eliminate glare from nonmetallic surfaces and also to darken blue skies without altering other colors.

Because they are not transparent, filters cut down the amount of light which travels to the film. Therefore you must compensate by applying a filter factor which is indicated in the instruction sheet that comes with the filter. For example, if a filter has a filter factor of 2, you must double the exposure. An advantage of the built-in, through-the-lens meters is that they compensate for the change in light level for you—they read the light after it has gone through the filter and indicate the appropriate exposure.

One of the nice things about Nikkor lenses is that most of those from 24 to 200mm have a threaded ring at the front which measures 52mm across. This means that you can buy one filter to fit all of your lenses. If all your filters are the same size, you can carry them around screwed into one another and protected by "stack caps." The latter are available from mail order houses like Spiratone in New York—see the back pages of any photo magazine. If you have lenses with different size front rings, you can buy *step-up* and *step-down rings* to make them accommodate one size filter. But again, these are extra accessories to bother with and carry around.

Lens Hoods

You'll need a *lens hood* for each of your lenses to keep the glancing sun from blinding them. You can get lens hoods that screw onto the lens; avoid the horrible reversible hoods. The latter reverse so that they can be stored on the lens when the camera is not in use, but their springs wear thin and they have a tendency to fall off the lens. I learned this lesson while covering a sensitive Washington, D.C. press conference. During one silent, tense moment, the hood slipped off my camera and went boyng, boyng, boyng, drawing pointed stares. If you've already got a reversible hood, you might try taping it to the lens.

Soft-Touch Release

One tool that can help overcome jerking the camera at the moment of exposure is the *soft-touch release*. It costs about $2 and if you own a Nikon, you'll need to buy one specifically engineered for that brand. The soft-touch release fits onto the shutter release and is designed to keep your finger up and away from the camera.

Close-Up Attachments

When your lens is attached directly to the camera, it can only focus to within a certain, minimum distance from your camera. Some lenses focus

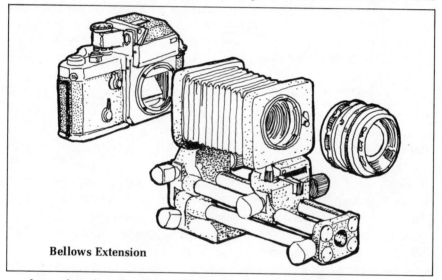

Bellows Extension

no closer than four feet, others three feet, and so on. *Extension tubes* and *bellows* are devices which you can put between the camera and the lens to allow you to get closer to the subject.

An extension tube is a thick ring which is fairly convenient to use and fits onto the camera easily. The bellows is adjustable so that it can place the lens at varying distances from the body; it is a much bigger, bulkier piece of equipment, but it can bring you a lot closer to the subject than the extension tube.

These devices are meant to be used exclusively for close-ups. When they are attached to the camera, you can't focus beyond a few feet from the lens.

Because these devices move the lens away from the body, they

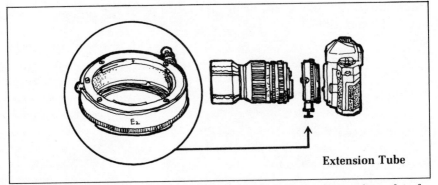

Extension Tube

require an increase in exposure. Again, the built-in meter does this for you. If you don't have a built-in, you can refer to the guidelines etched on the bellows or make an estimate—a real pain.

Focusing Screens

Some manufacturers, including Nikon, offer interchangeable ground glass, or *focusing screens*. There are about fifteen from which to choose, the majority of them used in such specialized fields as architectural photography and photomicrography. A number, however, provide alternatives for photographers with varying tastes in focusing guides.

The three commonly used focusing screens are the *split-image*, *microprism*, and the *matte center spot* screen. They differ simply in the type of focusing guide provided at the center of the screen. When a subject is out of focus with the split-image, any straight lines in that subject which fall in the center of the screen will not match up from top to bottom. With the microprism, out-of-focus subjects are fragmented into diamonds

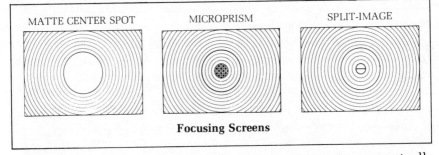

MATTE CENTER SPOT   MICROPRISM   SPLIT-IMAGE

Focusing Screens

which disappear when you focus. The matte center spot screen actually has no focusing aid and you've got to judge how sharp the subject looks.

The matte center spot is often preferred by working photographers because there's nothing in the viewfinder to distract them from composing the image. However, it's very difficult to use in low-light situations and with wide-angle lenses. With the split-image, the problem is that your subject must have a straight line in it and that half of the center spot goes dark if you are using a slow lens or shooting in dim light. The microprism seems to be a reasonable compromise.

Most focusing screens have *Fresnel rings* etched on the glass. These are concentric rings that radiate from the center to the outer edges. They are designed to increase the efficiency of the outer edges of the ground glass in transferring light to the viewfinder.

CARE AND MAINTENANCE

Once you have invested a few hundred dollars in equipment, you'll want to keep it. There are a number of common-sense precautions you can take to make sure that someone else doesn't walk off with it. Also, there are a few things you can do to keep it in good shape.

Please get your camera insured. Camera equipment can be included in the coverage provided by a homeowner's policy. If you use your camera as a professional tool, it is worth your while to purchase special insurance. Check with your insurance agent.

Don't leave your camera in the car, especially where it can be seen. It's particularly vulnerable to theft when left behind in a parked car near a camera shop; thieves haunt the stores looking for opportunities like that. Also, surprisingly enough, one of the most common ways to lose equipment is to leave it behind after a particularly nerve-wracking shoot.

It's a good idea to use an unobtrusive bag to carry your equipment instead of the traditional camera kit. A canvas bag works well, and Leitz makes a good one. Many working photographers use the everything-proof Halliburton suitcases which are made of aluminum and hold cameras and accessories in foam and rubber. But they are bulky and clumsy for fast-breaking situations.

Occasionally you will want to check the tiny screws on the outside of the camera and lens. If you use your equipment a lot, you should tighten them every so often, because they tend to work themselves loose. A jeweler's screwdriver is the best tool for this.

Another good tool is a paintbrush about 1½-2″ wide that can be used to dust off the cracks and crevices in the exterior of the camera body. Don't use the brush on the lens. In fact, you should really avoid cleaning the lens too much. Overcleaning is worse than having dust or fingerprints on the lens, and constant wiping or brushing can scratch the lens coating. Dust is fairly inconsequential—working photographers tend not to worry about the first layer or so. If your lens does get really dirty, you can use Kodak lens cleaner and tissue, but use them sparingly and follow the directions on the package. The idea is to avoid abrasion of the glass and coating.

KEEP YOUR CAMERA QUICK-DRAW

Most photographers are really into their equipment. They enjoy the gunslinger feel of it—the way it fits snugly in their hand and the way it moves with their body. If you want to keep your camera neat and quick-draw, first get rid of that hard, "never-ready" case they sold you. Get a soft leather strap like the Strapateer, with "split-O" rings to secure the camera. Beware of plastic straps; they handle like garden hoses. Also, it's best to get rid of the lens cap. It just slows you down. Most working photographers don't bother with a front lens cap, as the screw-in lens hood and skylight filter provide enough protection. If you have more than one lens, protect the rear element of any lens floating around in your camera bag by using a rear lens cap.

The point is that these cameras are tools, made to be used. They've lived through wars, incursions, and riots, and don't need to be wrapped up and protected between photos. Design your camera system to be clean, simple, and ready to use.

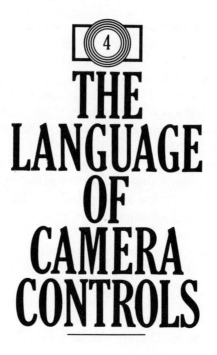

THE LANGUAGE OF CAMERA CONTROLS

The first step in gaining control of the camera is learning to think in the language of *f*/stops and shutter speeds. The terminology used in reference to these two controls rivals chess notation or classic Latin in its ability to create confusion. But once you get beyond the terminology there are only a few basic maneuvers involving the two controls, and they are very easy to understand and carry out.

The primary function of *f*/stops and shutter speeds is to regulate the amount of light which hits, or exposes, the film. Film responds properly when a certain amount of light strikes it. Yet the world we photograph varies considerably in the amount of light available at any given moment. When taking a picture, you first measure available light with your exposure meter and then manipulate *f*/stop and/or shutter speed to provide just the right amount of light needed for a proper exposure. (Techniques for using the exposure meter and learning to interpret the reading will be discussed thoroughly in Chapter 8.) In low-light situations, such as a dark café, the photographer will manipulate f/stop and shutter speed to allow the faint glow of light to hit the film for a long period of time. In bright-light situations, such as a sunny beach at midday, he restricts the incoming light so that the brilliant flash of sunlight strikes the film for a brief instant.

Various types of film differ in their response to light; some films need more light to obtain the proper exposure than others. The sensitivity of a film to light is called *film speed*, or *ASA* (a rating established by the American Standards Association). It is marked on each box of film and must be set on your exposure meter. The higher the ASA number, the greater the film's sensitivity and the less light it requires for proper exposure. Tri-X is a black and white film with ASA 400—a relatively fast film. Panatomic-X is a black and white film with ASA 32; it is less sensitive to light—a much slower film. Film speed's relationship to f/stop and shutter speed will be further discussed in this chapter and in Chapter 6.

THE RELATIONSHIP OF *F*/STOP, SHUTTER SPEED, AND ASA

There's a classic analogy used to describe camera controls: exposing film properly is like filling a glass of water from a tap. The glass represents the film. The capacity of the glass is the proper exposure, and the water from the faucet is light. It takes a certain amount of water to fill the glass, just as it takes a certain amount of light to expose the film. The extent to which you open the tap is analogous to choice of f/stop; the length of time you leave the tap open is comparable to shutter speed. You can fill the glass by opening the faucet all the way for a short time or by opening it just a bit for a longer time. In the same way, you may choose a wide-open aperture and a fast shutter speed or you can stop down the aperture all the way and select a slow shutter speed. (Remember that the integers on the aperture control ring and shutter speed dial refer to fractions, so the higher the integer, the less light admitted to the film.)

For example: a relatively slow shutter speed and small aperture would be a 4th of a second at f/16 (spoken "a fourth at sixteen")—a long trickle of light. However, the same amount of light would be admitted to the film by a setting of a 125th at f/2.8 ("a hundred and twenty-fifth at two eight")—a brief torrent of light. Exposure equals time multiplied by intensity ($E = T \times I$, where T is shutter speed and I is the brightness of the subject as modified by the f/stop). This is called the *Law of Reciprocity*.

In the following discussion, it will be helpful to follow the f/stop–shutter speed maneuvers with your camera in hand, actually referring to the dials on the camera. There's no need to count out f/stops and shutter speeds in your head; simply take advantage of the increments marked on your camera.

The essential thing to remember about f/stops and shutter speeds is that they have a one-to-one relationship. If you change the shutter speed one increment faster, you should change the f/stop one increment wider in order to let in the same amount of light and maintain the same exposure. For example, a 15th of a second at f/5.6 gives the same exposure as an 8th at f/8. Again, look at the f/stop and shutter speed dials on your camera and see this relationship as you turn the dials. Set them at a 15th at f/5.6. Change a 15th to an 8th, the next speed slower. Because there is a one-to-one relationship, you can maintain the same exposure by then changing the aperture to f/8, one stop smaller.

Try a 125th at f/2.8 on your camera. The following combinations will all give the same exposure: a 60th at f/4, a 30th at f/5.6, and a 15th at f/8. So will a progression of other combinations you can find by moving the dials one unit at a time in opposite directions.

Read those last two paragraphs again, looking at your camera for reference, until you understand this concept. If you own a hand-held exposure meter like the Gossen, you can see this relationship expressed clearly in the f/stop–shutter speed combinations marked on the calculator dial. (This is one advantage of the hand-held meters over the built-ins.) Press the depth-of-field preview button and look through the front of the lens. Watch the diaphragm close down or open up as you rotate the aperture control ring. To see shutter speed increase and decrease, open the back of the camera and watch the shutter move as you release the shutter at different speed settings.

A unit change in f/stop and/or shutter speed is called a *stop*. In the common parlance of photography, to let in more light you "open up" a stop or two or three or however many you decide upon. To let in less light you "stop down." The word "stop" is used whether you use the diaphragm or shutter speed to effect the change. If your camera is set for a 60th at f/4, you can open up one stop either by leaving the shutter speed at a 60th and changing the aperture to f/2.8 or by leaving the aperture at f/4 and changing the shutter speed to a 30th. In either case, you have let in one more stop of light. Every time you open up a stop, you let in twice as much light as before; every time you close down a stop, you let in half as much light.

At this point, you can see that there are only three basic maneuvers you can make with f/stop and shutter speed: by changing either one or both of the controls, you can admit more light to the camera, admit less light, or maintain the same amount of light.

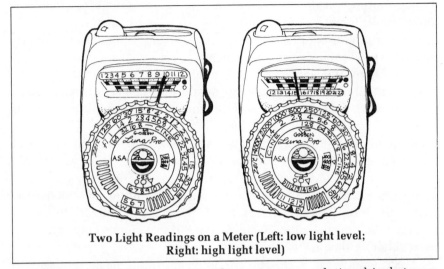

Two Light Readings on a Meter (Left: low light level; Right: high light level)

Film speed also figures into the one-to-one relationship between f/stop and shutter speed. Every time the ASA is halved, you need one more stop of light to expose that film properly. And conversely, each time you double the ASA, you need one less stop of light. For example, if the proper exposure for a film with ASA 400 is a 250th at f/8, then the equivalent exposure in the same lighting situation for a film with ASA 200 is a 250th at f/5.6. For film with ASA 100, it would be a 250th at f/4. This calculation is done for you when you set ASA on the meter.

HOW TO SELECT A SETTING

Your first step in choosing an f/stop–shutter speed combination is to determine the light level of the subject as indicated on your exposure meter. Again, the actual use of the meter and interpretation of light readings are dealt with at length in Chapter 8.

When taking a light reading with the built-in meter you'll see that there are any number of f/stop–shutter speed combinations that will keep the needle centered, indicating proper exposure. If you're using a hand-held meter you'll see at a glance on the dial a number of f/stop–shutter speed settings. These stops are all equivalent and are possibilities from which you can choose a setting. At certain light levels—very bright or very dark—and with certain film speeds there will be only a few practical combinations from which to choose, while at others there will be a broad selection.

Which Shutter Speed Do You Want?

The first thing you should consider in making a choice is shutter speed.

Higher shutter speeds are needed to counteract the effects of *camera shake*. Shake is the single most pervasive problem in achieving a sharp image; with hand-held cameras, in almost every photograph there are signs of at least some camera movement.

The higher the shutter speed, the less time there is for shake to be recorded on film. But high speeds are not the only answer to the vibration problem, and a large portion of the next chapter explains various techniques you can use to control it.

Camera shake is a serious problem at speeds below a 30th and less of a problem at speeds of a 125th and up, depending on the lens you are using. Telephoto lenses magnify your shake transgressions and wide-angles minimize them. A rule of thumb is to use a shutter speed at least as high as the focal length of the lens: a 60th for the 50mm, 125th for the 105mm, 250th for the 200mm, and so on. But experience may show you are steadier or shakier than this rule assumes.

For camera work without a tripod or electronic flash, the issue of shutter speed is so important that you must tailor your shooting around it. You just won't come back with the picture unless you use a shutter speed to suit the conditions. For example, if you are going to photograph backstage, you can assume that you'll have a problem getting enough light for proper exposure. The faster the film, the higher the shutter speeds you can use; so you should bring fast film with you—for example, Tri-X, a very fast, general purpose film. If you think you'll be shooting slower than a 30th, then carry a tripod or electronic flash with you.

Another consideration in choosing shutter speed is the desire to intentionally blur or freeze your subject in motion. If you want a moving subject blurred, it will take some experimentation with slower shutter speeds, and you should hold the camera steady. If you want the moving subject sharp and the background blurred, pan with the subject and again use slow shutter speeds. If it's stopped action you want, hummingbirds will require higher shutter speeds than slugs. And remember that a subject moving directly toward you will not require as high a shutter speed as something traveling across your field of vision. One technique for freezing motion is to try and capture the peak of action—for example, a high jumper exactly between up and down. Good luck.

Which *F*/Stop Should You Use?

When you change the size of the aperture, you do more than simply change the amount of light entering the camera. You change the way the final picture will look by changing the depth of field. A picture taken at $f/2.8$ will appear different from one taken at $f/16$; the former will look softer while the latter will be crisper. Thus, *f*/stops are graphic, artistic controls. But when high shutter speed is needed to counteract camera shake, *f*/stop necessarily becomes a secondary consideration.

Actually, choice of *f*/stop affects the appearance of a photograph in two ways: it influences depth of field and the lens' ability to resolve detail.

F/STOP AND DEPTH OF FIELD

Remember from the second chapter that depth of field varies with the size of the aperture, the focal length of the lens, the distance between subject and camera, and the size of the final print relative to the viewing distance. Therefore, choice of *f*/stop is simply one way in which you can alter depth of field.

There are tables which can tell you precisely how much depth of field you'll have with a particular lens focused at a specific distance from your subject and set at a given *f*/stop. But if you're a journalist standing five feet from a great picture, you don't stop to consult depth-of-field tables. There are more obvious considerations to be made first. You tend to work a certain distance from people—usually about seven feet away, sometimes an intimate five feet, and occasionally a cold ten or twelve feet. At these distances, the primary graphic choice is which focal length lens to use. Do you want a tight head shot or a more inclusive environmental portrait—telephoto, wide-angle, or in between? Having made that choice and needing enough shutter speed to fight camera shake, you'll find you're lucky indeed if you have a choice of three or four viable *f*/stop–shutter speed combinations. Now that possible range of combinations translates into a very subtle difference in image quality in the print. "Ah, yes, *f*/5.6 . . . I'd recognize it anywhere," is not a common observation. What is more apparent in the final print is your choice of focal length.

In practice, with a given lens, your choice of *f*/stop will influence the overall firmness or crispness of the image. When I use the terms "firm" and "crisp" I step away from classic photo language and probably horrify countless photographers who see depth of field in terms of mathematical formulas and calculations. It may be simplistic, but in my experience an understanding of depth of field as related to *f*/stop comes down to the knowledge that the *f*/stop you choose will determine how firm and crisp your image will be. If you want your picture to be amorphous and soft and gentle, you know that you should open the aperture as much as possible; if you want to firm up the lines and speak more strongly, you should stop down.

With an SLR camera there are two ways to check depth of field. The first is the depth-of-field *preview button,* which you can use to see the differences in crispness which various *f*/stops provide. (Remember that for ease of focusing, the lens remains wide open until you release the shutter.) The preview button manually stops down the camera to the aperture setting you have chosen, allowing you to see the effects on ground glass. For example, if you set the aperture at *f*/16, look through the viewfinder, and then push the preview button, the amorphous image on the ground glass will become firm and crisp. It will also look much darker, which is one problem with using this button. But please persevere—look through the darkness and watch the effect on the overall rendering of the image when you push and then release the button. Before you press the button, you are seeing the image with the aperture wide open. By pressing it, you get a view of the image at *f*/16. It helps to push the button several times in succession to see the difference in image quality. I use this device often, not only to see how the *f*/stop will render the image, but also as a substitute for squinting at the scene—to get an idea of the patterns of darks and lights in the picture and their relative strengths.

The second depth-of-field indicator is the set of colored lines matched up with the distance scale on the top of the lens near the focusing ring. The lines are color-coded to match the *f*/stop numbers on the lens and provide a rough guide to the depth of field at a given focus. This is the only immediate indicator of depth of field for the rangefinder user, but most rangefinder-users rely more on experience.

If you are photographing a moving subject and can predict its movements—for example, a sprinter at a track event—then you can determine a zone of focus using the distance scale and color-coded lines, and release the shutter when he passes through that zone.

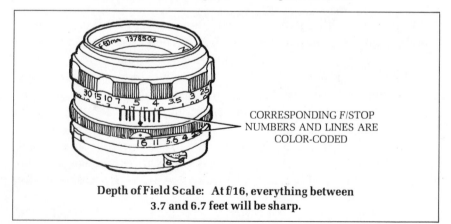

CORRESPONDING F/STOP NUMBERS AND LINES ARE COLOR-CODED

Depth of Field Scale: At f/16, everything between 3.7 and 6.7 feet will be sharp.

The colored lines and distance scale are based on the circles of confusion in an 8″x10″ print; also, they do not indicate abruptness of change in depth of field. If you are shooting with a wide-angle lens, the scale will tell you the zone that will be acceptably sharp; however, the area outside that zone will also be pretty sharp. With a telephoto lens, the depth of field indicated by the distance scale will be the only sharp part of the picture; the area outside the depth of field will become very unsharp quite abruptly. Looking at the distance scale will not tell you this.

The distance scale and lines are also useful in determining *hyper-focal distance*, the point at which to focus the lens for the most depth of field (to infinity) at any given *f*/stop. As you look down at the lens, put the infinity mark (∞) on the left indicator line that is colored the same as the *f*/stop you've chosen. The picture will be sharp from infinity to the distance indicated by the same colored line on the right. I can't remember when I used these color codes last.

F/STOP AND LENS PERFORMANCE

The second way in which *f*/stop helps determine image sharpness is through its relationship to lens performance. Every lens works best at a particular *f*/stop—usually two stops down from wide open. This is called the *optimum f/stop*. When a lens is used wide open, detail in the image is resolved relatively poorly in the center and even worse at the edges; the image is also low in apparent contrast and prone to degradation by flare and aberrations. This is because you are using the entire surface of the glass in the lens to conduct light. As you begin to stop down, however, the blades of the diaphragm restrict the path of the light through the optimum section of the glass, avoiding the extreme edges of the lens, where the glass is less precise optically. The result is an increase in the resolving ability of the lens. The corners of the film frame will never be as sharp as the center, but over the range of the three middle stops on your lens, you're getting the best possible definition and contrast. As you continue to stop the lens down to its smallest apertures, you again lose some definition because of *defraction*, or excessive bending of light rays traveling through a small hole.

A TRIP THROUGH THE LIGHT LEVELS

To start you thinking in *f*/stops and shutter speeds, and to give you an idea of what considerations you make as you choose an *f*/stop–shutter speed combination, we'll take a hypothetical journey through the light levels from darkness to bright sunlight.

I suggest you follow this journey with an exposure meter and a camera. Set the meter at ASA 400, the speed of Tri-X, used as an example because it is a popular film and has a long usable range. Although I'll be suggesting f/stop and shutter speed changes in terms of full stops, you should be aware that with f/stops you can make changes in terms of a fraction of a stop. For instance, you can set the control ring between f/5.6 and f/8. However, with all but the newest cameras, you must always change shutter speed by a full unit; you can't set the dial in between a 60th and a 125th, for example.

Start by adjusting your camera to a 30th at f/1.4—a setting appropriate with this film for the light level in a dark room. This is generally considered to be the lowest exposure feasible for hand-held work; lower exposures suggest a tripod to counteract the effects of shake. You're restricted to a 50mm or 35mm f/1.4 lens (if you can afford the latter), because there aren't any telephoto lenses as fast as f/1.4 and, if there were, the shutter speed would be too slow (remember the rule of thumb about using shutter speeds greater than the focal length of the lens). Also, there aren't any other wide-angles as fast as f/1.4. Actually, a 30th is a marginal shutter speed for a normal lens. Also, f/1.4 allows us the least possible definition of the image and a very limited depth of field.

Adjust the calculator dial to give you one more stop of light. Now you have a choice between a 60th at f/1.4 and a 30th at f/2. You are still basically restricted to 50mm and some shorter lenses, and your depth of field remains marginal. If I were confident of my ability to hold the camera still at a 30th, I'd go with a 30th at f/2 and thereby try to start improving the performance of the lens.

Go up another stop. This is a common light level indoors. Now you have a choice of a 125th at f/1.4, a 60th at f/2, and a 30th at f/2.8. Although you still can't use the f/2.5, 105mm lens, a 60th at f/2 with the 85mm might be passable. You are beginning to gain the option of greater depth of field and definition with the normal and shorter lenses because you have a choice of f/stops. You might consider using a 125th at f/1.4 to capture something fast and dark. Otherwise, a 60th at f/2 or a 30th at f/2.8 are both reasonable exposures.

Another stop gives you a 250th at f/1.4, 125th at f/2, 60th at f/2.8, and 30th at f/4. I'd forget the first choice unless you need the speed, because the f/stop has so little to offer. The latter three increments are all adequate. The f/2.8 setting will probably reflect the best image quality, assuming you hold the camera steady, because it is the optimum f/stop for the normal lens. If you are shooting with an f/2, 35mm lens, then f/4 would be the optimum setting and you can try the slower speed.

The sun has risen another notch and you have another stop to play with. There is a 500th at f/1.4, 250th at f/2, 125th at f/2.8, 60th at f/4, and

30th at *f*/5.6—five settings. I'd eliminate the first two stops unless I had a special purpose in mind; the rest are all valid, and you have the luxury of choosing, including the entry of a 125th at *f*/2.8, which is the minimum 105mm lens exposure. If you are using a 105mm lens, don't be afraid to use it wide open, at *f*/2.8. None of the brand-name moderate telephoto lenses look bad wide open, and the type of photo often associated with this lens is the soft portrait, which is ideally suited to the less sharply defined look of the wide open aperture.

Another stop up brings us to a 1000th at *f*/1.4, through five choices to a 30th at *f*/8, which you might use for a depth of field problem. This is an embarrassment of riches, including two usable telephoto settings.

The next stop affords us six settings, if your camera has a 2000th. We gain *f*/11 at a 30th, which is usable for the normal and wide-angle lenses. But you'd really have to need depth of field to choose this latter exposure; *f*/11 in the faster lenses begins to provide less definition, and a 30th is a risky shutter speed. At this light level, you get the choice of sharper *f*/stops for the 105mm lens; a 250th at *f*/4 is an ideal exposure for that lens.

One more stop and you lose *f*/2 and gain *f*/16. Any of the available settings is good for the normal and wide-angle lenses, especially a 125th at *f*/8 and a 250th at *f*/5.6. A 500th at *f*/4 will deliver absolutely optimum sharpness from that 105mm, and a 1000th at *f*/2.8 is a good setting for freezing motion.

From now on, each stop increase in light will rob your range of choices by one stop. Higher and higher light levels force you to use the smaller *f*/stops to avoid overexposing the film.

The next light level gives us a 1000th at *f*/4 at one end—a fine exposure for fighting shake and attaining optimum definition—and a 60th at *f*/16 at the other. Generally speaking, the latter setting is a degrading one. Most modern lenses stop at *f*/16 or *f*/22 because the definition of the image at the next stops down is of such poor quality. (There are exceptions. The longer telephotos are efficient down to *f*/32. The high quality Nikkor 55mm Macro is so well engineered that the tiny aperture does not detract from image sharpness. Some huge lenses that are made for 8x10 or larger cameras don't even start until *f*/11, with *f*/22 optimum and *f*/90 the limit. Photographers such as Edward Weston and Ansel Adams, who used large view cameras and small stops, were members of "The *f*/64 Club.")

The next four stop increases push us further and further until we are left with a 1000th at *f*/16, a most restrictive position. This situation occurs with Tri-X in bright sunlight, as in a beach scene or on the glaring streets of Los Angeles. With slower films, you won't run out of choices at this high level of light. For example, Kodachrome, with its ASA of 25, would give you a five-stop range, from a 30th at $f/22$ to a 1000th at $f/4$.

If you see a trend in all of these selections, it should be toward the higher shutter speed and optimum f/stop. Where there are several choices, the final selection should be made on the basis of aesthetic considerations. For once you have reached a shutter speed fast enough to deal with camera shake and have a choice of middle-range f/stops, you are free to play with depth of field, altering the crispness of image to suit the particular photograph.

SHARPNESS—AN OVERVIEW

It's important to realize that holding the camera steady and choosing the proper f/stop are not the only elements which will affect the clarity of the final print. Sharpness is not something that can be measured with complete objectivity; it is dependent on psychological as well as physical variables. Some photographs strike the eye as sharp because of the juxtaposition and quality of the light or the texture of the subject, even though the lens and film did not perform as well as they might have. For instance, a photo of harsh sunlight glancing along the slats of a picket fence feels sharper than a shot of undulating sand dunes in a fog. You expect sharp edges on the fence, and the rapid changes from white slats to dark spaces seem sharper than the gradual luminescence of the fog. It is the impression of sharpness that helps make the picture of the fence appear more clearly defined than that of the dunes.

Sharpness of image is not necessarily something you'll need to achieve in every photograph. Some pictures that aren't sharp work perfectly well. It depends on the particular subject and the mood you want to communicate. For example, if you are shooting machinery, you will probably want a sharp image. People looking at machines expect to see milled, planed edges and sharp, clear details. If the picture is unsharp, it probably will be disturbing. However, if you are taking a picture of a diaphanous maiden running through the forest, you may not want her to appear sharp. So use your intuition when you approach a picture and manipulate the factors which control sharpness.

In general, most photographs you take will be less than perfectly sharp. Perfect sharpness is likely to occur only under the most controlled conditions. To give you an idea of just how sharp your pictures can be and what is involved in exacting maximum sharpness from your camera, I'm going to recommend a test. Once you've seen how sharp a picture taken under good conditions can look, you'll understand how much camera shake and other factors can degrade an image.

Ideally, you'd want to use a high-speed commercial *strobe* for this test—an electronic flash which can give off light for a two thousandth of a second, virtually freezing motion. The camera catches the subject only during this brief instant of illumination, and in this instant there is no time for shake to be recorded. If for some reason you can't raise the money necessary to purchase one of these strobes or are unable to rent or borrow one, you can take the poor man's test, using the sun. This is probably more practical, since you are interested in seeing what your camera can do under the finest conditions you are likely to encounter in the real world.

For a subject, try a weathered, rugged male who hasn't shaved for a few days. You'll want the wrinkles and detail around his eyes, the pores in his skin, and each hair in his beard to be sharp. You'll need a bright day, your camera, a meter, Tri-X or Plus-X film, a telephoto lens if you have one (a normal if you don't), a substantial tripod, and a barn. If you

Sharpness Test

don't have a barn, look for a building that shades you and your subject from the direct rays of the sun so that you have a full, open sky behind you. The surface of the barn provides a warm, semidark backdrop to complement your subject's skin textures. Don't use a brick building, for its out-of-focus roughness would only compete with the face. A concrete wall wouldn't be good either because its light color would tend to wash out the overall impression of tones, hence sharpness.

You'll be taking a straight-on, full-face portrait. Set the camera on the tripod and position your friend so that he is comfortably immobile—for instance, sitting on a stool or leaning back against the wall. Your exposure should be about a 500th at *f*/5.6, just right for the optimum *f*/stop if you are using a telephoto lens. The combination of high shutter speed and tripod will hold shake to a minimum. Focus very carefully on the *catch lights* (reflections of the light source, in this case skylight) in his eyes and shoot off a few frames.

Does the final print look sharp? It should. You have maximized the physical and psychological factors that produce sharpness.

At this point, you should be conversant in the language of f/stops and shutter speeds and understand their one-to-one relationship to each other and to ASA. Hopefully, you've got a grasp on their influence over the final print, especially the f/stop's aesthetic impact and shutter speed's ability to counteract blur from camera shake. And after that trip through the light levels, you should also have an idea of the kind of decisions that go into selecting one setting over another. Chapter 8 deals exclusively with exposure and will provide the method for choosing the proper setting to achieve the proper exposure.

5
CAMERA
TECHNIQUE

I n one sense, film carries out its image-making function completely
oblivious of the photographer's intentions. As yet, there is no complete explanation for silver halides' reaction to light, but the transfor-
mation to metallic silver occurs time and time again, despite our
ignorance of the process. So in a philosophical sense, photography exists
by itself as an optical/chemical process. While the photographer can
achieve a high degree of control over it, he can never totally master it.

Even a skilled photographer armed with all the technology available today realizes that there is room for variation in every step of the
photographic process and that he can only control the variation to a
certain extent. There are so many steps in the process, each one exerting
its own particular influence over the final print, that he needs a bit of intuition to keep them all in rein. The studio photographer, with a large
format camera, controlled lighting, and all the other advantages of
a studio situation, has a relatively high degree of control. The photojournalist, working with available light and fleeting situations, has a
much more difficult time regulating all the variables. But no matter what

the photographic style, the photographer never really knows precisely how all the various factors will add up in the final print.

LEARNING TO SET THE TRAP

For the photojournalist, truly alive photographs are very often happy accidents resulting from well-laid traps.

A trap is well set when the photographer is familiar with his subject and his equipment. He can handle the camera confidently so that almost every shot is technically lucid. He understands that the camera sees the world in a special way and is aware of the limitations of his own perception. He uses all of this information to stalk the exciting picture.

For our purposes, then, camera technique is setting the trap. More explicitly, it is the whole process of taking a picture up to and including releasing the shutter. Once you become more comfortable with your camera, you will be able to eliminate or minimize the reasons for disappointment and allow for the happy accidents—the spontaneity that makes great 35mm photography. Camera technique is learning to take care of each technical problem, so that when that shot comes by you'll be prepared.

In addition to technique, your mind's eye and the way you see the world will influence the appearance of the final print. This is the province of you the artist and is outside the realm of this book. Nevertheless, you have a style, an individuality, which is brought to bear at the moment of exposure. Part of this whole you, for example, is the extent of your knowledge about graphic communication. If you are a visual sophisticate, if you know your own eye and what you want in a picture, you'll have certain expectations about the results—and you'll know enough to be often disappointed. If, on the other hand, you consider yourself a complete beginner, unsure of your intentions and unschooled in the wiles of art, initially you'll photograph out of a fog, almost by trial and error. Gradually your technique will improve and your style will begin to reveal itself. Whatever the extent of your graphic knowledge, though, the point remains that your personality, education, environment, breakfast, even your glands, your dreams, your sense of the instant, and your astrological sign—everything you are—will influence your photographic style.

INVESTING A LOT OF TIME AND EFFORT
FOR SMALL, IMPORTANT RETURNS

In striving for quality in your photographs, you will find that the search is governed by the law of diminishing returns. Anybody can pick up a camera, follow the instruction book, and take perfectly respectable, ordinary shapshots. But realizing the full potential of your medium requires a lot more effort, and the returns will come gradually and subtly. You will find that some gains are rather immediate—for example, refinements in technique that minimize camera shake. However, once you have reached a high level of mediocrity, additional improvements in technique will only gradually translate into improvements in the final print.

OVERCOMING YOUR FEARS ABOUT THE CAMERA

The first step in establishing a good working relationship with your camera is to take it off its pedestal. You may have spent several hundred dollars for it, but it is money wasted if you treat your camera too delicately and protectively.

One reason a camera is so expensive is that it is engineered to withstand a good deal of use and punishment. Remember that these machines have recorded human endeavor in the most uninhabitable corners of the world. They have worked in swamps, jungles, deserts, the arctic, even on the moon. And believe me, they are severely abused by people who use them every day as professional tools.

So get over the fear of hurting the camera. Pick it up, turn it around in your hands, feel it. It's a great machine. It's like a solid piece of sculpture, with ins and outs and weight and balance.

You'll want to spend many hours practicing without film in the camera until you begin to feel at ease with it and all the mechanical aspects of technique become second nature. This dry shooting won't hurt the camera, and there's a great deal of confidence and agility to be gained.

You'll also have to overcome any hesitation to expend film. There's a natural reluctance at first to committing yourself on film, and beyond that, you may find yourself wondering what's worthy of being recorded. Practicing without film in the camera can help you overcome this kind of block; if you feel comfortable with the camera in your hand you'll be more likely to use it. Maybe you can think of using the camera the way a painter uses a sketchbook to explore themes, an approach that will mean shooting a lot of film. You'd be surprised at how many rolls of film photographers use to explore every angle of a situation. This is not to say that shooting a generous amount will insure getting a good photo; even if your technique is good, a thousand frames of a dull situation won't add up to one good picture.

It has been said that batting averages are for baseball players, not photographers. You can't think in terms of getting one good picture every fifteen frames or every two hundred. But you should give yourself as many chances as possible under the circumstances to catch that elusive, spectacular moment. As far as I'm concerned, with the 35mm camera, overshooting is the name of the game.

HAND-HELD TECHNIQUE

Hand-held technique is a journalistic style of photography; it is fast-moving and demands a blending of man and machine. Technique deals with how to move with the camera, how to think on your feet with the machine, and how to use your trigger finger. If the photographer holds the camera in his hand, it becomes part of him as he moves and relates to the subject; this contrasts with the working style of a studio photographer, who sets up his camera on a tripod and then slowly builds a picture.

As a human being, you've got a certain body language, a special way of facing others, of holding your shoulders and your arms and the rest of your body. If you are shooting with the camera in your hands, your body language is transmitted through the picture. You have to become so comfortable with the camera that it does not impede your body language, but instead flows with it.

How you feel about your subjects is also transmitted through the picture—whether you honestly empathize with them. If you approach people with respect and show them that you do not intend to manipulate them, then this will be communicated in your photographs. This is an essential concept when photographing people.

Squeezing the Trigger

As mentioned earlier, camera shake is the major difficulty to overcome in shooting, especially when you hold the camera in your hand. The most immediate problem is a tendency to punch the shutter release instead of squeezing it. Perhaps the best way to counteract this tendency to punch is to concentrate on squeezing. Keep the pressure from your finger smooth and steady as you press down; it takes about a pound of pressure. You want to depress the button in a controlled squeeze.

Dry shooting will help you get over the tendency to punch the trigger. Practice until the squeeze becomes a habit. You'll notice that there's about 2mm of slack when you press the button; learn to take up the slack with a smooth, continuous motion. Train your finger to do this now, because later, in the midst of a fast-moving situation, you won't be able to think consciously about controlling the movement of your finger.

Another technique to dampen camera movement caused by pressing the shutter is to apply counter-pressure. However you hold the camera, some part of your hand should be directly opposite the release button, so that you can apply pressure about equal to the amount needed to depress the release.

Shooting Horizontals

Learn how to build a firm, comfortable human base to support the camera. Experiment with various pockets of hand and face in which the camera can sit. Try cradling the camera in the palm of your left hand, with the pinky finger on the base plate, directly under the shutter release. This applies counterpressure to the motion of the trigger finger. The other fingers should be up around the lens. All of the weight of the camera is in your left hand.

I am right-eyed, so I grasp the right side of the camera with my right hand; the prism housing on top of the camera presses into the bone over

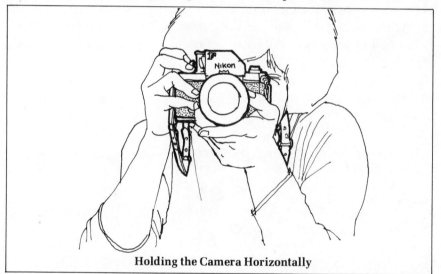

Holding the Camera Horizontally

my right eye. Snuggle the top of the camera as much as possible into the bridge of your forehead and nose—lean it right up against the bones.

If you want to shoot with the camera held level, your head should be tilted and twisted comfortably to the left a little, with your left eye down behind the back of the camera. This eye will squint while you are shooting; if you find that it gets tired, try letting it open, but keep it well behind the camera where it cannot see the subject or anything else.

If your hand position feels awkward, then make adjustments until holding the camera is comfortable for you. The most important thing to remember here is to hold the camera solidly cradled in your hand. Your arms and the palms of your hands should be doing most of the support work; the fingers should be relatively free to operate the focusing ring, *f*/stop and shutter speed controls, and shutter release.

If you want to point the camera up or down, move the whole assemblage by bending your neck, keeping the camera firmly against your face. The term "spot weld" is a good way to describe the connection you should set up between your face and the camera. If I'm working hard and steady during a shooting session, when I'm finished the bridge of my nose is red and sore from the pressure of the camera and I usually have the impression of the prism stamped into my eyebrow.

If you wear glasses, you've got a problem. I've tried shooting with sunglasses, and the only thing I could figure out was to press the glasses up against my face so that there was no slack. Probably the best suggestion is to buy a special viewfinder attachment that takes the place of glasses. This attachment, called a *diopter correction lens,* is available for almost all 35mm cameras.

When using a long lens, let the fingers of the left hand slide out and under to add support to the lens. But try to keep your pinky under the

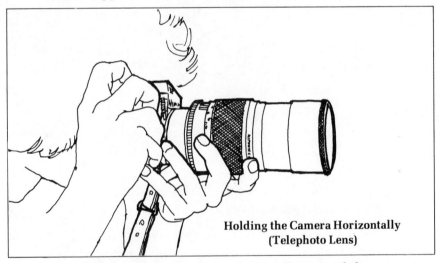

**Holding the Camera Horizontally
(Telephoto Lens)**

base plate. Because of the telephoto's additional susceptibility to camera shake, support is extra crucial here.

The whole idea is to cradle the machine in a solid, interconnected bed of flesh and bone. It might take some experimenting to find the right positions, angles, and nooks.

Shooting Verticals
When you shoot a vertical picture the principle is the same. You'll have

to make the changes in your hand structure, but they should be minimal, as you'll constantly switch back and forth between horizontal and vertical shots.

The back of the camera should be flat against your forehead, with the shutter release on the down side. (While this is my preference and it works if you're right-eyed, most photographers shoot with the shutter release up.) Your left hand presses the top half of the camera against

**Holding the Camera
Vertically**

your forehead and operates the focusing and aperture ring while the thumb of your right hand operates the shutter release. The fingers of your right hand or the palm of your left hand should apply pressure to oppose the force of the shutter release when it is pressed.

When shooting verticals, you'll have to take the camera away from your face to cock it. This interruption is a big reason for using the motor drive.

How to Hold the Rest of Your Body

Your stance should be basically that of a boxer. Plant your feet firmly apart, with the right one slightly ahead of the left, in a rock-solid balance. Your elbows should rest comfortably against your chest, unless there is a table or some other solid object nearby to lean on. Try to keep the camera securely over your center of gravity. If you want to lower the camera, don't bend over—simply spread your feet and lower your torso by bending your knees. Any time you are so off balance that someone could push you over, you are not giving the camera a chance.

Think of yourself as a tripod. If you want to move the camera closer to the subject, don't bend nearer, step forward. If you find it necessary to bend or kneel, experiment until you find a secure position. When you are bending or kneeling, try to use your knee as a support for your elbow. Or even better, sit with your feet wide in front of you, knees raised, and elbows resting firmly just outside the kneecaps.

If you've ever been taught to fire a rifle, you'll see that all the same principles of positioning your body apply.

A photographer who shoots everything from a stand-up-and-shoot-it-straight-on pose is robbing himself of a whole range of possibilities. Position is everything. Take advantage of the mobility of the small camera by moving your body and exploring various angles and levels. A mere shift of two inches to the side and a half inch down might move the background into perfect harmony with the subject, or it might emphasize the graceful line formed by the curve of her shoulder and the drape of her scarf. Your own body language will have a great deal to do with the message or mood of your pictures. If, for example, you step up boldly and address the subject, the photo will reflect that boldness. If you are shy and shoot from a less conspicuous angle, your photo will speak of that. Exploring a subject photographically is like dancing— with your small camera you should be able to move freely—run and sway and dip—and work a whole variety of angles.

Breathing While You Shoot

The movement of your body as you inhale and exhale can also add to camera shake, not only because of chest expansion, but also because of its effect on nerves and heartbeat. The idea is to suspend your body movement without tension and center your concentration into the viewfinder—a relaxed but intense concentration. The instant before you are ready to squeeze the release, hold your breath. Your lungs should only be half full, which is more comfortable. Then squeeze off your shot.

Now that you've got your hand-held technique comfortable, the idea is to practice until it becomes completely natural. Later on there'll be no time to stop and concentrate on the positioning of your hands and body, the way in which you release the shutter, or the correct time to take a breath. Find the most comfortable and efficient methods for you and try them out again and again until they become automatic.

USING A TRIPOD

On the one hand, the cumbersome tripod is the very antithesis of the mobile 35mm camera; on the other, it extends considerably the capabilities of the camera, allowing the photographer to shoot with slower shutter speeds and to record static subjects with great precision.

Normally, the photographer who shoots static subjects like still lifes, landscapes, or set-ups doesn't need the mobility of the 35mm camera and might prefer to use a larger camera for the sake of the image quality offered by large negatives. Nevertheless, the 35mm camera does deliver an image of supreme quality when used on a tripod, and there are definite advantages to choosing it over the larger cameras. For one thing, the 35mm offers a wider selection of lenses. Also, it's a much faster-working camera, even when used on a tripod. The 35mm photographer tries to give an exciting feeling to his pictures even when the camera is on a tripod. He does more than set up the camera; he explores all of the angles and variations.

Once you've put your camera on a tripod, you shouldn't assume that you've automatically solved all of your shake problems. If you're shooting with a slow shutter speed and you are photographing a static subject, you can take several precautions to dampen any camera vibration.

First, be sure to use as much tripod leg extension as possible as opposed to using the center column, because the center column is shaky when extended. Let the camera settle before you trip the shutter. Although a *cable release* is often used to trigger the shutter so that the camera is not jostled as it rests on the tripod, I've occasionally gotten along without one by using the self-timer. The latter allows ten to fifteen seconds before it trips the shutter automatically, providing time for the camera to settle. With many cameras you can lock the mirror in place during long exposures as an additional safeguard against camera vibration.

If, however, you are using a tripod to shoot an action situation, the self-timer or cable release will be too clumsy for your purposes. You'll probably want to capture a certain expression or gesture, and you'll have to be ready to trip the shutter quickly. You might as well keep your hands on the camera once you've focused and lean into the tripod to dampen the vibration as you press the shutter release.

If you find yourself in a marginal situation calling for a tripod, but haven't got one, natural supports are invaluable. Use your ingenuity and take advantage of whatever is available to support your camera. You can eliminate shake from your body by leaning against a wall; if there's a doorway, you can brace yourself against the doorjamb. If your subject is sitting across the table from you, use the table top as a support for your elbows. If you want to shoot with a long lens in a dark room, you can sit backward in a chair and rest the lens on the chair back. Motor drives help combat camera shake because their additional weight dampens vibrations, and you make exposures with a microswitch which requires very slight pressure.

FOCUSING

With the SLR, focusing depends on your ability to judge sharpness with your eye. The shorter or slower the lens, or the darker the situation, the more difficult focusing will be. Also, with a telephoto lens, moving subjects tend to jump in and out of the depth of field, requiring constant adjustment. For SLR cameras there is an intuitive focusing technique called *racking*. This involves rotating the focusing ring back and forth with your fingers, taking it in ever-decreasing arcs until the image is at its sharpest.

Most focusing is done in the matte center ring of the ground glass; the special microprism or split-image fields at exact center are used in difficult situations. You will find that your ability to focus will improve with time. Train yourself to concentrate on focusing, because it is easy to get sloppy about it even after you've got it mastered.

To judge whether an unsharp image has been caused by focusing problems or camera shake, take a good look at the print. If the entire picture is blurred, the problem is camera shake; if a part of the image is not sharp and should be but there are some sharp areas, then you have misfocused.

The question of where to focus is for the most part an aesthetic one. However, with ground-glass viewing you will find that it is easiest to focus on highlight—places in the picture which are lit by gleaming, shining lights.

When you photograph a person at close range, almost without exception you will want to focus on the catchlights, or reflections of light sources, in his or her eyes. (If you can't see the catchlights, sometimes you can find a glisten on the person's bottom eyelids.) If the nose is sharp and the eyes are blurred, chances are the picture won't work. However, if the image is almost completely out of focus but the eyes are sharp, the picture is seen as sharp.

USING THE VIEWFINDER

As you dry shoot, you should spend some time gazing at the world around you through the viewfinder, learning the tricks that a viewfinder and your own eyes can play on you.

It is impossible to *see* everything that appears in the viewfinder. The passing action goes by too quickly and your eyes and brain have a tendency to fill out images or eliminate things that you don't want to see.

In your eagerness to catch the squashed beer can, you may overlook that roly-poly child in the corner of the frame. But the film and the camera make no such oversights—they won't clean up the scene for you. It will take some mistakes and concentration on your part to keep you alert for that baby that may mess up a good shot.

Look *at* the viewfinder as if it were a little picture rather than *through* it, as if it were an aiming device. Also, as you look at the viewfinder, let your eyes wander over the entire rectangle and note the relationship of your subject to the borders. In the beginning, you may tend to isolate the subject in the center of the viewfinder; the result is pictures of tiny people in the middle of vast fields. Counteract this problem by stepping up closer so that the composition fills the frame. You are already working with a small piece of film, and if you have to crop it and enlarge only a part of the picture, the quality of the image will suffer from this additional enlargement. If you are shooting slides, you won't even have the option of cropping the film in the enlarger (although you can recopy that portion of the slide which you want), and you will have to learn to crop in the camera.

When arranging your composition, be aware of the pattern created by blocks of light and dark. One way to check this out is by squinting at the scene. If you're holding the camera to your eye, the depth-of-field button will do the same thing for you. While this isn't the primary function of the preview button, it's often a real help in composing.

Yet another aesthetic consideration to keep in mind is the plane of focus. The plane of focus is parallel to the back of the camera; you can visualize it as a pane of glass which intersects the scene. Notice what objects in the scene are intersected by it as you move the camera off its perpendicular axis. You may want to tilt the camera so as to capture in sharp focus—with the plane of focus—a number of objects at varying distances from you. Or you may want to emphasize certain lines in the picture by placing them in the plane of focus. For example, the edge of a round table will create a powerful curving line through the frame when it is sharply focused. If you tilt the camera so that the edge is less sharp and the salami on the table is within the plane of focus, the salami will become prominent.

You should be aware, though, that this shift in camera position will distort the image, primarily by converging vertical lines in the scene. If you want to keep square objects square, you should hold the back of the camera perpendicular to the ground. Pick a doorway and look at it straight on from eye level. Now tilt the camera upward. As you change the angle notice how the door seems to fall away from you; if you tilt downward, the door will seem to fall toward you. When you hold the camera flat and level, distortion is at an absolute minimum. The more you tilt the camera away from its level position, the more extreme the distortion becomes. You will find that you can keep a 24mm lens pretty quiet by shooting level, or you can tilt it and get results like a screaming 18mm. Become aware of this distortion as you practice, because you probably won't notice it when you are in a hurry, shooting with film in the camera.

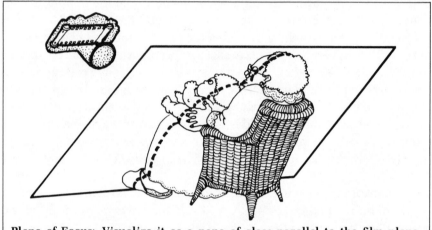

Plane of Focus: Visualize it as a pane of glass parallel to the film plane.

Perhaps you won't always want to avoid it—you may want to use it to converge or diverge lines and make them more loud and powerful—the point is that you should learn to see distortion and control it for your own purposes.

When looking through the viewfinder, you should also become aware of the way subject-to-camera distance can distort your subject. Even with an SLR, this isn't easy to see. If you are using a 50mm lens for a portrait and get up close to your subject, you may not notice that his nose has become somewhat bulbous since you know the subject well and assume that you know what he looks like in the viewfinder. Only later, when you get to the darkroom and develop the print, will you see the bizarre nose. The telephoto lens is not so prone to this sort of distortion because you tend to use it at a greater distance, but you won't always want to use the longer lens to counteract the problem. You should learn to see the more obvious distortions and to expect the more subtle ones so that you can eliminate or use them as you choose.

One more consideration to keep in mind while you are looking through the viewfinder is the *aspect ratio* (or ratio of width to length) of the final print. While each 35mm frame has an aspect ratio of 2:3, the standard-sized print (8"x10") has an aspect ratio of 4:5. This means that if you try to print the whole frame of a 35mm negative onto an 8"x10" piece of paper, you'll get a blank border along the bottom. While some photographers crop the outer edges of the 35mm negative to make the ratio right for the paper, others print entire negatives, leaving the blank space on the paper. If you do the former, you'll want to make sure that there is nothing important at the very edges of your frame that you will cut out when cropping.

TESTING

Photographers spend a certain amount of time in slump periods when they don't have assignments or don't have a project which really intrigues them. At these times you might want to keep busy by conducting tests and learning more about equipment and materials. If you do find yourself with free time, you should consider trying visual, technical, and chemical experiments which demonstrate to you the capabilities of your medium.

You may want to experiment with depth of field. Put your camera on a tripod and shoot the same photograph using four different f/stops. Keep a record of what you've done and then study the finished prints to see how they differ.

Tests are also a good way to finish off those last five frames of film in your camera. You may want to fire off five frames at a 60th just to see how much shake that speed will give you. Another thing you can do is experiment with your lenses, especially the ones you rarely use. Take a normal to lunch—explore with it, see what it does to various situations, learn where it will work best. Develop the ability to look at a scene and know what lens you will need to cover it.

As you develop discipline as a photographer and learn to get the most out of your equipment by dry shooting and experimenting, you will begin to break through the cloud of photo hassle. Your technique will improve gradually, you will begin to gain a certain amount of control over the camera, and you will finally come to express your own particular style.

FILM

The type of film you use is another in the series of variables that affect the texture and impact of your final print. Once you have opted for 35mm film, you have pretty much eliminated the possibility of super-precise detail, which the larger film formats like 4x5 afford. However, there are still a number of choices to be made. Films vary in their sensitivity to light, in their ability to resolve fine detail, and in their ability to record subtle changes in tone from black to white. Depending on how they are exposed, developed, and printed, the resulting photographs display a wide range of moods and textures, from very delicate and finely detailed prints to extremely high-contrast, gritty black and white photos.

WHAT IS FILM?
Black and White

A strip of 35mm film is composed of several micro-thin layers. Black and white film has at least three layers, of which the first and thickest is acetate, an oil product which serves as a base. It is dyed grey in order to stifle *halation*, a scattering of light around any light sources in a photograph; halation is caused by strong, direct light rays bouncing off the film backing. The second layer is an adhesive which bonds the *emulsion,* or thin third layer, onto the rest of the film. The emulsion is the most important layer—this is where the photographic image is formed. It is a gelatinous substance made up of processed cow cartilage in which particles of a silver compound are suspended.

The silver compound in the emulsion consists of special light-sensitive particles called *silver halides.* Millions of these particles are randomly scattered through each square millimeter of emulsion. When cones of light strike them from the lens, their structure changes and they become chemically unstable. At this point, the film is said to hold a *latent image.* When brought into contact with developer, the halides change again and become pure, black metallic silver, creating a visible image on the film. This process is the very heart of photography and remains basically a mystery.

It takes a specific amount of light to alter the halide and bring it to its unstable state. This is an either/or proposition: the halide is either altered or it isn't; it cannot be partially altered. In general, the larger the halide, the less light is needed to bring about the change. Film emulsion contains halides of varying sizes. In portions of the negative struck by many rays of light, all of the halides are altered; but in portions struck by a lesser amount of light, only the larger halides are altered.

A film's sensitivity to light, or film speed, is determined by the proportion of large to small halides. Kodak Tri-X, a very fast, general purpose black and white film, has a preponderance of larger halides. Panatomic-X, a much slower black and white film, has a greater proportion of smaller halides. The faster the film, the larger its halides, and the thicker its emulsion; and conversely, the slower the film, the smaller the halides, and the thinner the layer of emulsion.

When film is bathed in developer, this chemical eats away at the halides, reducing them to silver in pure, element form. During the process the developer leaves behind little streams of metallic silver which clump together. Seen under the microscope, the clumped streams of silver look like fuzz balls. The larger the halides, the more these streams of silver tend to clump together during developing. A single *grain* in a photograph represents a clump of these silver filaments—a grain is not an individual converted halide, as many people believe. It's especially easy to see individual grains in the broad grey areas of a print, as opposed to the dark areas where they are densely packed.

The size and texture of the silver clumps determine the grain characteristics of a film; films are characterized as fine-grained or coarse-grained. The faster black and white films, such as Tri-X, which have

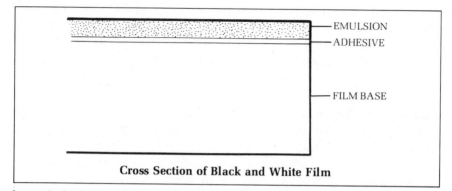

EMULSION
ADHESIVE

FILM BASE

Cross Section of Black and White Film

larger halides and thus larger clumps of silver filaments, exhibit a coarser grain structure than the slower black and white films. (However, what's considered coarse grain today was considered fine grain just ten years ago.) Also, the large clumps of silver filament make for a less smooth transition, or *gradation*, of tones from black to white and less precise recording of detail than is possible with the more numerous smaller clumps of fine-grained, slower films. Thus, high speed and extremely fine grain cannot coexist in one film; when selecting a film you must choose between them.

Another factor which influences grain is your choice of developer. Different developers will produce slightly different grain structures in a given film because their varying formulas lead to different clumping patterns.

After the developer has turned the halides into metallic silver, the film is placed in a fixer, or hypo, which makes the image permanent and dissolves away all the halides which were not altered by the light. The areas of the negative in which few or none of the halides were altered are now transparent. The areas in which a large portion of the halides were altered now contain a heavy concentration of silver and make up the black portions of the negative.

To restate the process: light renders silver halides unstable, forming a latent image on the film. This latent image is made visible by the developer and made permanent by the fixer.

THE H&D CURVE

The greater the amount of light which strikes a portion of the negative, the denser the deposit of metallic silver in that portion of the negative. For instance, light which bounces off the shadow side of a dark tree will produce a correspondingly thin deposit of silver on the film, and that part of the negative will be relatively transparent. Light bouncing off the brightly lit chrome trim of a car will produce a thick deposit of silver on the negative; that part of the negative will be almost opaque. Because the print is the positive version of the negative, the thin silver deposits, or transparent areas of the negative, will show up as dark areas in the print; the thick silver deposits, or opaque areas of the negative, will show up as light areas in the print.

Developing and exposure are two sides of the same coin; they are inseparable. No matter how much light has struck the film, you cannot have any metallic silver density until the film has been developed. Length of developing time does affect the density of the negative, but for now we'll assume that developing time is held constant and look at the effect of exposure more closely.

The relationship between silver density and exposure for a given film at a given developing time is graphically represented by the *H&D Curve* (developed by Hurter and Driffield in 1890 and sometimes called the characteristic curve or D-log E curve; it is based on logarithms). The

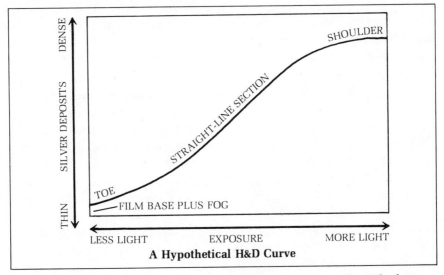

A Hypothetical H&D Curve

shape and angle of this curve varies slightly from film to film. The bottom of the curve is called its toe and represents the shadow areas of the negative. The middle portion, or straight-line section, theoretically represents the mid-range tones in the print; actually, almost all of the tones in your prints will fall in this section of the curve. The top part of the curve is called its shoulder and represents the highlight areas of the picture.

Let's see what happens to density as we go up the curve, or increase exposure. The first point of the toe represents *film base plus fog*. Film backing has its own minute density even without exposure, and beyond that it also has a relatively insignificant silver density created by the action of the developing process. Thus when film which has not been exposed to light is developed, it will not be purely transparent but will have a minute density. This minute density is film base plus fog and covers the entire film surface, even out to the sprockets.

The threshold is the point at which there is just enough light from the lens to transform the larger silver halides. On the curve, this corresponds to the beginning of the toe. At this point, however, an increase in the amount of light will not bring a proportionate increase in silver density. Farther up the toe is the *effective threshold* of the film, the point at which an increase in light will make a significant difference in the tone of the print. Depending on the type of photographic paper you use, it's possible that the threshold and effective threshold will coincide.

As you proceed up the straight-line portion of the curve, you'll see that for every jump in the amount of light from the lens, there is a corresponding, proportionate jump in silver density. This one-to-one relationship between exposure and density continues until you reach the shoulder of the curve. Again, this straight-line section of the curve is where most of the tones in your print are reproduced.

In the shoulder, a jump in the amount of light produces compressed increases in silver density. The tip of the shoulder represents the maximum density of silver deposits possible on the film.

Now let's look at development's influence on the curve. Basically, developing affects the angle of the straight-line portion of the curve, causing it to pivot on the toe. Remember that the toe of the curve represents the shadow areas of the photograph, where a relatively small number of halides have been converted by exposure to light. This means that development stops after a short period of time in this section of the curve because there are relatively few halides to be developed, or converted to metallic silver. Once this finite number of halides has been converted, no amount of additional developing beyond the standard recommended time will produce greater image density in the shadow areas of the picture.

As you climb up the toe, there are many more halides in the film which have been exposed. This means that the longer you develop the film, the denser you will make the highlight areas of the photograph—to a point. It also means that the upper portions of the curve have a greater potential for density. When you get up toward the shoulder section of the curve, increases in developing time will bring very large, disproportionate jumps in density. Thus, when you increase developing time in the darkroom beyond the standard time, the increase will have the biggest influence on the highlight areas of the picture.

Because developing time has little effect on the shadow portions of your print, you've got to expose them properly in order to record them correctly on film. Later, when you are developing the film, you can alter the density of the highlight areas (make them lighter or darker) by in-

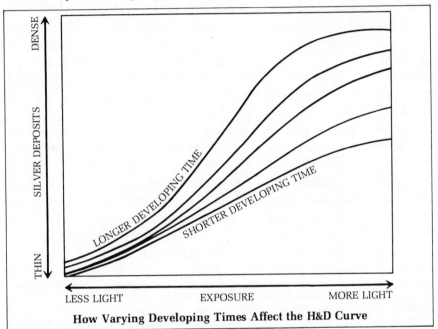

How Varying Developing Times Affect the H&D Curve

creasing or decreasing developing time. So a basic rule of thumb in photography is to expose for the shadow areas of the scene and develop for the highlights.

Another implication of this curve is that developing time affects contrast, or the degree of difference between darks and lights in the picture. Because developing can extend the highlights and make them lighter, it can make the difference between dark and light tones greater. The difference between the thickest and thinnest deposits of silver in a negative is referred to as *gamma* and is represented by the angle of the straight-line section of the H&D Curve.

An additional consideration is that longer developing times favor increased clumping of silver filaments and thus cause greater graininess. The longer the developing time, the greater the contrast and graininess of a picture.

Color Film

There are two types of color film: positive and negative. With *positive* film, most often called transparency film, the film you use in the camera becomes the final picture; it is developed, cut up, and placed in cardboard mounts to produce slides. Transparency films have names ending with chrome (for example, Kodachrome). With negative film, a color negative contains the complements of the colors photographed, and a print which records the original color of the subject is made from the negative.

Light produces color in film in the following way. A beam of white light—sunlight, for example—actually contains all of the colors of the spectrum. When the white light passes through an exposed and developed color slide, a certain mixture of colored light rays are subtracted from the beam of white light and we see the remaining colors in the light coming through the slide.

There are three primary colors in light: blue, green, and red (as opposed to the primary colors in pigments). Their complementary, or "subtractive," colors are yellow, magenta, and cyan. If a beam of white light is passed through a transparency composed of overlapping layers of yellow and magenta, the transparency will absorb the blue and green light rays and allow red to pass through, and you will see the transparency as red. In general then, when you look at a color slide through which a beam of white light is passing, a certain mixture of colors is subtracted by the yellow, magenta, and cyan dyes, and you see a mixture of

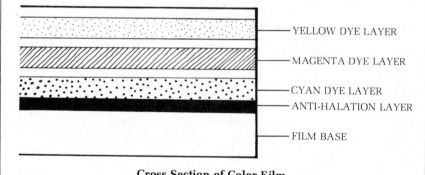

Cross Section of Color Film

these three subtractive dyes' opposite colors (red, green, and blue). All the colors you see on the film are a mixture of these three primary colors.

Color film has an anti-halation base and an adhesive layer. However, unlike black and white film, it has three separate layers of emulsion. Each layer is black and white negative emulsion, but each emulsion layer is sensitive to red, green, or blue light. Color slide film is developed twice. The first time it is put into the developer, the three emulsion layers become negatives. Between the first and second developing processes, the silver which was not exposed in the camera is exposed through chemicals or light, and thus forms a positive image. During the second developing process, the positive silver image is coupled with dyes of complementary color (yellow, magenta, and cyan). Next, all silver is washed out of the three layers of emulsion, leaving three superimposed layers of positive images on the film in yellow, magenta, and cyan dyes. When white light passes through the slide, you see a mixture of red, green, and blue light.

Color negative film works differently. It is processed into a negative—each layer of emulsion is a negative composed of complementary colors (yellow, magenta, and cyan). When the negative is placed in the enlarger, white light is passed through it, and the complementary colors subtract red, green, and blue. For example, a red apple reproduced on the negative will be cyan. When the light passes through cyan, red is absorbed by the cyan, and green and blue are allowed to pass through. Thus you see the apple in the negative as blue-green (cyan). The negative image is then projected onto a piece of photographic paper which also contains three layers of emulsion. Each layer of emulsion contains color dyes of complementary colors, so it reverses the negative and produces an image of the apple in its original red color.

This is a very complex and clever process, only briefly explained here. If you would like a more detailed explanation, you can refer to the Time–Life book, *Color*.

TYPES OF FILM

Although there are myriad 35mm films available, it's best if you choose one or two general purpose films for your work. Only rarely will you find it necessary to venture into the area of special purpose films. Pick one film and learn its subtleties; later, you may find a need for other films.

Film is getting better and better all the time, and for consistency of quality you just can't beat the Great Yellow Father. Kodak makes super film; in fact, I've never heard of a bad roll from Kodak. If a picture doesn't come out right, you can't blame them. You will find that they do not shout about improvements in their film. Kodak-watchers look for very slight changes in wording in the instruction sheet that accompanies each roll; one or two word changes in the description of a film indicate thousands of hours of research and gradual development.

Black and White Films

Tri-X is by far the most popular general purpose black and white film. In the instruction sheet, Kodak calls it a "high-speed film used for low-light situations." However, what Kodak calls bright light is actually extreme glare, so Tri-X is suitable for a wide range of lighting conditions. I think this film is great. I've shot thousands and thousands of rolls of it, and I've got no complaints. Its official ASA is 400, but by increasing developing time you can use it effectively with an ASA of 800 set on your exposure meter. However, in the past few years, people have come to realize that it performs excellently when it is developed for a shorter time and the meter is set at ASA 200. Tri-X at ASA 200 produces soft, silvery images with a full, beautiful transition of tones.

Plus-X is a good film with an ASA of 125. It is almost as sharp and grainless as the slower Panatomic-X and almost as usable as Tri-X in daylight situations. A photographer working in a studio situation or shooting a relatively controlled outdoor setting (e.g., fashion work) might use this film.

Panatomic-X is the next step down in speed and is remarkable in its ability to retain detail and produce fine gradation. It has an ASA of 32, but because of the developers that are generally used with this film, it is often shot at ASA 64 or 80.

These three films are all general purpose films, with continuous tones from black to white. All of them are *panchromatic,* which means that they are almost equally sensitive to all colors of the spectrum. Although the slower films are less grainy, it is false economy to use them just to gain sharpness—you lose shutter speed and your ability to make use of the optimum aperture.

Among the less widely used special purpose films are *High Contrast Copy* (or *High Con Copy*), the darling of the slow-speed, fine-grained films, and *Recording Film,* an ultra-high-speed panchromatic film.

Kodak High Con Copy, when used with its normal developer, reduces everything to pure black and white. It is designed for reproducing documents and has an ASA of 6. However, these days High Con Copy is often used as a continuous-tone film: a developer called H&W Control can be used with it to take advantage of a fluke in its chemistry and produce excellent gradation.

Extremely slow films such as High Con Copy require a tripod. And if you have to go to the trouble of using a tripod and are really worried about getting a truly fine-grained image with extremely subtle transition of tones, you might as well use a 4x5 camera. Photography is more than a contest to see who can get the sharpest image from the smallest negative. The 35mm films lose gradation in enlargement, no matter how fine-grained they may be. Although you can get a picture with high-quality 35mm film which resembles in sharpness and grain characteristics the product of a 4x5 camera, you just can't get the same subtle transition of tones with the smaller negative.

At the other end of the film-speed spectrum is Kodak's *Recording Film*, which has a basic ASA of 2000 and can be used as high as 8000 with appropriate developing. It was originally designed by Kodak for use as a police surveillance film. If you are photographing in caves or intentionally seeking grain, this is the film to use.

This is by no means a complete list of the black and white films available, but for the most part they're the ones you are likely to use in day-to-day situations.

Color Films

Almost all commercial color work is done with transparencies. Perhaps the only substantial commercial use of color negative film is wedding photography, where the client is given prints. This type of film is often used in situations where you plan to retouch the photograph in some way.

Color film is specially manufactured to suit the source of light. When choosing color film, you should consider the type of light with which you'll be shooting. Natural and artificial light vary in color; daylight is a blue light, whereas the tungsten light produced by regular light bulbs is a yellow-orange. (Color temperature is expressed in a measure called *degrees Kelvin*. Daylight averages about 5500 degrees Kelvin, studio tungsten bulbs approximately 3200, and electronic strobes about 6000.) When your eye views the outdoors and then the artificially lit indoors, it adjusts to the change in color temperature and you don't notice the difference. But color film does see the difference. If you use tungsten film when shooting outdoors, your photographs will be blue; if you use daylight film to shoot indoors, the images will be orange. So tungsten film must be used with tungsten light, and daylight film with natural light. However, you can buy conversion filters which enable you to use tungsten film for natural light and daylight film for tungsten light. These filters add density to the lens, requiring a substantial increase in exposure, and as a result are not used very often. If you are shooting a scene lit by both natural and tungsten light, it's better to use daylight film.

Fluorescent light has a special characteristic color which produces green images on film; pictures taken under fluorescent light look as though they were taken under water. You can get fluorescent filters to counteract this, and even though they require additional exposure, it's essential to use them. An FL-B filter corrects tungsten film for use under fluorescents, while FL-D corrects daylight film. Because fluorescent lights vary in the amount of green they produce on film, these filters are only partially effective. For color photographers, fluorescent lights are a big problem.

Two of the more common color negative films are *Kodacolor*, with an ASA of 80, and *CPS*, which has an ASA of 100. Although occasionally used commercially, these films have a relatively poor grain structure and are generally considered amateur films. Their main advantage is that they can be printed in a home darkroom.

Kodachrome is a transparency film which has always been considered one of the finest films available anywhere, in any format. In some cases, photographers choose the 35mm format over the 2¼ or 4x5 in order to use this beautiful film. It is one of the main reasons for the advance of 35mm photography, and its extremely fine grain makes it one of the sharpest films in the world. However, every few years Kodak decides to "improve" Kodachrome, causing great consternation among the photographers who have come to love it. The newly developed *Kodachrome 25* represents an improvement that worries many photographers. Its color seems to be off. But, knowing Kodak, by the time you read this book, it should have the extremely accurate and beautiful color rendition that is typical of Kodachrome. Kodachrome 25 comes in Daylight and Type A, both with an ASA of 25. Type A is designed for use with 3400-degree photofloods (see Chapter 7). *Kodachrome 64*, a companion film which used to be known for its relatively garish color rendition, has recently been improved significantly.

Only corporations directly franchised by Eastman Kodak can develop Kodachrome; the equipment required to develop this film costs hundreds of thousands of dollars, and Kodak has patented the Kodachrome developing process so that it is not in the public domain.

Anybody, however, can go down to the camera store and buy the chemistry to develop *Ektachrome*, another good transparency film. There is *Ektachrome-X*, with an ASA of 64; *High-Speed Ektachrome Daylight*, with an ASA of 160; and *High-Speed Ektachrome Tungsten*, which has an ASA of 125 and is intended for use with tungsten light. Like the black and white films, the ASA of Ektachrome can be increased, while Kodachrome's cannot. The labs will increase High-Speed Ektachrome as far as ASA 400, but once again you should keep in mind that an increase in film speed is accompanied by some loss in gradation and color rendition. Nevertheless, for the journalist working in low-light situations, Ektachrome used at either 160 or 400 is a life-saver.

There is no great advantage to processing color film yourself. Color developing takes fourteen different steps and nearly sixty minutes, and the color labs can do as good a job as you can in following the fairly rigid procedure.

Because color films make use of dyes, the accuracy of their color depends partially on the way the dyes have been combined. Different films are known to render certain colors especially well while others are infamous for their tendency to render certain colors poorly. For instance, Ektachrome is known not only for its vibrant blues but also for its tendency to emphasize blues; Kodachrome, on the other hand, has been admired for its particularly beautiful reds and pastels along with its accurate overall color rendition.

BUYING FILM IN BULK

You may want to buy film in bulk, which can save you quite a bit of money. A word of caution, though: buying film in bulk is a lot less convenient than purchasing preloaded cassettes.

A single roll of Tri-X (36 exposures) costs about $1.50. However, you can go to any professional camera store and buy 27½ feet (5 rolls) for $3.35, 50 feet (9 rolls) for $5.50, and 100 feet (18 rolls) for less than $10.

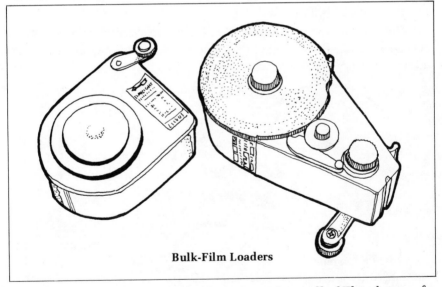

Bulk-Film Loaders

You can also save a lot on color films. A 100-foot roll of Ektachrome, for instance, costs about $30. If you bought 18 preloaded rolls you'd pay about $60.

In order to use these large quantities of film, you must have a *bulk-film loader*, a light-tight box with a crank and film-feed mechanism that loads your big roll onto small, reusable *cassettes*. These cassettes are similar to ones in which preloaded film is packed, but they have an easily removable cap. Kodak sells cassettes for about 25 cents apiece, and you can pick up a bulk-film loader for $12 or $15. There are two kinds of film loaders on the market: one is gear-driven, the other is not. The gear-driven type counts off frames more accurately.

Loading Bulk Film into Cassettes

Film is placed in the film-loader in total darkness. After you have closed the film compartment (making sure that a short tail of film extends from the light-tight slot) you can put the lights back on. Carefully cut the tail straight across with scissors—you'll be winding it onto a cassette, and if you cut the film at an angle it will be difficult to wind it smoothly. Take a piece of tape—any kind will do—and lay it squarely on the cassette spool so that it fastens the film to the spool.

Since you're doing all of this in the light now, the tail end of the film has been exposed and will develop black. Thus, when shooting bulk-loaded film, you usually will find that the last half of the final frame is struck with light. Try to keep this in mind so that you won't use the last frame and lose a beautiful shot. It's easy to forget, though, and this is one liability of using bulk-loaded film.

Once the film is taped to the spool, slip the cassette case over it, put the cap on, place the cassette in the loader, and give the crank a half-turn

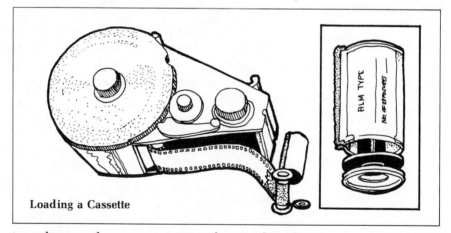

Loading a Cassette

to make sure the cassette is seated properly. After the cassette is in the loader and the outer door is closed, you can wind the film.

The gear-driven film loaders have a counter device that clicks off each frame; on the others, you'll find a chart that tells you how many times to turn the crank for a certain number of frames (for instance, if you want 36 frames you turn the crank 32 times). In my experience it's impossible to be consistently accurate in counting the frames with the latter method.

Once you've wound off approximately 36 frames, open the door, pop out the film cassette, and pull a few more inches of film through the film-compartment slot to give yourself a trailer; then cut the film off

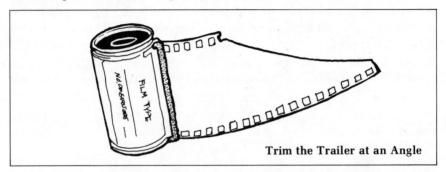

Trim the Trailer at an Angle

squarely. Next cut a long triangle out of the trailer coming from the cassette; this will give you a narrow end to fit in the small slot in the receiving spool of your camera.

If you buy film in 27½-foot lengths it will have narrow strips every 5½ feet, so you won't have to cut out triangles. If you miscount the frames, the narrow strip can end up in the middle of your shooting roll, and unless you pull the film out of the loader or the cassette, thereby exposing it, there's no way of knowing exactly where the narrow strip is. The 50- and 100-foot rolls don't have this nifty feature.

When carrying bulk-loaded film in your camera bag, try not to leave the cassettes lying loose in the bottom of the bag. They pop open. When I used to be really conscientious about bulk-loading, I'd load up about eighteen rolls and place them in the little film cans that preloaded film comes in (these accumulate quickly when you are not bulk-loading) and then seal the cans with masking tape. This way I could reach into my bag and know in an instant which rolls were fresh.

Kodak recommends that you use the cassettes once and then throw them out, but you begin to lose the financial benefit of bulk-loading when you're always buying new cassettes. If you're careful and keep them clean, you should be able to reuse them quite a few times. Store them in a plastic bag or box and examine them occasionally for signs of wear that might indicate light leaks. Another problem to watch for is dirt, which builds up on the felt lip of a cassette and scratches your negatives. I've had cassettes that have lasted for as long as a year, but sometimes you don't see trouble until it's too late.

The main problem with bulk-loading is that it's a hassle to load film all the time—it's a lot more convenient to use preloaded rolls. And the reusable cassettes do occasionally pry open, leaving an entire roll light-struck.

Furthermore, none of the film-loaders has a really accurate system for counting off frames. You may get 34 frames on a cassette one time and 38 the next, and you never know which will be the final, light-struck frame. It's not advisable to have more than 36 frames to a roll because on the Nikor developing reel a longer strip of film tends to unravel or get damaged. Also, you can't get more than 35 frames on an 8″x10″ contact sheet, and it's really a bother to put those one or two extra frames on a whole new sheet of paper.

So why bulk-load? Because it is so much cheaper than buying individual rolls and encourages you to shoot large quantities of film. I have to admit, though, that I don't bulk-load at all anymore.

ODDS AND ENDS

Manufacturers warn you that once film has been exposed it should not be stored too long before developing. This is because the halides are unstable and factors such as heat may degrade the latent image. Actually, black and white film can be stored indefinitely. Color film is less stable, however, and should be developed within twenty-four hours in order to obtain maximum results. After a day has passed, there's no difference in the image if you wait as long as a month. But if you wait any longer, you'll find that the dyes have faded and the pictures appear washed out.

There may be certain cases in which you'll want to make identifying marks on the film cassette: for instance, an indication of the ASA at which the film was shot or a word about the subject matter. Perhaps you'll want to number the rolls for one assignment. An old *Time–Life* trick is to not rewind the film all the way into the cassette, but rather to leave a short trailer outside the cassette. Identifying notes can then be written with a pen on the emulsion side of the trailer. I find this practice disconcerting. Having a cassette totally rewound is the best way of knowing that the roll has been exposed. If you want to make identifying marks, you can use a felt-tipped indelible marker on the outside of the cassette.

You now have an idea of the types of 35mm film available and the general characteristics of these films. The next step is to choose one of these films and learn about it first-hand.

LIGHT

I t just so happens that the chemistry of light and silver interacting produces very beautiful images. That is one important reason why photography has become such a popular medium. More than an industrial or commercial tool useful because of its ability to record detail, photography is an art form because of the lovely and exciting ways that silver renders light.

Learning to look at light and coming to understand what it can do on film is like learning to listen to music—appreciating its elusiveness, its intricacies, and its infinite variation within the confines of certain principles can be an incredible joy. Light is the language of photography: it describes form and texture and mood—the way light is reflected from an object tells us that it is round or shiny or coarse; the way it illuminates a scene can speak of dark, obscure feelings or lucid, serene attitudes. Light can be alive, subtle, shimmering, changing, warm, harsh, cold, gay, majestic—also dull, clunky, scattered, grating, harsh, and garish. Light is an element in the composition of a picture and can become the subject of the picture.

In black and white photography, light is almost everything. The placement and quality of the highlights, shade, and cast shadows de-lineate form and texture. Objects are distinguished or separated from each other in the photograph by differences in tone from black through grey to white. In color photography, objects are also distinguished from each other by variations in color. A red apple seen against a green leaf may produce a startling contrast when shot in color, but if the leaf and apple are lit evenly and have the same color intensity, their tones will blend together when shot in black and white. Thus, when using black and white film, a photographer must learn to previsualize the scene in terms of how it will look in black and white in a photograph.

This chapter, then, is aimed at explaining the language of light—how to speak clearly with it and how to use it expressively. In particular, it deals with *available light,* the existing light that journalists use and occasionally supplement in order to capture that elusive moment. Also included in the chapter is a brief description of artificial lighting in controlled, studio situations.

Because light is so variable, keep in mind that any principles offered here are merely guidelines, or handy ways of looking at light. Most important, you should be sensitive to the feeling or emotion that light communicates—the impression that it gives. Above all, you should use your intuition in dealing with it.

FILM SEES DIFFERENTLY

In photography, light is represented by metallic silver on photographic paper. So learning to previsualize how a scene will look in a black and white photographic print involves learning the way in which silver responds to light.

The photographic process has certain limitations. It can only record a finite range of light values from the real world. Your eye can see a tre-mendous range of light values at a glance, but at a given exposure, film can only see a limited range.

In a high-contrast situation, film cannot handle the extremes of light and dark. In other words, the shadows in the scene fall below the toe of the H&D Curve, and the highlights fall above the shoulder. An example is the situation of a person with a brightly lit window behind him. The glass behind the subject may glow with radiant light, appearing to create a particularly dramatic effect. As you view the scene without the camera, your eye adjusts to the differing light levels: when you look at the window, your pupils contract; when you look at the subject, your pupils dilate to take in the light from the much darker face. But as said earlier, film, at a given exposure, does not have this flexibility. If the window is exposed properly, the face is recorded as black, or as a silhouette, in the photograph; if the face is exposed properly, the window becomes so bright in the photograph that part of the picture becomes blasted out with light and shows no detail.

In a low-contrast situation, where there are only a few different light levels, your eye fills in information about the scene by recognizing color differences. But, recalling the apple and leaf example, if apple and leaf are evenly lit and have the same color intensity, they will be recorded as similar tones in the black and white photograph. The photographic image will have a narrow, dull range of greys.

These types of situations can be handled to a certain extent with exposure, developing, and printing techniques which will be explained in later chapters.

GUIDELINES IN LEARNING TO LOOK AT LIGHT
Direct and Reflected Light

Contrast depends on the type and intensity of light which falls upon a scene and the kind of surface upon which the light falls. Subjects are lit by direct and reflected light. *Direct light* strikes the subject straight from the source of light, while *reflected light* strikes the subject after bouncing off other surfaces first. Most scenes are lit by a combination of direct and reflected light, or only reflected light. It's theoretically possible for a subject to be lit only with direct light. An object placed inside a black velvet box and illuminated by a small, pinpoint light source would be

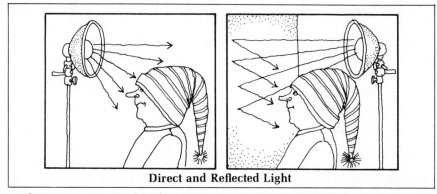

Direct and Reflected Light

such a situation. The black velvet would effectively kill almost all reflection from the object, so the shadow side of the object would receive very little light. There would be an extreme contrast between the shadow side of the object and the lit side of the object.

If the box were white instead of black velvet, then many of the light rays from the source would bounce off the object and then off the walls of the box. The light bounced off the walls would be a relatively direction-less light which would provide illumination to the shadow side of the object. With the shadow side of the object partially lit by the reflected light, the contrast between the shadow side and the directly lit, or high-light, side would be much less.

If the light source were aimed into the box so that it struck only a wall and not the object, the object would be lit entirely by reflected light from the wall. Again, this would be a low-contrast situation because there would not be any extremely dark shadows.

If the light source could be aimed so that all of the walls were evenly lit and the object were not struck with direct light, the object would be illuminated with enveloping, apparently directionless light. There would be no shadows and very little contrast.

Often in studio lighting you'll hear the terms *main* and *fill light*, and these concepts apply to available light also. A main light is a light source which illuminates the subject with directional light, producing high-lights and shadows. A fill light provides illumination for the shadow side of the subject, to reduce the contrast. If you are shooting outdoors, the sun provides direct, main lighting. Some of sun's rays will not strike the subject directly; they will bounce off the atmosphere, buildings, ground, and other surfaces and then hit the subject as fill lighting.

If you are shooting on a sunny day, but the subject is shielded from the direct rays of the sun, then he is entirely lit by reflected light, or *skylight*. Kodak calls this type of light "open shade."

If you are shooting outdoors when the sun is shielded by a heavy bank of clouds, the sunlight is *diffused*. Diffused light has qualities very similar to those of reflected light in that it can be soft and enveloping and it fills in shadows. Sunlight is not the only light that can be diffused; any light transmitted through a translucent material (a frosted window, for example) is diffused.

The direction from which light strikes your subject plays an impor-tant part in revealing the subject's form. It's the direction of light which places the highlight, shade, and cast shadow on the subject. *Frontal lighting*—that is, light which comes from behind the photographer and falls on the front of the subject—is the simplest light and probably the dullest. Highlights fall on the rounded parts of the subject closest to the photographer (nose, chin, and so on); the cast shadows are small and do little to reveal form. One of the most familiar—and least flattering—uses of frontal lighting is the direct flash snapshot. Most family albums are testaments to the difficulties of illuminating a scene with a single small flash. This type of picture has a characteristic look: everything in the foreground is overexposed; the background is underexposed because of the rapid fall-off of light; shadows are harsh and the faces gleam with tiny, compacted highlights. We've come to accept direct flash snapshots as a part of our culture, but beautiful, informative light they're not.

Lights which come from either side of the subject create highlights on the side closest to the light source; the opposite side of the subject is in cast shadow. *Side lighting* does more than frontal lighting to reveal form but has a tendency to divide the subject in half. *Forty-five-degree lighting*—light projected at a 45-degree angle from the center axis of the subject and from a location above the subject's eye level—is very commonly used for portraits. This type of lighting creates upside-down triangular highlights on the subject's cheeks and a cast shadow to the side of the nose, pointing toward the corner of the mouth. The placement of the shadows and highlights makes this 45-degree lighting very effective in revealing form. *Top lighting*, which is projected from above the subject, will illuminate the hair, forehead, and bridge of the nose and will create dark eye sockets. It reveals form in a choppy sort of way and is not very flattering.

Probably the most romantic and beautiful of all light is *backlighting*, or illumination which comes from behind the subject and effectively separates it from the background. If there is adequate reflected fill light and the sun or source of illumination is behind the subject, the backlight can create a halo, placing accent highlights on the subject's hair. A major consideration in backlighting is the amount of reflected light available to illuminate the front of the subject. If there is none, the picture may become a black silhouette. You'll also have to be careful that the light doesn't beam directly into the camera, creating unwanted *flare*, or bursts of light in the image. (Sometimes you might want flares, for they can be very beautiful. They are a phenomenon unique to photography and are the result of light, silver, and lens interacting. Flare is usually caused when a light source is included in the picture.) With the SLR camera, as opposed to the rangefinder, you can see in the viewfinder what the flare is doing to the image and thus you can control it by blocking the light source in some way. Often you can avoid flare by having someone hold a card above the lens to help shade it from direct beams of light. (You'll need to do this even though you have a lens shade on the camera.) Because the fill light which illuminates the front of the subject is usually directionless, very little form is revealed with backlighting.

The characteristics of a surface determine the way in which light will be reflected from it. A very dark surface, like the black velvet, would reflect about 2 percent of the light rays striking it. A white surface reflects most of the light which hits it. Caucasian skin reflects approximately 35 percent. A matte or irregular texture, like fabric, will scatter light in many directions, while a shiny or smooth surface reflects most light in the same direction. Specular, or mirror-like, surfaces reflect light rays in such a tight bundle that the image of the light source can be seen clearly in the surface.

The Angle of Acceptance Equals the Angle of Reflectance

The angle at which a light ray strikes the surface is identical to the angle at which it is reflected from the surface. This is how a mirror works and also explains why irregular surfaces scatter light. Because the minute curves in the surface of a piece of fabric intercept the many rays from a light source at different angles, they bounce the rays at a corresponding variety of angles—and the angle of reflectance of each ray is equal to its original angle of acceptance. A knowledge of this angle-of-acceptance-and-reflectance principle can be a real help in revealing texture, controlling glare, emphasizing highlights, and distinguishing objects from one another.

Find a table near a light source like a window; you'll see the light source reflected in the surface of the table. Using the above principle, you can either remove the pool of light completely or change its position so that it becomes useful. You can do away with the pool by changing the

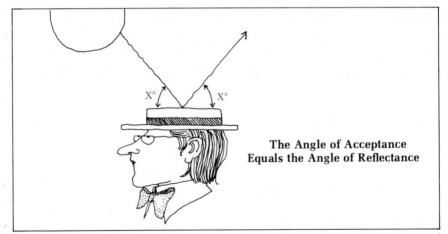

**The Angle of Acceptance
Equals the Angle of Reflectance**

position of the camera so that it is out of the path of the light rays bouncing from the surface. In other situations you may want to use the reflected light to set off a darker object on the dark table and insure a lucid separation of tones in the print. Separation of tones is the key to black and white photography—light against dark against light. You can place the highlight where you want it by changing your position slightly. If you move to the right, the highlight moves to the right; if you move to the left, the highlight will do the same. If you lower your position, the highlight creeps toward you; if you raise your position, the highlight moves away from you.

Another example of the law governing angles of acceptance and reflectance can be seen in the *Limb Effect,* a principle which explains how

The Limb Effect

we are able to distinguish the shape of a three-dimensional object lit with direct, frontal light. You can see this effect if you hold an egg in front of a white wall and position yourself so that there is a light source behind you (ideally, the light should come from over your shoulder at eye level). The part of the egg closest to your eye will appear the brightest. This is where the light strikes the egg and bounces back directly into your eye. The edges of the egg will appear darker, not because they are in shadow, but because a good deal of the light that strikes those areas bounces off toward other parts of the room instead of back to your eye. If it were not for this effect, the egg would appear one-dimensional. This helps explain how we perceive round objects as round and why we are able to distinguish the white egg from the white wall.

Quality of Shadows and Highlights

The softness of a shadow and the broadness of a highlight are proportionate to the relative size of the light source. That is to say, a pinpoint source creates sharply defined shadows and tight highlights while a large source creates less defined shadows and broad highlights which tend to blend into each other. Outdoors, this can be seen clearly in the way direct sunlight produces small highlights and sharp shadows. In this case, the sun can be considered a distant and therefore relatively small light source. But if the sun is behind the clouds, and sunlight is diffused through them, then the whole sky becomes a huge light source and the resulting shadows are very soft and the highlights very broad. When light is bounced off a large wall to illuminate a subject, the wall is considered a large light source.

Here "the size of the light source" means the actual physical dimensions of the light source in conjunction with its distance from the subject.

The Size of a Light Source is Relative to its Distance from the Subject.

We all know that the sun is huge, but because it is so far away it is considered a small light source. So the closer a light source is to the subject, the bigger it is.

One application of this law can be seen in the way studio photographers light silverware for commercial photographs. Because they are shooting highly polished objects and want to convey the rich, shimmering quality of the silverware, they use broad light sources which create large, smooth highlights. These large highlights cover and illuminate the entire surface of the knives, forks, and spoons. Since the silverware is lit from all possible sides by a dome of light, the size of the light source relative to the subject is infinitely large. If they were to use small light sources, the silverware would be splotched with small *specular highlights,* which duplicate the shape of the light source.

To achieve the desired effect, the photographer places the silverware on a table and then builds a tent of paper, parachute material, or acetate over it. Light rays are shined through the surface of the tent from the outside or are aimed up into the tent, where they bounce around. The whole tent becomes a light source filled with broad, luminescent light. The reflection of the light source delineates the form of the silverware with long, beautiful highlights that describe the ins and outs of the surfaces. A hole is cut in the tent for the camera, and the photographer may take hours to position the camera and lights to pick up just the right amount of highlight. Sometimes, just to break the continuous glow of the shiny surface, he may hang a few black strips of paper inside the tent, which are then reflected in the knife or fork.

In the silverware example, we have demonstrated how a large light source can be used to reveal the texture of shiny surfaces by providing broad highlights. A small, glancing source of illumination can be used to reveal textures of a different sort. If you want to bring out the weave of a fabric such as burlap, for example, you can cross-light it with a small, direct light. This will create tiny highlights and sharp shadows in the hills and valleys of the material.

Inverse Square Law

Another principle of physics that's basic to photography is the *Inverse Square Law*, which states that the intensity of illumination is inversely proportional to the square of the distance from the source. In practical terms, what this means is that as you move away from a given light source, the intensity of the light diminishes quite rapidly (in an inverse geometric progression). The law holds true for a beam of light, which spreads as it leaves the light source; it does not hold true for a single light ray. The Inverse Square Law also explains the fact that the farther away

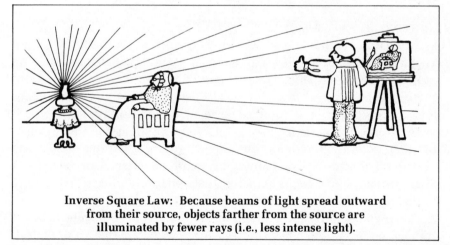

**Inverse Square Law: Because beams of light spread outward
from their source, objects farther from the source are
illuminated by fewer rays (i.e., less intense light).**

you get from the light source, the more even the lighting (for instance, the difference in intensity of light at distances of two and four feet is much greater than the difference at distances of twelve and fourteen feet). This is a major principle in photography. The fact that light falls off in an inverse geometric progression as you travel from the light source is the basis for most of photo math. For example, the same law that applies to light flowing through a window applies to light traveling through the lens of the camera. $F/5.6$ on a long lens is a larger diameter than $f/5.6$ on a short lens because light must travel farther through the lens.

The Inverse Square Law is an extremely valuable concept, especially when you are shooting indoors. For example, let's say you're taking a picture of two people sitting next to each other and lit from the side by a nearby window. The person nearer to the window is illuminated by a more intense light than the other person, even though the two people are sitting close together. This is a situation which is not immediately evident to your eye, but is obvious on film. Thus, if you were to take a picture of them, the resulting photograph would show two faces very differently lit. However, the farther you move the two subjects away from the window, the more evenly they will be illuminated. With black and white film, you can correct the unevenness in lighting with manipulations during the printing process. In color photography, you must add supplemental fill light at the time the picture is taken; you can't make corrections when printing.

The law applies to situations where the light source is relatively close. If you are outdoors with the sun as your main light source, the fact that one object is closer to the sun than another will not mean that the two will appear to be lit differently in the resulting print.

LIGHTING SITUATIONS

As you gain experience, you'll learn to predict when the film will not react well to particular types of lighting, and you'll probably return again and again to those situations that are particularly conducive to successful photos. At first, you'll probably want to shoot everything that catches your eye, giving little thought to the aesthetics of light. But soon you'll begin to recognize certain characteristic lighting situations and the qualities they impart to the final print. Some lighting situations are flat and unexpressive, some rich and luminous, some opalescent, some crisp, and others garish. You'll begin to realize that certain lighting situations are inherently beautiful, while others aren't.

One workable lighting situation that you'll run into repeatedly is indirect daylight from a nearby large window, where the window itself becomes the source of light but is not necessarily included in the photograph. With a bit of experience, you'll learn how to position the subject to make the best use of this beautiful illumination. The best way to get this experience is to find someone willing to stand near the window and move around for you, so that you can see the changing light. If you can't find someone to do this, you might use a hand-held mirror and watch yourself as you move around near the window.

Other very workable lighting situations occur late in the afternoon through sunset, or a few minutes before and after sunrise, when the light is soft, the highlights broad, and the shadows long, gentle, and compositionally unifying. Storm light or light modified by clouds or inclement weather conditions are also satisfying. Backlighting is almost always beautiful, wherever you find it. In fact, if in doubt, use backlight—given enough fill. Different parts of the world have their own characteristic lighting because of variations in latitude and prevalent atmospheric conditions; some areas of the world have more beautiful lighting than others. Los Angeles, with its bright glare and smog, is awful; Wales, with its frequent rainfall and high latitude, tends to have lush, luminous light.

If there are situations in which light, optics, and silver combine to produce pleasing images, there are also situations which tend to produce aesthetically unpleasing photographs or difficult technical problems. We have already discussed the problem involved in photographing a person seated in front of a brightly lit window, where the window is included in the picture. Another difficult lighting situation is posed by noonday sun.

In general, direct sunlight tends to be unattractive in silver. The two just don't interact well. Direct sunlight tends to be very splotchy, particularly if photographed in black and white. Take a look at a city street when the sun is high and the sky is clear; you will see that parts of cars and buildings are brightly lit and glaring, while other corners and crevices are hidden in dark shadows. The effect is grating and harsh on film.

Direct sunlight is especially bad when you are photographing people. When the sun is overhead at midday, direct sunlight creates impenetrably dark eye sockets and puts glowing noses on unsuspecting victims. Another problem is the subject's natural desire to squint under these conditions.

Architectural photography is one area in which direct sunlight works well. If you shoot a building on a clear, sunny day, the contrast imparted by the direct light glancing across the features of the building will give sharp lines and bold patterns.

Often you'll run into *mixed-light situations*, where important action or detail falls within both deep shadow and bright highlight areas of the scene. While it is difficult to expose and print this type of picture and retain all of the important information, it can be done. Often, mixed-light situations can be very beautiful, and with experience you'll learn to deal with them.

Although you'll find that certain situations recur again and again— some that are inherently workable and some that are not—it becomes apparent that light is infinitely variable. Within such broad categories as backlighting, window lighting, and the vast spectrum of outdoor light-ing, there are endless possibilities for variation. As you learn to pre-visualize how light and silver will interact in a specific lighting situation, you will gain the ability to go beyond simple lighting solutions and begin to work creatively with the drama and subtleties of light.

ARTIFICIAL STUDIO LIGHT

It's my feeling that natural light is potentially more alive than studio light. But lighting in a studio can be clean and controllable, and you can use artificial light to illuminate just about anything. If your job is to take a picture of a stereo or a tape recorder for a catalogue, you're probably not looking for alive and beautiful light. You need informative, clean, direct light that reveals the form and detail of your product—and it's much easier to achieve that with studio light than with available light. In addition, if you are doing fashion or food photography, time is an impor-tant factor. With studio lighting, you know that the light will be right when the food is finished cooking or when the high-priced models report for work; you are not a slave to the unpredictable fluctuations of natural light.

There is a great deal to be gained from studying studio lighting technique. However, since this book as a whole and this chapter in particular are geared to available light photography, our discussion of studio technique is necessarily brief.

Artificial Lighting Tools

The studio photographer uses a variety of tools, both in the studio and on location. *Reflector floods* are 500-watt incandescent bulbs that are mush-room shaped. They are simple and cheap. The inside of a reflector flood lamp is a reflective silver which bounces the light forward from the filament into a wide beam. The lamp can be screwed into a socket that has a clamp attached, thus enabling you to attach the reflector flood to a door or table, or any available projecting surface. When aimed directly at the subject, these lamps produce harsh, awful light not unlike direct sun-light, but if they are bounced off ceilings, walls, or corners, they can provide soft, flattering light or serve as fill light. *Photoflood lamps* are also 500-watt; they are used with metal bowls that act as reflectors.

A *focusing spotlight* is a light bulb placed in a casing with a parabolic reflector and a special lens which projects the light in a controlled beam. You'll often see them on movie sets or at supermarket openings. All of the light rays are tightly focused by the parabolic reflector and lens, and as a result these spotlights have a unique property: their light does not fall off in an inverse geometric progression. *Rim kickers* are spotlights or any other type of lamp used for backlighting—to give your hair some glow if you're a person, or to throw a little halo around your whipped cream if you're a sundae.

Quartz iodide lamps are most often used on movie sets; they consist of a filament in a small glass tube set within a complex metal fixture. They

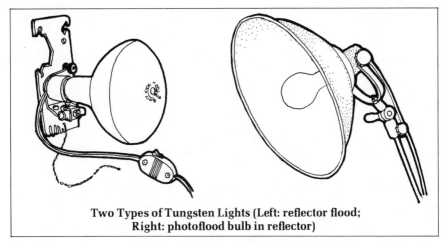

**Two Types of Tungsten Lights (Left: reflector flood;
Right: photoflood bulb in reflector)**

deliver much more light for their size than the floods and spotlights do, and are best used when bounced. This is the type of lamp that you see TV cameramen carrying around on a handle.

Strobes, or electronic flash lamps, provide light by firing through a glass tube an enormous charge of electricity which has been built up and

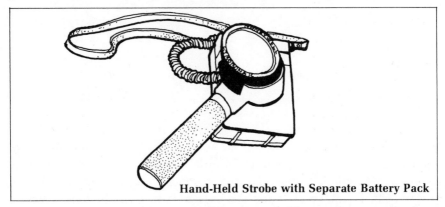

Hand-Held Strobe with Separate Battery Pack

stored in a capacitor. They provide a powerful burst of extremely short duration. This brief flash freezes the motion of your subject. Strobes are powered either by batteries or AC outlets and come in a variety of forms. The small, amateur units attach to the camera and have self-contained batteries that require recharging. They are relatively weak in light output and the interval between flashes, or capacitor recycling time, is fairly long—ten or fifteen seconds. The working photojournalist doesn't have time to wait around; he uses a hand-held strobe that recycles within a second. These professional strobes are powered by separate, dry-cell battery packs worn over the shoulder or hooked to your belt. They cost

Large Commercial Strobe with AC Power Pack

about $150. The third general type of strobe is the relatively unportable commercial model. This type is usually AC, but sometimes both AC and battery-powered. One or more strobe lampheads are attached with a cord to the large, heavy power pack. These units cost hundreds and sometimes thousands of dollars and can operate at as much as 2000 watt-seconds of power. The better commercial strobes contain a small, incandescent *modeling light* which gives off much less light than the strobe itself and reveals how the strobe will illuminate the subject. The strobe must be synchronized with the camera shutter so that the flash occurs when the shutter is fully open; this means that with the focal plane shutters, the fastest shutter speed you can use is a 60th. (At faster speeds, the film is exposed by a moving slit so that the frame is never completely open.) The exact time of the shutter speed is not critical when you shoot with an electronic strobe: the flash goes off in a millisecond, in the middle of the shutter movement, and the light picked up in that millisecond exposes the film.

When using a strobe unit, you have two options for determining exposure. One is the electronic flash meter, which is pretty expensive (starting at just under $100), but essential if you do a lot of strobe work. The other is the use of *strobe guide numbers,* an exposure method based on the inverse square law. These numbers are used in conjunction with strobe-to-subject distance to figure the correct *f*/stop. One reason they aren't dependable is that they don't take into account the size and tonal qualities of the room in which you are shooting. As a matter of fact, advertised strobe guide numbers are as accurate as car manufacturers' claims about gas mileage.

Strobes have pretty much eliminated the use of flash bulbs in photography. The only time you'll see a flashbulb now is on the top of an Instamatic.

Two recent developments in strobe technology are the solid-state sensors and the use of the *bare tube.* The sensors shut off the strobe when the appropriate light level has been reached; this is automatic exposure. The bare tube is used by press photographers in fast-moving situations where they must get the picture regardless of the light quality. In the past, photographers used direct flash in this type of situation, but the bare tube, which is attached to the strobe unit, is preferred now because it spreads light in all directions from its source and provides a softer light. Bare tubes are also used occasionally by fashion photographers working outdoors, to provide a blink of fill light.

It's possible to modify all studio lights with a number of different accessories. *Barn doors* are black metal flaps that look like the blinders on a horse; they limit the flow of light from a lamp. *Snoots* are black metal tubes which create a narrow but unfocused beam of light. A *scrim* is any translucent material placed over the light to diffuse it—often spun glass or wire screens and sometimes parachute material. Any of the studio lights can be bounced off reflective surfaces to achieve a softer effect. In studio lighting, these surfaces are *flats,* which are big movable walls, or customized *umbrellas.* Because they are portable and reflect light so beautifully, umbrellas are extremely popular. The light bouncing out of an oversized white- or silver-lined umbrella creates a large reflective source of light, with soft shadows and broad highlights.

Reflector floods, photofloods, and focusing spotlights are all tungsten lights; they produce a light that is 3200 degrees Kelvin and call for Type B color film. Quartz iodide light and some reflector floods

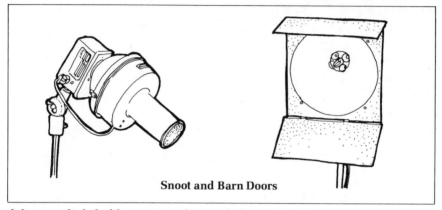

Snoot and Barn Doors

deliver a slightly bluer, 3400-degree light, and call for filtration. Strobes are matched to daylight.

Schools of Lighting

Within the context of studio photography, it seems to me that there are several different schools of lighting. One is the Kodak style; another good name for it is "catalogue lighting." These techniques are used most often for portraiture and product photography. Basically, this type of lighting involves the use of standard formulas and the results are predictable and dry. For example, Kodak offers all sorts of valuable information on standard situations: "How to light a black telephone: Here's how Bell photographers dealt with the problems of a black, shiny surface. . . ." I don't want to put down Kodak—they do provide a lot of important "how-to" data. But theirs is a whole different world from that of the New York fashion photographer or the Hollywood cinematographer. When the Kodak photographer lights, he definitely wears a tie, has clean fingernails, and doesn't run around eating cheese danish.

The New York fashion photographers are especially distinctive for their imagination and ability to make light alive and exciting. Some of the photos in the ads of *Vogue* and *Harper's Bazaar*, from the standpoint of technical lighting, are incredible masterworks.

The key to the fashion school is the use of bounced, or indirect, light. The fashion photographers usually take light and bounce it into an umbrella or off a white flat. This way the subject is lit by the more flattering indirect light. Umbrella lighting is an invention of the New York school. If you leaf through a *Vogue* or *Harper's Bazaar* and look at the catchlights in the models' eyes, you will often see white circles with black dots inside them. These catchlights are reflections of umbrellas with lights aimed inside them. The roundness and size of the umbrella allow the light to wrap around the subject and fill in the area surrounding it, giving a particularly luminous quality.

In natural lighting, one of the most beautiful types of light is the classical painter's frosted and slanted northern skylight, of Parisian garret fame. The studio photographer's huge *bank light* is an imitation of this classic light. This is a frame hung with as many as twenty lights; recently New York fashion photographers have begun to use as bank lights huge movable walls of specially filtered fluorescent light.

Working out of their two-story brownstones with custom-made ten-foot by ten-foot neon fantasticks and thousand-dollar multistrobes, these photographers have taken the art of studio lighting to a much higher plane than the catalogue school.

As for the Hollywood school, an entire vocabulary and equipment industry have been built around the special requirements of motion-picture lighting. On the movie set, the person in charge of lighting is the director of photography, who must deal with all the lighting problems of

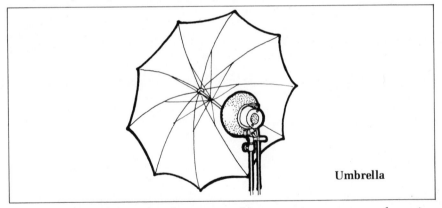

Umbrella

the still photographer plus those created by a moving camera and moving subjects. He is assisted by the gaffer, who rigs the lights. The "Best Boy" helps rig the lights and adjusts them to the gaffer's specifications. An electrician is also on hand to run the light cables. Movie production depends on tight and even lighting, and on some sets you'll see an entire ceiling filled with lights used to produce precisely the right amount of exposure.

I can't urge you enough to look at light and begin to think of the ways in which you can use it. When you walk into a room or get on a bus, whether you're going to take a picture or not, train yourself to look at the light—what direction is it coming from, what and where is the source, how do the reflective surfaces alter it, what is the general contrast? And most important, what are the emotional and aesthetic qualities of the light? Pick up magazines and look for catchlights in the models' eyes—figure out the direction, size, and type of light source from the shape, size, and placement of the highlights and shadows. How do the shadows and highlights reveal form? Look at the works of master painters—Rembrandt, Vermeer, Degas—and see how they used light. Take a look at the work of great photographers such as Ansel Adams, Richard Avedon, Bruce Davidson, and W. Eugene Smith, and see how they have made use of light.

Light is one of the foundations of photography. With it, you can reveal detail and capture the feeling of that elusive moment. And, armed with an appreciation of what light can do and an understanding of how it works, you can work wonders with silver.

EXPOSURE

Long before anyone devised photo math, the H & D Curve, and exposure meters, there were beautiful pictures being taken. Technological refinements came along later, developed by photographers who wanted more predictable results. But in those early days, in the 1800s, the photographer used a camera without once checking a light meter, and his technique was essentially trial and error.

As phototechnology has grown over the years, unfortunately so has the potential for confusion. Faced with a morass of charts, logarithms, and jargon, many a would-be photographer has turned and run. And probably the most abused victim of all the hocus-pocus photo language has been exposure: the technique for measuring light and choosing an f/stop–shutter speed combination appropriate for the range of light levels.

Today, with the built-in, through-the-lens exposure meters, most of the difficulty surrounding exposure has been eliminated. In practice, all you have to do is center the needle in the meter and shoot, open up in light situations, or close down in dark ones. It's as easy as that. Furthermore, in evenly lit, low-contrast situations, black and white film allows you approximately a three-stop latitude. That is, you can be a stop underexposed and as much as one or two stops overexposed and still achieve an acceptable print by working it out in the darkroom. In the more difficult, contrasty situations, though, you have to be more precise in selecting an *f*/stop–shutter combination.

So exposure can be pretty easy. Nevertheless, you should take the time to develop in your head a visual model of how it works. In pursuit of that, we'll use Ansel Adams' Zone System. As with every other aspect of photography, exposure is a visual process, and dealing with it verbally can be pretty tricky. To date, Adams' zones are the most efficient semantic tool for handling the relationship among light levels in the real world, *f*/stops, shutter speeds, the H & D Curve, and the final print. The zones serve as an aid in previsualizing how the scene in front of you will translate into the photographic print. A knowledge of these zones enables you to make intelligent decisions in selecting exposures.

WHY WORRY SO MUCH ABOUT EXPOSURE?

What would happen if you always accepted the meter reading—just centered the needle on your built-in meter and shot without making any adjustments? You'd probably get a lot of OK photographs; approximately seventy-five percent of your negatives would be adequately exposed if you were shooting black and white film. Of the remaining photographs, maybe half could be adjusted during printing, because you have a three-stop latitude with black and white film. So why worry about being precise in your choice of *f*/stop and shutter speed with all these things going for you?

For one thing, choosing the best exposure allows you to record as much information as possible in the negative. If you overexpose or overdevelop, you lose gradation and detail in the highlights; however, if you underexpose, shadow detail will be lost forever. Through certain corrective printing techniques, you'll be able to get an image from negatives which have been underexposed, but they won't look very good and it will be an exasperating process. Maybe you won't want all that tonal information when it comes down to making a print; you may decide to go for a stark black and white picture. But you should have as much tonal information as possible in the negative so that all your options are open. Once you've lost it in the negative, there's no way to restore tonal information to the print.

Secondly, if you've exposed the film properly, you've maximized its ability to give smooth, subtle gradation of tones from black to white, and you've maximized the sharpness and grain characteristics inherent in the negative.

Also, precision in exposure makes darkroom work a lot easier. After thousands of photographs, that's an advantage. Of course, if you're there when Jack Ruby pulls out his gun, your major consideration is speed, not beauty. Later, if you find that the exposure is three stops over, I'm sure that you can still carve an image out of the negative.

If you're shooting color transparencies, exposure is crucial: color film has much less latitude. Exposure affects not only the lightness or darkness of the transparency, but color saturation as well. Overexposure washes out the colors, and severe underexposure mutes them. If the transparency is a little too dark or light, this can be corrected to a certain extent by copying the film. But selection of exposure is the final control the photographer can exert over color saturation: a variation of a half-stop one way or the other makes a big difference and cannot be corrected. If you are using color film and have a chance, try exposures at half-stop intervals up or down from the exposure you think is best. This is called *bracketing*. In black and white photography, if you must err in exposure, it's best to do it on the side of overexposure; in color photography, you should err on the side of underexposure—once the color is washed out, you'll never regain it.

COMMON SOURCES OF EXPOSURE MISTAKES

Lack of confidence and understanding is the most common cause of mistakes in exposure: hopefully this chapter and some experience will

Exposure Problems: Watch out for unwanted glare in your meter reading.

alleviate that. One common mistake is incorrectly pointing the meter when taking a light reading—and the easiest way to correct this is to use a built-in meter. With the hand-held meters, there's an enormous difficulty in knowing exactly what the meter is reading; if by chance you've aimed it in such a way that you pick up a bit of unwanted glare, your reading will be thrown off considerably. With a built-in meter, you know exactly what is read, including that glare, because you see it in the viewfinder. Also, if you are using a hand-held meter you tend to hold it close to the subject, and it's hard to avoid throwing your own cast shadow over the area which

Exposure Problems: Avoid taking a reading of your own cast shadow.

you are reading; again, the built-in meter is usually free of this difficulty.

Making dumb mistakes in transferring the information from your hand-held meter to the *f*/stop and shutter speed controls on your camera is another common problem. On the built-in meter there are no figures to read and thus less chance for this type of error.

All sorts of outside influences and variations in photochemistry also contribute to the problem of achieving a well-exposed image. It's one thing to say that the light measures so much, that you're going to expose at exactly a 60th, and that you'll get precisely the result you want—but the conditions necessary to get exactly what you want every time just don't happen consistently in day-to-day photography. For example, your exposure meter may be slightly less than accurate, which is common, and your camera's shutter speed may vary more than 20 percent from the indicated setting (20 percent is considered the maximum acceptable variation). In addition, if you're not familiar with the subject you're shooting, if you've never shot under those particular conditions before, you can only make an educated guess at how those conditions will affect the outcome. As said earlier, photography is not an exact science, and at times it can be really frustrating to deal with all of these variables. However, with experience you'll become familiar with various types of photographic situations and begin to recognize those that seem inherently photogenic. As you return to them, you'll learn what exposure methods work best for your favorite window-lit portraits or Heathcliff-on-the-moors studies. To use another rifle term, you could think of adjusting to equipment inaccuracies and evaluating the scene in terms of Kentucky windage—taking aim at the target, judging how hard the wind is blowing, and compensating by moving the gun barrel into the wind a bit—or in your case, maybe opening up half a stop.

TRANSLATING THE SCENE TO PHOTOGRAPHIC PAPER

On any piece of black and white photographic paper, the relationship between the "pure white" and the "pure black" of the paper is fixed; no amount of sunlight is going to give you a white that is whiter than the pure white of the paper and no hollow, deep pit is going to produce a black that is darker than the ultimate possible black of the paper. This fixed range from ultimate black to ultimate white is the world of the print.

But in the world around us there are thousands of levels of darks and lights; the range of light levels in the actual world is much greater than the range that can be recorded as tones in a photographic print. Thus the photographer translates the range of the real world into the more limited world of the print.

Exposure, then, is dealing with the incredible range of light levels in the real world and converting them into the very finite range of blacks and whites and greys of a photograph. If you are dealing with an extreme range of light levels, you'll have to contract the range or sacrifice one end of the continuum; if you are dealing with a very narrow range of light levels, you'll want to expand them so that they read a full range of tones between black and white in the print, rather than only a few dull greys. Once you get the hang of exposure, you can choose the particular f/stop-shutter speed combination that will give you the range of blacks and whites you desire.

DIVIDING THE PRINT INTO ZONES

In Chapter 6, we mentioned the H & D Curve, a graphic representation of the relationship between clear areas of the negative (dark tones in the print) and dense silver deposits on the negative (highlights in the print). Ansel Adams established a system, or language, which defines the black, grey, and white tones possible on photographic paper, and now we can relate the H & D Curve more specifically to these tones in the print.

Adams divided the H&D Curve into ten zones. Zone 0 is the equivalent of film base plus fog, or the very bottom of the curve; thus Zone 0 is the blackest tone possible on photo paper. Zone 9 represents the shoulder of the curve, or dense silver deposits; so Zone 9 is the whitest tone possible on the paper. Zone 5 falls in the middle of this continuum and represents that silver density which produces a middle grey in the print.

Each zone represents a stop difference in exposure on the H&D Curve. If you increase exposure by one stop, you admit more light to the film and make the tone one zone lighter. For example, if you increase exposure one stop more than the exposure which produced Zone 5, you will have a correspondingly denser deposit of silver on the negative and in the print a lighter tone of grey, which represents Zone 6. Another stop increase in exposure will give you an even lighter grey in the print, and an increase in exposure of four stops above the Zone 5 exposure would give you Zone 9, or white. If you decrease the exposure for Zone 5 by one

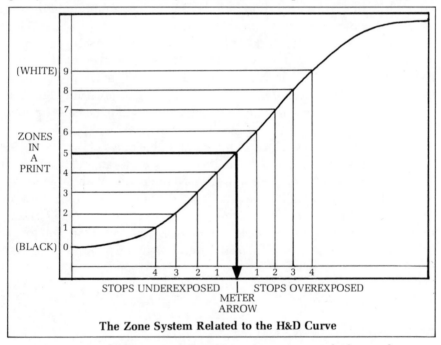

The Zone System Related to the H&D Curve

stop, you get a darker tone of grey in the print, and if you decrease exposure for Zone 5 by four stops, you get black.

Adams related the *Zone System* to the real world by noting that certain objects tend to fall into certain zones. For instance, Caucasian skin in frontal light, or soft, diffused or reflected light, is more or less the same tone of grey in most photographs—the tone of grey represented by Zone 6. Here, then, are the ten zones or shades of grey, as they relate to objects in the real world and to the print:

Zone Zero: a hollow, empty black which you might get if you were to photograph the inside of a cave or a fold in a man's dark suit; often a hole without light rather than a black surface. It is also called *key black*.

Zone One: the first hint of tone above film base plus fog in the negative; in 35mm photography this zone is actually recorded as black in the print.

Zone Two: the first hint of texture in dark grey, with minimal detail showing; an example would be a dark sweater.

Zone Three: a grey with adequate texture; might correspond to a dark beard with detail in the hair visible.

Zone Four: a tone of grey that is equivalent to Caucasian skin seen in cast shadow or the shadow areas in landscapes.

Zone Five: middle grey, which could correspond to grey stone, weathered wood, or the deepest blue part of a sky seen in the print. Kodak makes middle grey cards which you can purchase. Darker complexions often fall in this zone.

Zone Six: a lighter grey equivalent to Caucasian skin which is frontally lit or seen in very soft light. Cast shadows on snow are usually recorded as this tone.

Zone Seven: a light grey that corresponds to very light skin or a sidewalk in sunlight.

Zone Eight: a glowing white tone that still has some detail, corresponding to a white highlight—for example, sun on a white pillar.

Zone Nine: a pure white; the equivalent of a field of snow seen in bright light. Areas of the print which fall in Zone 9 are said to be *key white.*

Any objects in the real world which fall in light levels above Zone 9 begin to be *blocked up* and fall into the shoulder of the H & D Curve; in an unmanipulated print they are recorded as Zone 9 or white.

With 4x5 film, Adams is able to achieve each of the ten zones as fairly distinct categories; the large film format is capable of extremely full and fine gradation. However, with 35mm film, you'll find that tones become compacted at the extreme ends of the zone continuum—in practice, there are only very subtle differences between Zones 0, 1, and 2. In reality, you'll be using Zones 3 through 7 most of the time. They are the "meat" of the Zone System, and the other zones are the "seasoning." Thus, as said in Chapter 6, most of the zones in your prints will fall in the straight-line section of the H&D Curve.

Every exposure meter is keyed to Zone 5, the middle grey. This means that if you were to use the exposure meter to take a reading of any smooth, evenly toned surface in the scene, the resulting exposure would produce a Zone 5 tone in the print no matter what the original tone (if the print were printed at a standard time.) If you were to take individual photographs of three cards—one white, one middle grey, and one pure black, expose each one as the meter indicated, and develop and print them properly, the resulting prints would all be the same middle grey. Needless to say, then, there are times when you do not want to go by the exposure meter reading, when you want the lights to be light and the darks to be dark.

TWO WAYS TO PUT THE ZONE SYSTEM TO USE

Using your knowledge of the Zone System, there are two ways you can measure a scene in terms of exposure. One is to measure a particular dark or light area in the scene and think of it in terms of its logical zone. The other, less classic method is to average all of the light levels for a general zonal impression of the scene.

Placing

There may be one part of the scene which is predominant—for instance, a snowfield—or an area which is particularly important to you—maybe a person's face. In these cases you'll want to be sure that this part of the scene falls into the proper zone. If you are concerned about getting tonal detail in an extreme area of light or dark, you'll want to take precautions to insure that you get the proper exposure for that area. You can pick out the most important part of the scene, place it where you want it on the zone scale, and let the rest of the scene fall where it may in terms of zones.

Note that the placement of one area of a scene into a zone determines the zones into which the other areas will fall. For example, let's say you're photographing a man wearing a dark suit and white shirt. He is standing with his back to a dingy wall. For the purposes of this discussion, we'll assume you're using a hand-held meter to take readings of individual areas of the scene. Later you'll see how a built-in meter can also be used. On the hand-held meter, his face reads 15, his suit reads 12, his shirt reads 17, and the wall reads 14. Now you decide that the face is the most important part of the scene, and you want to be sure that it falls in the proper zone. You know that the correct zone for a frontally lit Caucasian face is Zone 6. So let's see where the other readings fall in terms of zones:

Zones	Zero	One	Two	Three	Four	Five	Six	Seven	Eight	Nine
Integers	9	10	11	12	13	14	15	16	17	18

The suit would fall in Zone 3, and thus in the print would be a dark grey with adequate texture. His shirt would fall in Zone 8, in the print a glowing white with some detail. The wall falls in Zone 5, a middle grey.

These all seem like appropriate placements for his clothing, face, and the wall, so you decide to expose the film with this zone placement. You would put the number 14 on the meter at the calculator dial arrow and use the corresponding f/stops and shutter speeds to choose an exposure. The reason you place 14 at the arrow is that you know 14 corresponds to Zone 5, and that the arrow on the meter represents Zone 5.

In practice, you won't want to write down all of this information and look at it each time you expose a scene. A quick way to place the face, or whatever you feel is the most important area of the scene, is to take a

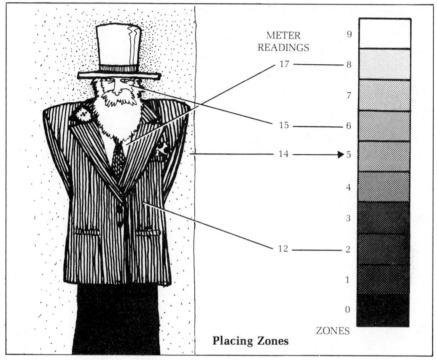

Placing Zones

reading of it, then decide what zone it belongs in. Knowing that the meter will give you Zone 5, count the number of stops which you must stop down or open up from Zone 5 in order to place the face correctly. In this case, you know that the face should be placed one stop above Zone 5. So you place the arrow on the meter one stop below the integer which represents the face (15)—you place the arrow on 14. Then you read off the resulting f/stop–shutter speed combinations on the calculator dial and choose a combination.

Here's another example, in which the zones fall over a wider range and make it more difficult to choose an exposure. Using the Zone System, you should be able to previsualize the possible ways in which this scene can be recorded in the print. Let's say you're photographing light transmitted through the kitchen window and exploring the way it falls on the window sill. The window pane gives a meter reading of 21 and the sill is 15. The pane is the part of the scene which you find most important, you decide that you want it recorded as a detailed light grey, and you place it in Zone 7. Now working down from Zone 7, you place the other meter integers on the zone scale:

						▼				
Zones:	Zero	One	Two	Three	Four	Five	Six	Seven	Eight	Nine
Integers:	14	15	16	17	18	19	20	21	22	23

As you work your way down the zone scale, you'll find that 19 on the meter falls at Zone 5. So you set the arrow on the meter dial at 19. As you continue to work your way down the zones, you'll find that 15 falls in Zone 1. This would make the window sill black, sacrificing all detail in this area of the picture. But if the sill isn't important to you and this is the effect you want, you'd set the meter at 19 and choose from among the corresponding f/stop-shutter speed combinations.

What if you feel that the window sill is the most significant part of the picture and you'd like it to give the impression of whiteness in the final print? Place 15 in Zone 7 and see what happens:

						▼				
Zones:	Zero	One	Two	Three	Four	Five	Six	Seven	Eight	Nine
Integers:	8	9	10	11	12	13	14	15	16	17

You'll find that 21 doesn't even fit into the zone scale, and you can figure that the window pane would be terribly blocked up in the print.

Perhaps the best solution would be to place the window pane in Zone 8, sacrificing some highlight detail and causing the window sill to fall in Zone 3, which would at least give you enough detail to see that it is a window sill.

The built-in meter is more tricky to use for this kind of zone placement than the hand-held meter. When using the built-in, first you have to isolate the area you are placing by finding it in the viewfinder. Then you center the needle to find Zone 5. Next you click off the stops on either the shutter speed or f/stop dials to reach the zone you want—open up one stop to place the area in Zone 6, and two stops for Zone 7; or stop down one stop to place it in Zone 4 and two stops to place it in Zone 3. If you want to do this for several different parts of the scene, it becomes a bit complex and unwieldy because you have to retain and count f/stops, shutter speeds, and zones in your head.

Averaging

Going around placing zones all the time is time-consuming, and you can use your knowledge of how the Zone System works in order to streamline the procedure. Wherever you're sitting right now, take a look at the scene around you. Chances are that there is a mixture of darks and lights. Since you're reading, there's probably a bit more light than dark. Visualize the darks and lights around you as they would appear in a black and white watercolor. What would happen if the paint were still wet and you ran it all together? Are there equal amounts of dark and light, so that the resulting blend would be a middle grey, or Zone 5? (The people who designed exposure meters figured that most scenes will average out to Zone 5, and this is why meters are keyed to this zone). If the room is quite bright, the blend might average out to a lighter mixture which approximates Zone 6. Learning to look at a scene and judge the blend is one of the basic tricks of selecting the right exposure when using the averaging method.

Let's say the scene averages out to approximately Zone 6. You've taken a meter reading with your built-in and determined what exposure will give you that average middle grey. Since each zone corresponds to a stop, you can open up the camera a stop and this will place the scene in Zone 6, or in other words, this will expose the scene to an average of Zone 6. Open up two stops if your subject is really pretty light, and this will place it in Zone 7.

On the other hand, you may be shooting in dim, shadowy conditions. The meter tells you how to produce an average middle grey scene, but you know that in reality the scene should be darker. So you stop down, perhaps averaging the scene to Zone 4.

Basically, exposure averaging is as simple as that. The meter gives you a reading for middle grey, you judge whether the scene should average to middle grey or not and make the appropriate adjustment. Let's say that you get a reading of 16 on your hand-held meter. You've looked at the scene and decided that it doesn't average to middle grey, but instead should be a whole lot brighter. Then you would open up two stops by setting the meter at 14 and selecting from among the f/stop–shutter speed combinations for the integer 14.

In a fast-moving situation with a built-in meter, it's best to find a part of the scene which seems to average to Zone 5; expose for that part of the scene and hope that everything else will fall into place. For instance, if you are photographing a person, you might be able to place the view-finder so that her face (which is light) takes up half of the viewfinder and her blouse (which is dark) takes up the other half; the scene will then av-

erage to Zone 5. Now you can center the needle and choose an appropriate exposure; then you can compose your picture and shoot. It's easiest
to do this sort of thing if you're using a mid-range telephoto lens, like the
85mm or 105mm. You'll find that you can isolate areas with these lenses
more precisely. Your ability to isolate areas for averaging is the key to
proper exposure with the built-in meter.

   As said before, a scene is middle grey if it is a fairly even mix of darks
and lights. However, very intense highlights like glinting sunlight or
light bulbs will have a greater influence on the blend than blacks; if these

**Averaging with a Built-In Meter: Isolate an area that seems to be
middle grey or an equal mixture of darks and lights.**

highlights are unimportant, isolate them out of the viewfinder and average the rest of the scene. You'll find that it's hard to eliminate these
distracting highlights with a wide-angle lens attached to the camera. You
should switch lenses to do your averaging—that's why it's handy to carry
more than one camera body with lenses attached; the meter body should
have the telephoto. If the highlights are significant to you, you can place
them individually in zones, and let the rest of the picture fall into the
logical zones, or tones. This is a much more exacting and time-
consuming procedure, but certain situations will require this precise
treatment, as we've said. From the Zone System point of view, zone
placement, rather than averaging, is the classic method of determining
exposure.

   In the field, you'll find yourself using a combination of zone placement, averaging, intuition, and experience. When averaging, you'll
probably come to find that most scenes average to Zones 4, 5, and 6, and
that you are averaging fairly expansive areas of the scene. If there are

areas which you want to place in Zones 3 or 7, they will tend to be small, specific areas. Areas which correspond to Zones 0, 1, 2, 8, and 9 are usually so tiny that they are difficult to read with anything but a spot meter.

If there are people in the picture, the best policy is to go with their faces and expose them in Zone 6 if they are properly lit. Human skin is the easiest thing for your eye to recognize in a print, and if you can place the skin tone in the appropriate zone, everything should fall in place logically.

High-contrast situations, because they go beyond the ten-zone range of the print, are the most difficult situations to expose properly. When it's important to get detail in both the highlights and the shadows of a contrasty situation, using the placement method and the hand-held meter is probably the safest alternative. But you may find that you'll have to give up either the highlights or the shadows. Low-contrast situations, like a piece of driftwood on an overcast beach, fall easily within the ten-zone range of the print, and it's much easier to select an exposure. A one-stop error in either direction won't be serious, and you can use the averaging method.

INTERPRETING EXPOSURE

Part of the problem in determining exposure is defining exactly what is meant by white and black and dealing with the relativity of tones. For example, your subject is sitting in the shadows and smiling; in the print his teeth are light grey. But if you were to ask someone looking at the print what color the subject's teeth are, he would probably say "white." A lot of the difficulty arises from our psychological interpretation of words and colors. The subject's teeth will appear white to you no matter how grey they are, because you "know" those teeth are white. Also consider this: in what zone would you place the reflection of a white table in a shiny black telephone? Much of the problem has to do with the fact that whites, blacks, and greys are relative. A grey card against a white field looks darker than the same grey card against a black field.

In the beginning, deciding what zone to place something in won't be easy. Let's take the example of Caucasian faces; they are not always logically presented when placed in Zone 6. It depends on the mood, the lighting, and the importance of the face. If the person is seated in shadows and you wish to convey a somber mood, you might place the face in Zone 4 or 5. If the face isn't so important and another part of the scene is, you may even go to the extreme of placing it in Zone 3. If you are having difficulty making a decision, judge the face in relationship to other parts of the scene. If the wall behind the person is light and you decide to place the face in Zone 6, will this drive the wall to an overly bright Zone 8? If that's the case, it probably would be best to settle on Zone 5 for the face and Zone 7 for the wall.

If you're having trouble placing a face or any other center of interest, it might also help you to first establish the extremes of dark and light in the scene—the important shadows and highlights in the picture you want. Then you will know the zonal context within which the face should logically fall. One quick way of determining the extremes is to scan the scene with a hand-held meter. The moving needle will show you the extremes of light levels and the number of stops between them.

Photographs are rarely comprised of large, flat areas that say "Place me in Zone 6." More often, they are a conglomeration of details, textures, and uneven light that does not immediately fall into a particular zone.

Exposure then, is a matter of interpretation; you interpret what is of interest in the scene and then choose an exposure that will communicate your impression. You may want to experiment and try a number of different exposures, giving different parts of the scene varying importance. Let's say you're doing a face shot of a woman wearing a scarf. Light shines through the scarf from behind, making a beautiful pattern on the cloth. Meanwhile, her face is rather dark. Now you could expose for the face, placing it in Zone 5 and produce a nice, ordinary picture of the face with the light through the scarf blocked up. Or you might expose for the highlight in the scarf and let that be the subject of your picture, with the face less prominent in the shadows. In either case, it is up to you to previsualize the final picture and make your decision in terms of that conception.

THE EFFECT OF DEVELOPING ON ZONES

Another tool in exposure is manipulation of developing time. Let's return to the H&D Curve. Remember that longer developing time increases silver density in the shadow zones very little, in the middle zones moderately, and in the highlight zones a lot.

If you have a scene which is very low-contrast, or has only a few zones, you can extend the range of these zones by underexposing and overdeveloping. Underexposing will push the shadow values farther down the curve, and overdeveloping will push the highlight values farther up the curve. The result is a higher-contrast image, or a bigger difference between highlights and shadows. Thus the zones are extended to fill out the H&D Curve.

If you have a scene which is very high-contrast, or has more than ten zones, you can compact these zones to fit the H&D Curve by overexposing and underdeveloping. Overexposing will make the shadows lighter, and underdeveloping will make the highlights less blocked up. The result is a lower-contrast image, with a smaller difference between highlights and shadows. Thus the zones are compressed to fill the H&D Curve.

A photographer who exposes and develops each picture individually, as with 4x5 film, can make these sorts of exposure and developing adjustments to control contrast in each picture. However, with 35mm film, this usually is not done because all the pictures on one roll of film are developed at the same time. You handle high- and low-contrast situations by selecting different contrast grades of paper, as explained in Chapter 11. For instance, you would print a high-contrast negative on low-contrast paper.

If, however, all of the pictures on a roll of film are high-contrast, you may choose to overexpose and underdevelop the entire roll. If all the pictures are shot in a low-contrast situation, you can underexpose and overdevelop—this, in effect, is what you do when you shoot film at a higher ASA.

You might also choose to use the higher ASA if the lighting conditions were so dim that you couldn't get the shutter speed you needed; doubling the ASA setting would give you one more stop of exposure. But if you double the ASA setting on the meter, you are effectively underexposing the film and must overdevelop to compensate. So you use this ASA knowing that you are driving the detailed shadows into black and the detailed light tones into blocked-up highlights. Shooting film at a higher ASA and then overdeveloping it is called *pushing*.

If you push film in a dimly lit situation that is low-contrast, you've done no harm because you've increased the range of the narrow span of shadows and highlights. However, in a dimly lit situation that is high-contrast, you lose detail in both the shadows and highlights if you push the film, and you must be sure that the necessary information is conveyed in the middle tones.

Some photojournalists push their film most of the time so they can have the security of knowing that they've got a faster shutter speed with which to play. But because the gradation and grain structure suffer, as does the film's ability to get detail in the shadows, I'd steer away from this practice.

EXPOSURE EXAMPLES

It may be helpful to go over a variety of possible situations so that you'll become familiar with exposure techniques in practice.

Low Contrast

Perhaps the easiest scene to photograph in terms of choosing exposure would be one with very low contrast, or just a few tones. For example, you may have a grey horse against a grey weathered barn on a hazy day. There are few shadows and they are not very sharp; the grey of the horse is maybe a zone lighter than the grey of the barn. So basically you've got two tones with which to work—horse and barn. You can place these tones anywhere between Zones 3 and 7 and still get detail for each area of the scene. Choice of exposure here is not critical; you can go with the Zone 5 meter reading, open up a few stops, or stop down if you wish.

High Contrast

But what if you are in the operating room photographing open heart surgery? Hopefully this won't be your first time out. You'll probably find that the operating table is brightly lit and that the light drops off dramatically as you move away from the table. If you're lucky, you'll have a spot meter to take readings off the surgeon's hands and the patient, or if you have a long lens and a built-in meter you can get in close that way. In either case, you'll find that the range of tones exceeds the ten-zone range of your film; the meter should tell you that it will be impossible to get detail for both the dark background and the brightly lit table in the same picture. Even the doctor's face may be too dark to get detail in the same shot as his hands under the lights. So you'll have to make a choice; place either the hands or the face in the appropriate zone, and let the rest of the picture fall into place. Probably the best solution would be to put the face in Zone 4. The hands will block up some—later, in the chapter on printing, we'll discuss how you can try to correct this by manipulating the image. If you expose for the hands, the detail in the face will be permanently lost.

Performer on a Dark Stage

It can be difficult to get a good exposure for a performer on a darkly lit stage or for any other situation where there's a small but important area with one light level surrounded by a large field of an entirely different light level—in other words, a white spot in a black field or a black spot in a white field. In the case of the dark stage, most of the picture will be black, with only small areas like hands and face adequately lit. This is an ideal situation for a spot meter—you'd aim at the performer's face and then place the resulting reading in the correct zone. You could also try to get backstage before the performance and take meter readings, even ask the technicians to turn up the lights some. But basically, in a strange situation like this, you'd want to pick out something on the stage that looks like middle grey or flesh tone, and using a telephoto lens or spot meter, zero in on it and take a reading. Then you'd let all the other areas of the stage fall into place around the reading for that area.

Highlight within a Highlight

Let's say you've got your eye on a white ocean liner on the bay. Its upper-most deck shines even more brightly than the white decks below, and to capture this white highlight within a white highlight you'd have to expose very carefully. If you were to overexpose, the whites of the ship would block up and you'd no longer be able to see the difference between the two whites.

You've got to carefully place both of the whites. Take a reading of the darker white and place it in Zone 6 or 7; the other white will fall into place.

Learning the language of the Zone System is valuable if you can set it clearly in your mind and then forget about it. Zones are just words and should not be blocks to taking pictures. The whole idea is to free your mind so that you can use your light meter and expose with reference to the way you want the image to look on paper. If my explanation of the Zone System has not quite clarified the matter for you, you may want to refer to photo magazines on the market. Every three months or so, at least one of them will run a story on the Zone System—usually a variation on an article that has been run again and again. I know that I found different interpretations of Adams' words very helpful in getting a handle on his system, and if you see another explanation elsewhere, don't hesitate to look at it.

Previsualization is a key element to using the Zone System, and it means learning to look at the setting as if it were a photograph and not a reality. Instead of seeing the colors and hearing the sounds, try to see the scene as a two-dimensional black and white picture. Some people believe that coming to know how a scene will appear in the print is a transcendental, religious experience. I just think it's an ability that you acquire with practice.

9

THE DARKROOM

S o there you are with several rolls of exposed film. Now you must decide whether to do your own darkroom work or let someone else do it for you. While the way in which a roll of film is developed certainly affects the way the image will appear in the final print, the developing process is standardized and routine, with little room for creativity. In the printing process, however, there's enormous opportunity to manipulate the image and emphasize your personal vision. In fact, I'd say that as much as fifty percent of the impact of the final print is achieved in the darkroom. Even if a home darkroom is unfeasible for you, it's worth your while to go through the process or have a knowledge of it so that you can better understand what's at stake.

Many working photographers send their black and white pictures to a custom lab or hire a technician whom they can bend to their style. Color photographers are even more likely to send work out, as color film is more complicated to develop. In addition, there's little creative leeway in the processing of color slides. There are a number of new color processing techniques which have been developed for the home darkroom, but from a commercial standpoint, these are not viable alternatives. Professional labs, with their access to extremely sophisticated equipment, can do a much better job. As with the rest of the book, the emphasis here will be on black and white processing.

Once you have decided to try your own darkroom work, you have several choices. You can rent or arrange to use a darkroom and buy chemicals, paper, and some tools. Rentals are often available through schools, camera shops, photo supply houses, or municipal parks and recreation departments. If you think you'll be developing and printing fairly often, you can buy an enlarger and a bit more equipment for a couple of hundred dollars and establish a temporary darkroom in your bathroom or kitchen that can be set up and then dismantled after each session. And if you're really committed, you can build a permanent darkroom in your home, spending anywhere from several huɪdred to several thousand dollars. However, one of the main points of this chapter is that you don't have to spend thousands.

Some technicians spend their lives in the darkroom. They tend to look pale and a little gnarled and shriveled. You would too if you spent most of your time in a dank, sunless cell. Because printing is so important to me, I spend hours cooped up in that room, even though I'd rather be elsewhere. For that reason, I've made a real effort to make the place as warm and comfortable as it can be. If you only go into your lab once or twice a month to do a couple of prints, then you'll probably concentrate on the prints and the ambiance of the room won't bother you so much. But if you pass numerous hours in the darkroom each week, it can be a stone drag. I remember hearing somewhere that the first time you see a print come up in the developer, it's a tremendous thrill. But I'd say that after the 800th print or so, a lot of the thrill is gone. At that point, you might want to furnish your work area with a few diversions—radio, stereo, and even TV—which we'll discuss later in the chapter.

Throughout this book, the aim has been to make it as easy as possible for you to produce pictures. The planning and construction of your darkroom is no exception. If your darkroom is ill-planned, drab, and uncomfortable, it can be a detriment to your perseverance in creative printing and can also make your work much more prone to error.

It's also disheartening if you find that the camera store salesman has sold you a lot of darkroom equipment that neither improves the quality of the final image nor makes getting there any easier; hopefully this chapter and your own thorough planning will help you avoid that kind of waste. This isn't to say that gadgets aren't fun—sometimes, working all the dials, I feel like a submarine captain—but in my darkroom the gadgets all serve some important function.

When planning your darkroom, you should keep in mind the two basic processes that take place there: developing negatives from exposed film and making prints from the negatives. These are really very separate processes, with their own specific requirements and equipment. There are also other considerations to keep in mind when making your plans. You'll have to figure on room for mixing and storing chemicals, enough counter space to stretch out a roll of film and cut it, and storage space for negatives and contact sheets. Also, you'll want to decide whether you'll wash negatives and prints in the darkroom, the kitchen, the bathroom, or some other room with plumbing.

We'll begin by discussing the specific equipment you'll need for developing and printing, and then describe how to set up a darkroom.

DEVELOPING SUPPLIES

In the course of developing your negatives, you'll need tanks and containers to submerge the rolls of film in developer, water, hypo, and hypo clearing agent. Additionally, you'll need film reels, a thermometer, a timer, washing and drying facilities, a squeegee, and mixing and storing equipment.

Tanks and Reels

Probably the best developer containers are the stainless steel cylinders made by Brooks, Honeywell-Nikor (not the same people who make Nikkor lenses), Kindermann, and Omega. Kindermann's has a rubber lid; the others have stainless steel lids. These *developing tanks* conduct temperature quickly, are easy to keep clean, and have a light-tight capacity which you may or may not want to use, depending on your developing technique. As explained later in this chapter and the next, I develop with the tanks open and the room light-tight.

The stainless steel tanks are designed to hold multiple reels of film, and are commonly available in two-, four-, and eight-reel capacities. It's not really worth it to buy a two-reel tank. The four-reeler is only a few dollars more and gives you a larger capacity, but can still be used to develop one roll.

The *film reels*, on which you load the film before submerging it in the tank, should also be stainless steel. Nikor makes reels without clips in the core, which in my opinion, is an advantage. I find the reels that have clips harder to use. (For a detailed description of how to load film reels, see Chapter 10.) Patterson and some other manufacturers make reels in plastic, but these are more vulnerable to injury. Also, plastic is more difficult to clean because it is porous and will absorb chemical residue from developer and hypo solutions. Stainless steel tanks and reels are more expensive, but they are a lifetime investment.

When you buy the larger tanks, you get a metal stem for lifting the reels in and out of the tanks; you can also buy the stems separately. The stems are especially important in the open-tank developing method. It's helpful if the stem is longer than the height of your containers so that you can get a good grip on it. Since developer is an alkaline solution, it's especially slippery, and if a relatively short stem gets wet, you'll have a hard time grasping it.

If you plan to use the open-tank method of developing, you'll need separate containers for water and hypo. Plastic half-gallon orange-juice containers will serve just fine—no need to put out cash for fancy tanks

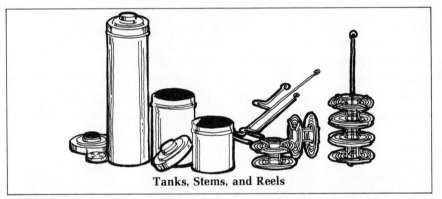

Tanks, Stems, and Reels

in this case. If you don't have the money for stainless steel tanks to hold developer, you can make do with the plastic orange-juice containers for that too. But keep in mind that the porous plastic will absorb chemicals and is difficult to clean. Thus you've got to be careful to use the same container for a particular chemical each time you develop—hypo in the pores of the plastic can contaminate a jug of developer. Also, plastic conducts heat and cold much more slowly than the stainless steel, and when you are trying to get a chemical to the right temperature, it will take you considerably longer if the tank is plastic.

Thermometer

Accurate temperature is crucial to the developing process, and you'll need a reliable, precise thermometer for determining whether your chemicals are at the proper temperature. Basically there are two types of photo thermometers from which to choose; the simple glass and mercury model and the more sophisticated bi-metal type. The latter, made by Weston and a number of other manufacturers, is much easier to use, for it reacts quickly to changes in heat and cold. However, the Weston-type does have a major drawback—it can become inaccurate without your knowing it.

Although the glass ones break easily, at least it is immediately apparent when they have done so. Since they are so fast-acting, you may want a Weston anyway; if so, it would be a good idea to stash away a mercury thermometer and use it regularly to check the accuracy of the Weston.

Watch out for those cheap little tray thermometers that cost a dollar or so. Their increments aren't accurate enough and they usually only

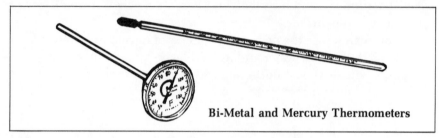

Bi-Metal and Mercury Thermometers

measure temperatures between 68 and 75 degrees. The Kodak color process thermometer, with mercury and a stainless steel backing, is probably the best thermometer you can get. However, it's very expensive—$28. The same model without the stainless steel backing costs only $5, but it's extremely fragile.

Timer

Exact timing is also a necessity when you are bathing film in developer, water, and fixative, so you'll need a timer marked in second increments as well as minutes. Since you'll be working in the dark, the big electric

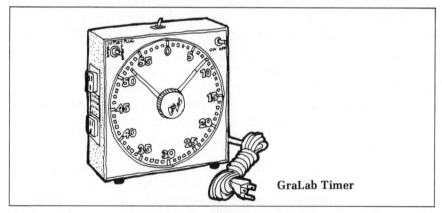

GraLab Timer

clocks with easy-to-read luminous dials and synchronous timing mechanisms make timing the easiest. The GraLab timer has always been a favorite, and recently Time-A-Lite came out with a similar model. The GraLab allows you to move the minute hand without disturbing the action of the second hand; this means you can segue from the timing of one film bath into the timing of another without missing a beat. For example, if the film is in the developer and the second hand is approaching 0, I can move the minute hand to 4 in preparation for the water bath. When the second hand hits 0, I dunk the reels in the water, and I don't have to reset the clock for the thirty-second rinse and the three-and-a-half minute hypo bath.

The GraLab is a fairly expensive item at $42, but is by far the best choice in developing timers. There are little wind-up clocks that are not nearly as efficient, and even these are fairly expensive—about $20. My two oldest photo possessions are the GraLab clock and a Nikor tank, and the clock has not gained or lost a second in eleven years. Furthermore, the GraLab can serve temporarily as an enlarging timer if you can't afford an additional clock for printing. Outlets on the GraLab enable you to plug in other electrical appliances, such as the enlarger, while the small wind-up clocks don't have this feature. However, timers which are designed specifically for enlarging are much better suited for this task because they are repeatable (see page 155) and some have tenth-of-a-second increments.

In a pinch, you might try using a regular alarm clock with a luminous dial for developing negatives, but it will be difficult. Most alarm clocks don't have accurate minute increments, and it's easy to lose track of how many times the second hand has gone around, especially if you're a little batty from sitting in the darkroom a while; they are also hard to see in the dark. I wouldn't consider these clocks accurate if you are working with a developing time of less than ten minutes.

Film-Drying Supplies
Once the negatives are processed and washed, you'll need space and equipment for drying. I use rubber *squeegees* to swab the film; see Chap-

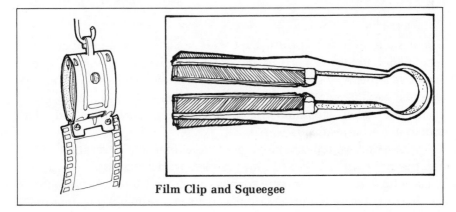

Film Clip and Squeegee

ter 10 for special recommendations on what to buy and how to store them.

It's worth investing in *film-drying clips* to hang the film, even though clothes pins will do. I would not recommend any type of forced-heat drying apparatus.

Mixing and Storing Your Supplies

Mixing and storing requirements vary with the type of developer that you choose. Some developers are stored between use in a corked gallon jug while others are mixed and then discarded after use. If you select the first kind, the replenishable developers, you'll need a dark-glass gallon jug for the main solution—a wine jug is good—and a quart bottle for the replenisher. You'll also need a one-gallon container for your hypo clearing agent and others for miscellaneous chemicals, but these don't have to be glass. Glass is dangerous in the darkroom, and you'll have to be careful.

For measuring chemicals, you'll need a one-quart graduate. You can spend a lot of money for a stainless steel or plastic Kodak graduate, or you can mark off 32 ounces on an orange-juice container. For chemicals which must be measured out in very small amounts, like replenishers or one-shot developers, you should have a graduate marked in very small increments from a half ounce to five ounces.

A glass rod is good for stirring chemicals, and the Kodak paddle stirrer can't be beat. Avoid wooden sticks.

PRINTING SUPPLIES

Setting up your darkroom for printing requires a more substantial investment. The main cost will be the enlarger; other items include an easel, timer, negative cleaner, grain focuser, trays, tongs, safelights, dodgers and burners, washing and drying facilities, and a few other odds and ends.

Enlarger

The basic item in your printing set-up is the *enlarger*, a piece of equipment which holds the negative and projects it through a lens onto photosensitive paper to make a print. Elaborate professional enlargers can cost as much as $600 or $700, and even my bottom-of-the-line Omega B-22 costs about $200. This model is classified as an amateur or "popular" unit, but it is quite adequate.

There are two types of enlargers, one with a condenser light source and the other with a diffused, soft-light set-up. The condenser is the one to use with 35mm film; its lamp consists of a frosted bulb and two or three condensing lenses. It creates a tightly focused stream of light and directs it through the negative holder. Enlargers are adaptable to different film formats, and you can buy lenses and negative carriers appropriate for 35mm, 2¼, and—with larger enlargers—4x5 as well.

Omega is the most popular brand of enlarger, and I chose the B-22 in particular because it allows me to use variable contrast filters in the lamphead (see Chapter 11). With all enlargers, you can mount contrast filters under the lens so that they intercept the light after it has passed

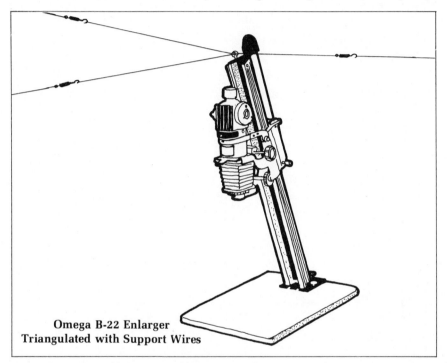

Omega B-22 Enlarger
Triangulated with Support Wires

through the lens. But I change filters in the middle of enlarging, and the only way to do this without shifting the focus and ruining image quality is to place the filter in a filter drawer between the negative and the light source.

You should occasionally check the alignment of the enlarger head. The negative holder must be parallel with the surface onto which the enlarged image is projected; otherwise, the image won't be sharp corner to corner. If you see the grain dissolving into mush in the corners of your prints, you'll know you have this problem. Enlargers are factory aligned, but they slip out of alignment with use. You can check out the alignment yourself with a carpenter's level, making sure that the negative holder is parallel with the baseboard. If you do find that the head is out of alignment, loosen the screws and very carefully work it back. While alignment is quite important, it isn't the sort of thing that should be a constant worry, especially when the enlarger is new.

My first enlarger was a Bessler 23C, which always seemed to drift out of focus. The Bessler has a filter drawer mounted between the negative carrier and the lens. Changing filters during printing with this arrangement will cause a sharpness-destroying image shift.

Another prominent brand is the Italian-made Durst, which is an expensive and well-made unit. It delivers sharp prints as easily as the Omega.

A baseboard is attached to most enlargers, serving as a support and providing a surface to hold the easel. The B-22, like many enlargers, is designed so that you can unscrew the enlarger from the baseboard, turn it around, and position it so that you can make giant blow-ups on the floor. In addition, the Omega B-22 comes in two column lengths: regular and extra-long. The latter allows you to make 16"x20" prints on the baseboard or countertop without turning the enlarger around. This little extra adds another twenty dollars or so to the price of the enlarger, but is worth it if you plan to do any 16x20s.

A wobbly enlarger can degrade the quality of a print, and it's been my experience that an enlarger will vibrate if you hit it or the counter, if you're changing filters, or if a truck rumbles past. For this reason, I've triangulated the center post to hold it steady, using piano wire, little turnbuckles, and hooks. Another alternative is to anchor the center post to a nearby shelf.

Lenses do not come with the enlarger, although sometimes the camera store will sell them in a package deal. I use Nikkor enlarging lenses, which are of the same high quality as the Nikkor camera lenses. For 35mm film, 50mm is generally the correct focal length. For 2¼ film you would use 90, 85, or 80mm. However, you could also use the latter lenses if you were making smaller, 5"x7" prints from 35mm negatives. When you make a 5"x7" enlargement using the 50mm lens, the enlarger head has to be moved quite close to the paper. This leaves only a little space between lens and paper in which to work, and this is a problem if you want to dodge and burn (see pages 202–03). In addition, the closer the enlarger head is to the paper, the more intense the light and the shorter the exposure time, which gives you very little time in which to play with the enlargement. If you want to hold back the corner of a print for ten percent of the exposure time and have only three seconds to work with, you'll find it pretty difficult. The longer lenses give you more exposure time and more distance between the paper and the enlarger head. If you only do 5"x7" prints occasionally, you probably won't want to invest in a special lens; instead, you can use neutral density filters. These clear grey filters cut down the intensity of the light and allow longer exposure times. They cost about $6 each.

As with camera lenses, enlarging lenses have optimum *f*/stops. On the Nikkor *f*/4, the optimum stops are *f*/5.6 and *f*/8. Nikkor also makes a more expensive *f*/2.8, but there's no need for speed in an enlarging lens—again, the more enlarging time the better, within limits.

Home color printing requires a more complicated enlarger head, and manufacturers have recently come out with a whole battery of elaborate heads to suit their regular models.

Easel

To hold the paper in place under the enlarger, you'll need an *easel*, and this too can be a pretty expensive item. Basically it is a heavy slab of

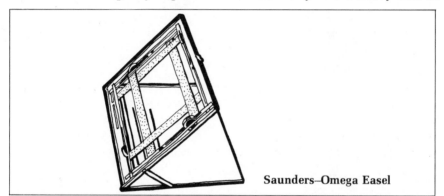

Saunders–Omega Easel

wood, metal, or some other material with metal bands that pin down the paper. You can pick up an adequate easel for about $80.

In addition to pinning down the paper, the bands frame the image. I like the easels with four movable bands that allow the image to be centered on the paper. Most easels have only two movable bands, which forces you to place smaller images in one corner of the paper. The Saunders–Omega has four bands and takes three different sized papers: 11"x14", 8"x10", and 5"x7". If the paper can be centered on the easel, you have more flexibility in placing the picture where you want it on the photo paper.

The 35mm enlarger projects a frame of film whose aspect ratio is 2:3, but the standard printing paper has a ratio of 4:5. If you use an easel with movable bands, you can arrange them to form the 2:3 aspect ratio, retaining the full, elongated 35mm shape.

The less expensive, so-called Speed Easels are poorly designed and tricky to use in the dark. The small 8"x10" easels which are also available are inflexible and not worth the lower price. For those who want prints that run to the edge of the paper, or *bleed*, there are borderless easels. These tack down the barest tip of the corner of the paper. If you usually make prints with borders but occasionally make bleed prints, you can improvise with Scotch Magic Transparent Tape. I've marked grids on the counter so that I know where to position the paper; I remove the easel and attach the tips of the paper to the counter with tape.

A Saunders–Omega that will hold a 16″x20″ piece of paper and has four adjustable bands will run about $200. If you do prints that large only occasionally, you can rig up a makeshift easel or borrow one.

To reveal the natural black border of each negative, you can carve a sixteenth of an inch from around the inside of the enlarger's negative carrier. The carrier is made of thin metal and can be easily cut. Some people like to carve it back far enough to show the film's sprocket holes, hoping to communicate a photographic purity, showing that the frame was not altered in any way and is seen in its entirety.

Negative Cleaners
The negative must be free of dust before printing. The best tool for removing dust is the Static Master Brush, a special brush that contains a replaceable piece of radioactive plutonium. As you run it lightly over the film in one direction, it eliminates the static electricity that attracts dust. Specially treated pieces of cloth are a less advisable alternative; they tend to retain pieces of dust which can scratch film the next time around. If you do have scratches on the negative, you can fill them in with a very, very thin coating of vaseline.

Grain Focuser
A crucial darkroom tool for 35mm work is the *grain focuser*, which

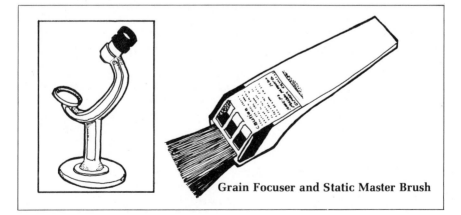

Grain Focuser and Static Master Brush

magnifies a small portion of the image and makes for precision focusing. Without it, you would merely judge with your eye whether the image projected onto the easel is in focus; with it, you can see grain patterns and focus until they are sharp. You focus with the lens stopped down, because with the lens wide-open you can't see the grain. (Meanwhile, you can prove to yourself the existence of optimum *f*/stops.) The classic grain focuser is a French product called the Scoponet, but there are several others, including one by Patterson. They cost about $30 and are worth the expense.

Enlarging Timer

As mentioned earlier, the GraLab clock can double as an enlarging timer if your budget is limited. However, the GraLab is not quite as precise as the clocks designed especially for enlarging work. An enlarging timer like the Heathkit solid-state model can time to a tenth of a second. Furthermore, most enlarging clocks are repeating timers: you set the dial to a specific interval, and each time you press the start button it turns on the enlarger light for that interval. A separate time/focus switch allows you to turn on the light manually so that it stays on while you focus and compose.

Time-A-Lite is the classic brand of enlarging timer; it is an electric clock with a sweep dial and costs about $70. More recently, the solid-state clock has gained popularity. Heathkit is probably the least expensive model, if you are willing to build it yourself. With no prior experience, I assembled the Heathkit in three days—two days to put it together and one day to correct my mistakes. It performs excellently.

The solid-state clocks have the advantage of tenth-of-a-second increments, while the electrics such as Time-A-Lite are measured off in whole second increments from 0 to 60. When you decide to increase printing time, you do so in percentages of the original time. For instance, if your printing time is 12 seconds and you want to increase it by 20 percent, it's much easier to measure those extra 2.4 seconds on a solid-state clock.

A little luxury that makes printing a lot easier is a foot switch hooked up in parallel with the time/focus switch. Usually you have to move your hands very quickly when burning in a print and it's awkward if you have to both turn on the switch and shield the paper at the same time. The foot switch frees your hands by turning on the light. You can pick up a heavy-duty waterproof switch at an industrial supply house, but you'll have to deal with the complicated wiring yourself.

The Time-A-Lite and Heathkit models have two outlets, one that can

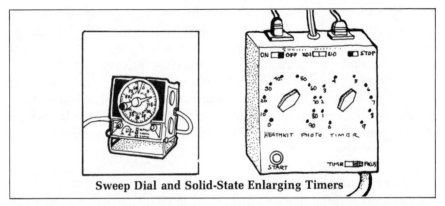

Sweep Dial and Solid-State Enlarging Timers

be used to link the clock with the safelights and another to connect it to the enlarger. Usually the safelights are plugged in so that they turn off when the enlarging lamp goes on. This makes focusing, dodging, and burning easier.

Safelights

When printing you'll be using *safelights;* these are regular bulbs in a casing with amber filters, producing a color of light to which photographic paper is not sensitive. Place one for your work around the enlarger, another near the developing tray so you can see the prints come up, and maybe a few more to even up illumination in the room and make it more pleasant. Each paper manufacturer makes a safelight which is supposed to work only with that particular brand of paper. But generally speaking, they are interchangeable and one brand is as good as another.

You can make sure that your safelights are not too strong with a very simple test. Turn out the room lights and turn on the safelights. Place any opaque object on top of a piece of photosensitive paper and wait about ten minutes; then develop the paper. If there's a slight grey tone on the paper where the object wasn't covering it, the safelights are too strong. You can correct this by moving the lights farther away from the enlarger or putting in lower wattage bulbs. Also, you might check to make sure the safelight filters aren't faded.

Some industrial darkrooms use safelights that put out a sodium vapor of safelight color; these are brighter than the conventional filtered lights and much more expensive. They are also more difficult to use because they can't be turned on and off with the enlarger; they are similar to fluorescent lights in that they take a while to start up.

Trays

You'll need at least four trays for printing: one each for developer, stop bath, and hypo, as well as a fourth for miscellaneous purposes, such as holding prints until they're ready for washing. Some rented darkrooms and larger labs have separate rooms for washing and drying. In this case, the fourth tray can be used to carry prints to the other room.

White, hard plastic trays are good; the alternatives are stainless steel, white enamel over metal, and the multicolored plastic trays. The stainless steel trays are extremely noisy—one more thing that can make life in a small darkroom depressing. Enamel trays can chip, and without the coating the exposed metal will rust. And rust in the darkroom can be a real problem.

Ribbing or a raised cross on the bottom of the tray is essential. Otherwise the print will settle to the bottom and cling there, making it

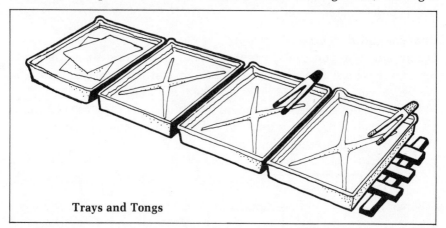

Trays and Tongs

very difficult to pick up with your tongs. It's also tricky to use tongs with the small 8″x10″ trays; there's no room to get a hold on the paper. The 11″x14″ trays are much easier to work with.

One mark of a permanent darkroom is a standing tray of printing hypo covered with another tray or some sort of lid. This way you avoid the hassle of pouring an 11″x14″ tray of hypo into a jug each time you finish printing.

Tongs

For years I used my hands to manipulate prints during developing. In fact, I felt you didn't get a "human" print unless you got up to your elbows in developer. Since then I've learned better. While some people are less susceptible than others, developer can cause skin problems. When I noticed that I was beginning to grow a second set of fingernails, I considered using rubber gloves, but gloves don't feel right to me. Bamboo tongs work well and they are cheap, but you may want to check out the metal and plastic ones. Basically, it comes down to what feels best to you. Whichever type you buy, be sure that they are rubber-tipped so that they grip the print and don't damage the surface of the paper.

You'll need two tongs, one for developer and another for everything else. It's important to keep them separate so that you won't contaminate the developer. Tongs have a variety of different colored handles for this reason.

If you can get used to tongs, then you won't have to wash and dry your hands so often during printing to avoid contamination. Acquiring dry, wrinkled hands is one more thing that can make darkroom work unpleasant. If you use your hands and aren't careful about washing them, you're liable to leave white fingerprints on the photograph with your hypo-contaminated fingers.

Dodgers and Burners

During printing you can alter the image by darkening some areas and lightening others. The tools used for this are called *dodgers* and *burners*. For an explanation of how these are used, see Chapter 11.

You can buy dodgers at a camera supply shop, but you can also make them yourself with stiff wire, black tape, and cardboard. Their stems should be about 8 inches long and it's handy to have circles of three

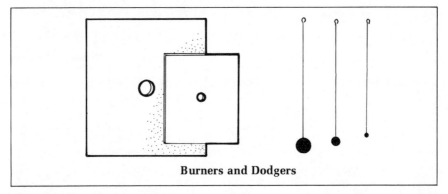

Burners and Dodgers

different sizes. A diameter of 1½ inches is good for work on 16"x20" prints, 1⅛ inches for 8"x10" prints, and ½ inch for small prints or for working on small areas of a larger print.

Burners can be made from the bottom of an 11"x14" box of photo paper with a ½" hole carved out of the middle. You wouldn't want the board much smaller than that, because as you move the hole to one corner of the image you want to shield the rest of the image from the enlarger light. Camera stores sell a burner made of safelight plastic with a half dozen holes of assorted shapes. I read about a photographer once who used this type of burner, but only when he was printing in his white tie and tails.

Dryers

Prints can be dried a number of ways: between blotters, on amateur electrical dryers, on racks, or on large, commercial, continuous-belt dryers.

Blotters are great if you live in the desert or only do a few prints a month. They take a long time, especially if you live in a humid climate.

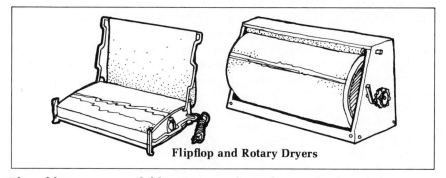

Flipflop and Rotary Dryers

Photo blotters are available at camera shops, but are fairly expensive.

There are two kinds of amateur dryers. One is the flipflop type, which is flat and has either one or two drying surfaces, or platens. Up to four prints are placed on the heating platen and then a canvas is stretched over them. This type of dryer costs about $30 and does the job, but with a large number of prints it will take a long time.

I use the other type, the amateur rotary dryer, a chrome-plated drum with a heating element inside. Prints are wrapped around the drum and held in place with canvas. This type of dryer costs approximately $250; I got a used one for $10. It holds six prints at a time and dries them in fif-teen minutes.

Commercial rotary dryers with the highest quality chrome plating go for as much as $800 or $900. They carry the prints on a belt which moves continuously and extremely slowly. This means that you have to attend them constantly, feeding them and then waiting for the prints to fall out one by one. With the small rotary dryers, you can feed them and then go away and do something else while the prints dry. For this reason, if I were to increase my drying capacity, I'd invest in several more rotary dryers instead of buying a large commercial one.

There is another drying method that allows you to do a large number of prints at one time. With plastic fly screening pinned to wooden frames, you can make a series of drying drawers or racks. The wet prints are placed on the screening and are held down by the drawer above them, which prevents curling. A hot-air blower can be used to circulate air through the whole set of racks. This is an excellent and relatively inexpensive method of drying. However, it does take up a lot of space.

The rotary dryers are designed with chrome facing so that you can *ferrotype* prints—that is, make them glossy. When a print is wet, its emulsion is soft and swollen. If you squeegee it perfectly, face down on the smooth surface, and then dry it on the chrome, it just might come out with a smooth, glossy finish. However, more and more, glossy prints seem to be a thing of the past. A glossy print used to be considered the only kind that would reproduce well in newspapers and magazines, but this is no longer true. In fact, most photos are printed on glossy paper but then dried with the emulsion side facing away from the chrome so that the finish is matte. Furthermore, the introduction of resin-coated paper has made it possible to avoid ferrotyping altogether.

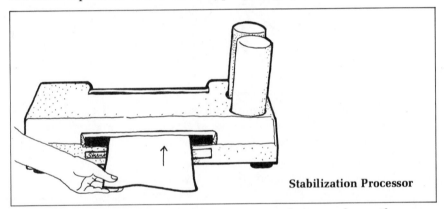

Stabilization Processor

Resin-coated paper, a relatively new product, produces the same high-gloss effect as the expensive chrome dryers and doesn't require a dryer at all. The paper is coated with a shell of plastic, and the emulsion sits on top. Thus the paper never accepts the water or chemicals; they soak into the emulsion but don't seep into the paper. Normal prints are washed for hours to remove chemicals which have seeped into the fibers of the paper. With this new paper, it only takes a few minutes to wash chemicals from the emulsion. Then you squeegee it and in a few minutes it is clean and dry. Although this paper eliminates a lot of the hassle involved in washing and drying, its surface leaves something to be desired. It feels almost like a laminated ID card. I use the resin-coated paper for contact prints, but prefer the regular papers for other prints.

While we're talking about eliminating cumbersome processes, we should mention the *stabilization processor*. This machine works like a copier; it develops prints quickly. Special chemically treated paper feeds into the machine, goes through a chemical solution, and comes out the other side as a damp/dry print. There's no need for trays or plumbing. At Associated Press, where they use this process, they haven't had a drop of water in their darkroom for years. However, stabilization prints don't seem to have the beauty and richness that the more traditional method provides. If you have a small darkroom, you might consider this process. Spiratone makes an adequate stabilization processor for $150; the next model, made by Kodak, jumps in price to $450. Stabilization prints will fade after two weeks or so, but you can fix them in hypo and wash them like normal prints to make them permanent.

BUILDING A DARKROOM
Selecting a Location

The less permanent your darkroom, the longer it will take you to set it up. If you're renting a room, you'll have to lug assorted chemicals, paper, tanks, timers, thermometer, tongs, contact glass, easel, grain focuser, and Static Master Brush and then set them up. If you are using a bathroom or kitchen, it'll take you about an hour to remove everything from the closet, lay it out, mix the chemicals, and make the room light-tight. Then you can start printing. And when you're finished you'll have to take it all down, clean it, and put it away. If you only develop and print once in a while or if you're just learning, that may suit you fine. With my permanent darkroom, I can walk in and have my first print in the developer in about five minutes. I know where everything in the room is and I do the developing and printing the same way each time.

If you find that you are doing more and more darkroom work, you'll probably come to the point where you'll want a permanent darkroom. You can partition off part of an attic, transform a large closet, or claim a room in your house or apartment. Darkrooms can be built anywhere. Early photographers prepared their film in light-tight tents on the Civil War battlefields; photographers today are offered floor plans for darkrooms in mobile homes.

No matter where you set up your first darkroom, it would probably be best to take a modular approach. A darkroom can grow and move with you, with equipment first used in the bathroom later incorporated into a permanent room. And once you have set aside space for a permanent darkroom, you can still keep it fairly mobile. For example, my sink and splashboard are not nailed down and can be removed with relatively little hassle the next time I move.

Taking a modular approach also means buying each piece of equipment with the idea that it is part of an evolving system. Even if you have a modest bathroom darkroom, it is worth your while to invest in a good enlarger and other quality tools. This way you won't have to lay out cash for better equipment when you set up a more permanent lab, and you'll have the benefit of reliable equipment right from the start.

A TEMPORARY LOCATION

A bathroom set-up gives you the advantage of running water close by. I know someone who placed the enlarger on the toilet and the trays on the floor—it was very cramped, but it did work. A workable arrangement is to build a shelf over the bathtub that can be lowered to hold the trays and add to this a small table to hold the enlarger. If you do set up in the bathroom, take some time to figure out where you can put the various tanks and trays and how to position them for the greatest convenience. In fact, in any darkroom set-up you choose, it's important to go over the developing and printing processes and then figure out how you'll arrange things. You may want to develop in the bathroom and take the negatives elsewhere to dry, you may want to make prints in the attic and carry water back and forth from the bathroom, or you may want to process the film in the kitchen and hang the negatives to dry over the bathtub. There are a lot of possibilities, and the decision should be based on what is most comfortable and feasible for you.

When I was going to school, I lived in a cheap hotel room. I put my enlarger on the floor and would sit cross-legged in front of it. When I moved to a larger place, I had a darkroom in the attic, but it was never light-tight enough for open-tank developing. So I would take my film, chemicals, timer, and tanks into a closet and tack up clothing all around the inside of the door to block out the light. After five minutes of this I'd get a little crazy, but I'd also get my film developed.

A PERMANENT LAB

Most often, people will select the basement, laundry room, or utility room for a permanent darkroom because the plumbing is there. My preference is a large closet or room in the house; basement or utility rooms are usually dingy and dank already without the help of chemicals and water.

However, I tend to be like the cook who leaves batter all over the walls. When I first started working in the darkroom, I would spill whole bottles of chemicals or would get distracted and turn around with the running hose in my hand—not the sort of thing you'd want to do in a nicely painted and equipped room. But I've found that it's worth paying attention to controlling splash so that I can work in a comfortable space rather than build my darkroom in what amounts to an indestructable cell. If you've done a print that is almost right and say to yourself, "Hell, I don't want to sit in this place another fifteen minutes doing it over again," then the darkroom is working against you.

Darkroom Construction
SHUTTING OUT THE LIGHT

If your darkroom has a window, there are a number of ways you can block out the light. The most Rube Goldberg way of doing it—temporary but effective—is to cover the window with aluminum foil and tape. The foil gets pinholes in it as it begins to crinkle and age, but in my attic darkroom I was able to sustain this type of light screen for a year by patching holes with pieces of masking tape. The edges of the window and the door can be sealed with weather stripping, which is available at most hardware stores.

Black plastic sheeting also makes a good blackout device and can be obtained from plastic supply firms. Or, if your landlord is amenable, you can paint over the window-glass.

Before you decide to seal off a window completely, you should consider the ventilation in the room. Moisture accumulation and the lack of circulation can make a darkroom stuffy. If you're working in a tempo-

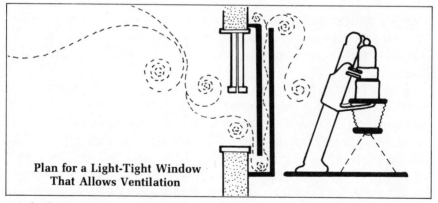

**Plan for a Light-Tight Window
That Allows Ventilation**

rary bathroom set-up, you'll want to open the door and walk out every so often. If you have a permanent darkroom with windows, you may want to construct a light-tight box over the window that allows air to circulate. Although there aren't any windows in my darkroom, I've improved ventilation by drilling holes through a closet wall into the next room and covering them with a light-trap box. An exhaust fan in the ceiling draws the air through the room. In my next darkroom, I hope to have air conditioning.

You can check your darkroom for light leaks after sitting in it for ten minutes. It takes that long for your eyes to adjust to utter darkness, and you'll be amazed at how much you can see after that amount of time.

WET AND DRY SIDES

Classically, darkrooms are divided into a wet side and a dry side to guard paper and negatives from chemical splash. On the wet side are the trays and chemicals, on the dry side the enlarger and space for loading reels and handling dry film. While there must be a separation between the wet and dry sides, the less distance between the two sides, the better. If you have to make a print, take it out of the easel and walk across the

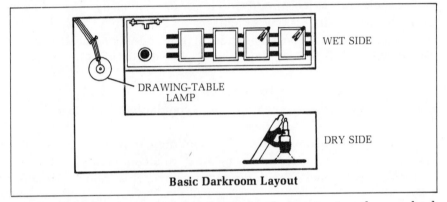

DRAWING-TABLE
LAMP

WET SIDE

DRY SIDE

Basic Darkroom Layout

room with it, sit down and develop it for three minutes, then go back across the room, chances are you won't want to make that trip often. It's infinitely easier to turn from the enlarger and have the trays right at your fingertips.

Counter space for the dry side can be made simply by utilizing any handy corner of the room and constructing a two-legged table against it. All you need is a piece of ½" plywood, three L-brackets, and some legs. In determining the size of the plywood, take into account space for loading reels, mounting the enlarger, and cutting the film. For the latter, you'll need enough countertop to hold 5½ feet of film. Cover the table with contact paper or Varathane to seal it. This is pretty bottom-of-the-line, and as you settle into darkroom work you may want to do some more sophisticated carpentry, including provisions for storage. Whatever you build, keep in mind that the lower the counter, the more the backache.

The wet side of the room doesn't necessarily have to include a sink; if you can't pipe water into the darkroom, you can carry it back and forth from another room in a tray. But this is awkward. A sink in the darkroom is a true convenience for draining liquids and containing splash. For thousands of dollars you can buy a stainless steel job, and for less you can purchase a molded plastic shell. But the least expensive option seems to be building one out of marine plywood. This should be a carefully carpentered trough which is glued and sealed at the seams and then coated with polyester resin. It's a two- or three-day project and requires some research, but it's well worth it.

In considering dimensions, take into account that you'll want at least enough room for four trays to sit side by side in the sink on a *duckboard*. The latter is a platform that holds the trays out of the bilge in the sink and prevents them from rounding at the bottom from the weight of water or chemicals. I made the duckboard in my sink from redwood fencing. The wood should be thick enough (at least ¾ inch) to support the trays when they are heavy with chemicals.

When I built my sink I mixed the polyester resin with powdered asbestos and used this mixture to build up the bottom so that liquids would flow toward the center, where the drain is. Mixing the resin correctly is important and seems to be the biggest problem with this type of sink. Before you mix the resin you should talk to a good plastics salesperson and make sure you know what you're doing. It's also important that you make the bottom smooth so that pools won't collect and make it difficult to keep the sink clean.

The drain in my sink was forced into a hole cut in the plywood and then sealed with plastic. In fact, I coated the whole inside of the drain

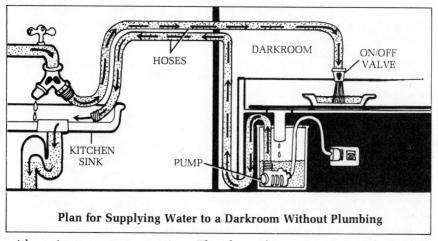

Plan for Supplying Water to a Darkroom Without Plumbing

with resin to prevent rusting. The drain fits into a pipe which then empties into a large plastic garbage pail under the sink.

Because there were no plumbing connections in my darkroom, I had to connect my sink to the water supply and drain in the kitchen via two rubber hoses. Maybe you can use this system as a model for your darkroom. Water pressure in my apartment building is low, so I've never had to worry about the hoses splitting. The new PVC plastic piping now used by some commercial plumbers is great. It can be cut with a knife and joined with glue, and is available at plumbing or building supply stores.

One hose brings water into the room and another takes it out. Fresh water comes through the hose into the darkroom sink, and an aereator at the end of the hose softens the flow and lessens the chance of splashing. I use a fish-pond pump in the pail beneath the sink to send water and chemicals back to the kitchen, and I turn it on and off several times during a darkroom session. (Most home darkrooms don't dump enough corrosive chemicals into the sewage system to affect the pipes, but if the plumbing in your building is really old and decrepit, you may damage it. It's a good idea to check this out.) Before I had the pump, I carried water in and out of the room in jugs—a real pain.

In the kitchen, one hose is attached to the faucet with a Y-shaped pipe (a garden supply appliance) so that I can get water in the kitchen for other purposes when the darkroom hose is connected. For connecting hoses to the faucet pipe and to other accessories, *snap connectors* found in hardware stores and also in camera shops under the name "Darkroom Plumber" are very handy. Screw connections take longer to hook up.

PRINT-WASHING FACILITIES

When washing prints, you'll need a continually moving supply of water that replenishes itself in the tray within four or five minutes. The Kodak Tray Siphon is a circulating device that continuously introduces a swirl-

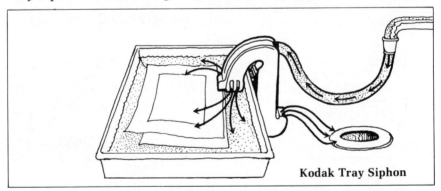

Kodak Tray Siphon

ing stream of fresh water into the tray while drawing out the old water. It costs only about $9 and lasts a lifetime. You can spend a great deal of money on special washing devices, but the Kodak Tray Siphon, when used with hypo clearing agent, is sufficient.

Hypo-laden water is heavier than regular water, so it sinks to the bottom of the washing tray. If you were to wash the prints by directing water into the tray with a hose and allowing it to flow out and over the sides, the hypo-laden water would stay in the bottom of the tray and the fresh water would skim across the top. Also, the print would flow out and over the sides of the tray. But the siphon keeps the water flowing through the entire tray. It comes with a fluted rubber cone that is supposed to hold it onto the faucet or hose; it does, until the water is turned on, so your best bet is to link it to the hose or faucet with a snap connector.

ELECTRICAL CONSIDERATIONS

Because of the water and other liquids in the darkroom, you should take special care in placing electrical outlets where they can't be easily splashed. Also, you should be aware of the variations in current that can affect enlarger performance. Probably the greatest difficulty with home darkroom electricity is the reduction in voltage when an appliance like the refrigerator switches on in the middle of a print. This can diminish your exposure time by seven or eight percent, causing an occasional unexplained lighter print. Although current regulation is a finer point of darkroom work, you may want to buy a voltage regulator to guard against dramatic current fluctuations.

ADDITIONAL TIPS

A *splashboard* above the sink keeps water and chemicals from dripping down behind the sink and also provides a surface upon which to squeegee prints. Formica is good, and you can also make a small splashboard from a sheet of plexiglass.

Watch out for the hard rubber squeegees with wooden handles designed for swabbing prints. The wood rots and splits and the rubber is held in place with metal staples that rust. Kodak's all-rubber squeegee is made of thick, hard rubber and is kind of brutal; the best alternative is probably a window-cleaning squeegee made of rubber with a coated aluminum handle.

A stool comes in handy for all those times when you are waiting around during processing. It works best if your room is small and you don't have to pull it out and reposition it each time you turn around. If the wet side and dry side are close enough, you can just turn in your seat.

A darkroom that can be kept clean easily is important, since you'll want negatives as free of dust and dirt as possible. For this reason, if possible, you should design the room to have few ledges and exposed pipes. You'll need a few storage areas, though, for filing negatives, contact sheets, prints, chemicals, and other accesories. You'll also need a special area for hanging the film strips up to dry; Chapter 10 describes an efficient set-up with hooks and a shelf. I would allow drying space for twice the capacity of your reels. While one batch is drying, you can clean and air dry the reels and soup another batch of film.

I'd recommend painting at least the area around the enlarger matte black. If you're doing a lot of dodging and burning, the enlarger lamp will bounce a significant amount of light off your hands and against the wall. From there it can reflect back onto the paper and fog the image.

Luminous tape sold in photo stores and hardware stores is another item that makes life in the darkroom easier. Since it is luminescent, you can use strips of it to help identify anything you'll be reaching for in the

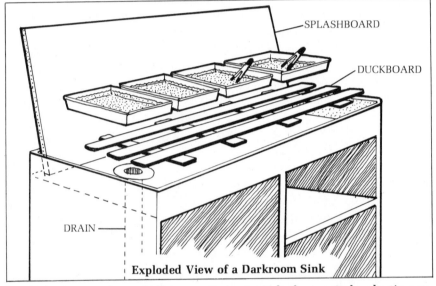

SPLASHBOARD

DUCKBOARD

DRAIN

Exploded View of a Darkroom Sink

dark—light switch, grain focuser, timer switch, foot switch, plastic containers, telephone handle, etc. However, the tape must be placed so that it is exposed to light when you turn on the regular lights in the room. The tape gets charged up this way so that it will glow in the dark.

You also might want to make labels for the orange-juice containers that hold hypo if you are using the open-tank method. With indelible ink or Dymotape you can mark the level to which hypo should be poured and the point beyond that to which the water should go. The same can be done with a jug of replenishable developer. With labels, you can avoid rereading the directions on the package each time you want to mix a solution.

Another handy item is a drawing board lamp that can be pulled over to illuminate either the wet or dry side of the darkroom. A lamp is especially useful for seeing dust on negatives.

For those middle-of-the-night sessions, you should have extra enlarger and safelight bulbs on hand. If a bulb should go out at 2 A.M. and you don't have another, you won't be able to pick up one at the corner liquor store.

If you use replenishable developer, you'll need at least one funnel for returning it to its jug. Be sure to use that funnel for developer only. Otherwise it may become contaminated with other chemicals and alter a perfectly good batch of developer. Also, with regard to pouring chemicals, there's a secret to emptying a large jug in a hurry without splash. Turn it upside-down and swirl it. This will create a whirlpool, with air traveling up through the center, allowing the liquid to flow out smoothly instead of going glug, glug, glug. It's tricks like this you dream up in the darkroom.

Once you've got your developing and printing routines down pat, you may want to introduce such diversions as radio, stereo, and TV. The lighted radio dial should be blocked out, and the TV screen should be covered with Rubylith, a deep red sheeting available from any art supply store. Headphones are usually pretty easy to bring into the lab if you don't want to hook up stereo speakers.

If you've got your splashing act under control, you might think about laying down indoor/outdoor carpeting. This adds warmth and comfort and makes life easier for your feet.

Additional suggestions for darkroom planning can be found in many of Kodak's publications. They often have specific design ideas, including suggestions for ventilation and light traps. Another source of ideas is the *Photo-Lab-Index,* which you can check at the library.

Striving for zero defect is an essential concept in darkroom work. There are so many little things that can drive you crazy and trip you up while developing and printing that it's wisest to design your room for greatest ease and efficiency. It may take you fifteen minutes to make each print. If at the end of that time you discover that the borders are off because the easel moved, you're going to have to do it all over again. You can avoid this type of aggravation by buying quality equipment—in this case, a substantial easel with rubber feet. And the same is true of all your other equipment. Intelligent planning and the choice of well-designed materials will save you considerable time and expense.

Whether your darkroom is permanent or temporary, you can approach zero defect by organizing the lab, stocking it with efficient equipment, and making it comfortable. The more efficient your darkroom, the freer you'll be to experiment and use your imagination to produce crisp and exciting prints.

10
DEVELOPING

Developing a roll of film is a simple, mechanical task, best performed as if you were a robot. There's no creativity here—just machine-like efficiency to achieve consistent results. But as dull as the actual task may be, it is a critical element in the photochemical process. The negative is the receptacle which stores information for the final print. And you only get one chance to develop, or *soup*, the negative.

While there are a number of significant variables in the developing process, the single most important factor is the overall care you devote to the task. The goal is an informative, clean negative—one that stores all the information accurately and completely. Care and precision in developing your negatives pays off in easy prints that fall onto the paper without all sorts of adjustments for developing mistakes.

One significant variable in developing is the length of time you soup a negative, as we've explained with the H&D Curve; if developer temperature and agitation are held constant, as I feel they always should be, then developing time will help determine image contrast. The longer you develop, the more contrasty the image will be. Unlike 4″x5″ film, where each negative can be developed individually at a custom time, with 35mm film you must soup an entire roll at once. This means that you've got to find one developing time that suits most of the pictures on the roll. If a few shots would have looked better with a longer or shorter developing time, you can make up for this in printing by selecting either different contrast grades of paper or different contrast filters for those particular shots. In general, however, you should try to attune developing time to suit your tastes in contrast and your choice of printing paper, which we'll discuss in the next chapter. The final test of a negative is how your print looks. Accurate judgment in developing and printing is acquired over the long term; it comes only with experience and through seeing other people's work. In the beginning, it's best to pick one developer and hold developing time constant, using the manufacturer's recommendation; as your ability to judge crystallizes, then you can toy with developing time.

Keeping things clean when developing is especially important. You're working with chemicals that can contaminate one another and the negatives, so you should go to lengths to make sure your hands and equipment are free of hypo before touching the developer. Also, dust or dirt on the negative will be magnified many times in the print. This doesn't mean that a dirty, stomped-on negative can't produce a beautiful picture; you'll just have to work on it a whole lot longer to get it right.

You're likely to find that it's a drag if you have to spend hours and hours in the darkroom. If you repeatedly have to take extra time when printing to correct errors that could have been avoided during developing, you'll resent it. After a while, the aggravation of correcting errors will detract from your ability to be creative when printing.

As in every stage of the photographic process, small errors and carelessness accumulate to subtly degrade the overall quality of the image, while attention to detail tends to enhance the quality.

Now that you've got the right perspective, it might be a relief to learn that serious errors in developing are rare. Basically it's an easy, safe process that's been done millions of times without problems. There are really only a few mistakes you can make that will destroy a negative or roll of film. Loading the developing tank reel incorrectly can crimp or buckle the film and leave scars on your negatives. Of course, turning on the light at the wrong time can obliterate an entire roll. Using the wrong bottle of chemicals is another possibility; I once developed five rolls of film in a developer solution that was mixed half and half with fixer from an unmarked bottle. That's the kind of mistake you make only once. If it's any comfort, Robert Cappa, one of the world's great photojournalists, covered the invasion of Normandy from the very first wave only to have the film destroyed by a darkroom technician in London. But if you're careful and think each step through, there's no reason you'll ever have to lose a picture through developing mistakes.

THE BIG PICTURE

Before examining the specifics of each step in developing, let's briefly run through the process. We'll assume you've got one or more Nikor reels, a tank and some accessory containers, developer and fixer properly mixed, thermometer, film-drying clips, and all the rest of the darkroom equipment mentioned in the last chapter.

In the dark, you open the film cassette with a can opener or Official Kodak Cassette Opener. Then you load the film onto the Nikor reel and drop it into a tank that has been filled with developer carefully adjusted to the correct temperature. Achieving and maintaining developer temperature is particularly important; with the other solutions it does not seem to be that critical.

The film is left in the developer for a specific amount of time— usually between three and seventeen minutes—and is agitated at regular intervals. The degree to which the film develops is a product of length of time in the soup, temperature, and agitation. If you increase any one of these, you extend the developing process and thereby intensify contrast in the image; but, as mentioned earlier, it's best to hold these constant.

At precisely the right moment, you transfer the film to a water rinse, or *stop bath*, and agitate it for about fifteen seconds to stop the action of the developer. Next you immerse the roll in fixer, or hypo, which completely stops the action of the developer. After about half a minute, the image is stable and you can turn on the lights. The hypo has "cleared" the image by removing from the emulsion all silver halides that were not converted into metallic silver by the developer—that is, the halides which were not affected by light at the moment of exposure or were not developed during the time the film was in the soup.

Depending on the type of hypo, the film usually remains in the solution for two to ten minutes. Then it is washed carefully to rinse out all traces of hypo left in the emulsion. (This step is often accomplished with the aid of a chemical *hypo clearing agent*.)

Now you're ready to take the film off the reel, squeegee it, and hang it to dry in a dust-free place. Once the film is dry, it is usually cut into five strips of seven frames each or seven strips of five frames each. This is in preparation for contacting, which will be discussed in Chapter 11.

CHOOSING A DEVELOPER

Browsing through the shelves of a well-stocked camera store is enough to send the uninitiated reeling from the darkroom forever. I count about thirty different developers for 35mm film, all of them claiming approximately the same thing in just about the same words: "Offers excellent gradation, sharpness and contrast, with fine grain; suitable for giant enlargements, while utilizing the maximum possible film speed." Surprisingly enough, they all deliver.

As a rule, though, most photographers stumble onto one developer that works well with their basic film and they stick with it. Keep in mind that choosing a developer is only a minor variable in the countless possible variations in producing a photographic print.

Of all the developers, approximately ten are realistic choices for Tri-X film; the others are designed for special-purpose films. Among the ten, it's really hard to discern any differences. Really hard. Kodak's D-76 is considered the classic developer. It is mid-range in the way it handles grain versus sharpness and is good for Tri-X, Plus-X, Panatomic-X, and all other normal black and white films. While some developers are proprietary—that is, patented or secret—D-76 is a public formula. So you can buy the component chemicals, make it up yourself, and vary the formula by adding a little bit more of this or that. Otherwise, you can get it already made in powder or liquid form.

One consideration in choosing a developer is the length of developing time specified by the manufacturer. I like Ethol UFG partly because it has a short time: three and a half minutes. This way, I don't have to sit around in the dark for fifteen or twenty minutes waiting for the film to soup. The drawback is that a ten-second mistake in timing represents a fairly significant chunk of my developing time—an error of 5 percent—whereas a ten-second error out of fifteen or twenty minutes would be negligible. D-76 has a developing time of seven and a half minutes—not too bad if you aren't as impatient as I am.

Another consideration in choosing a developer is the type of chemistry you prefer. Developers come in liquid or powder form and are either *one-shot* or *replenishable*. The one-shot developers are used once to soup the film and then thrown away. Usually they come in liquid concentrate form with instructions telling you what proportion of water to add. This type of developer gives you the advantage of a fresh solution every time, eliminating the possibility of weak development due to old or contaminated developer.

The replenishable developers come in liquid or powder form. You mix them with water and use the solution over and over again, each time adding a little fresh chemistry, which is called replenisher. The replenisher is a sister formula to the developer; for example, if you develop with D-76, you replenish with D-76R. Replenisher not only provides fresh chemistry, it also neutralizes the retarding effect of byproducts created by the action of the developer. The manufacturer supplies a separate can of replenisher along with the developer, and the replenisher is kept in a separate container once it has been mixed with water. You add a precise amount—usually half an ounce—to the main jug of developer for every roll of film you've souped. You'll find that after a while the main jug will get cloudy with silver particles. Though there's really no need to worry about them, you can filter them out if they bother you.

At one time I felt that all the solutions I used had to be pristine and never-before-used, but now I realize that replenishables work just as well. In fact, I've come around to seeing developer as an old, bubbling stockpot—if I can keep the solution alive and going, that's fine with me. However, there is a limit to how much you can replenish a developer. Usually you can use no more replenisher than an amount equal to the original quantity of developer solution. To be on the safe side, I toss my developer a little before this limit is reached.

For those interested in playing with the chemistry, there are probably thousands of developer formulas to tinker with. In addition to the thirty or so brands in the camera stores, you can find page upon page of developers listed in the *British Journal of Photography* and the *Photo-Lab-Index*. Of course, these publications include formulas for all types and formats of film. For example, you might find listed a formula numbered 2236 that calls for 6 grams of X chemical and 2.8 grams of Y chemical, which should produce in Z film emulsion a strikingly beautiful tonal quality. But keep in mind that if the refrigerator went on in your house and reduced the voltage to your enlarger while you were making a print, that would make more difference in the final print than would the use of formula 2236. I don't mean to say that the choice of developer is completely insignificant, but that the differences are very subtle.

As mentioned in the film chapter, different developers produce slightly different grain structures in a given film because their varying formulas lead to different silver clumping patterns. Kodak's Microdol-X, for instance, although advertised as a fine-grain developer, causes the silver to clump in such a way that the grains appear muted and image sharpness suffers. On the other hand, high-energy developers such as Acufine give the impression of enhanced sharpness by creating a more defined, "salt-and-pepper" grain structure. Most developers fall somewhere between these two types. In pursuit of the beauty of silver on paper, some people devote a great deal of time to experimenting with film/developer combinations. I don't want to discourage that, I just want to put it in the proper perspective.

SPECIFICS OF DEVELOPING

Now we'll discuss the developing process in detail, taking you each step of the way to the finished negative. Once again, I'd like to stress the importance of consistency; after you've experimented and chosen a developing time, you should do each step in the process in exactly the same way every time you develop. The less you change such variables as time, temperature, agitation, and chemicals, the more likely you'll be to achieve consistent results.

First of all, the darkroom should be clean. And so should your hands. Each time you finish mixing or pouring one of the chemicals, you should wash your hands. And when you're finally sitting there with your chemistry all together, the temperature of the developer correctly adjusted, and your empty reels in front of you, you should clean your hands again. Throughout the process, keep your fingers off the surface of the film so that body oils won't smudge it.

Before turning out the lights, take one last look around and make sure that your act is together. Run through the process in your mind and make sure the film, reels, stem, cassette opener, and scissors are placed so you can find them easily in the dark. Double-check to see that your solutions are all in the proper places and at the correct temperature and that your timer is set properly and plugged in. At this point, you might consider an emergency procedure in case of unforeseen difficulties. This planning might include figuring out what to do if you knock over a container or spill chemicals. For instance, know where you can get a paper towel to dry the tank in the dark and where you can find the lid to the tank so you can turn the lights on.

Preparing the Developer

The manufacturer gives you instructions on how to mix the developer, and you'll probably find that a large wine bottle is a good place to store it. Pay close attention to the wording of the instructions. Notice whether it says, "To X amount of developer add enough water to make one gallon," or "Add one gallon of water to X amount of developer." There's a difference. You might want to mark the one-gallon level on the jug with a piece of tape to facilitate measuring. Many manufacturers recommend using distilled water, and I go along with this. Tap water may be excessively acid or alkaline and thus upset the delicate pH of the developer.

Developer temperature is extremely important. In fact, to achieve consistent results, your measurement must be accurate to within half a degree. So pick a temperature as a standard and always develop at that temperature. The manufacturer will probably give you a few choices; for example, the worldwide standard for D-76 is 68 degrees. However, if you live in a warm climate and water from the tap runs consistently warmer, you may want to standardize it at a higher temperature and shorter developing time.

The stainless steel Nikor tanks conduct heat and cold very quickly, so it's easy to get the temperature of the developer exactly the way you want it. Plastic containers are considerably slower. You can submerge the tank of developer in a large bowl of warm water and swirl it around or chill it in a container of ice water. Once you've got the temperature right, it will stay pretty constant as long as you keep your hands off the tank. However, if it's 90 degrees or warmer in your darkroom and you've got a long developing time, the solution may end up a few degrees warmer by the end. Rolls that have been overcooked usually aren't ruined, they're just a little harder to print. Although you should try to be accurate to within half a degree from one darkroom session to the next in the interests of consistent, predictable results, you can still work with a negative that wasn't souped at the proper temperature.

Loading Nikor Reels

Normally you would begin your work in total darkness, but loading Nikor reels requires some practice. When you're learning, practice in the light with several unexposed rolls of film. This might seem wasteful, but it's better than blowing two or three rolls of exposed film by loading them incorrectly. Once you've got the feel of it, you'll probably never have problems loading again.

Using a can opener or Kodak opener, pop the lid off the film cassette—not the end that the spool protrudes from, but the other. Remove the film and cut off the first four inches or so; this is the amount that you used to load the film onto the camera's receiving spool and to get it moving on the sprockets. Be sure to cut it off squarely.

Now pick up the reel and see where the spirals stop. In the dark you'll have to do this by feeling them. In the core of the reel there's an open slot; insert the film there. (Some manufacturers are making reels with a clip in the slot to hold the film. I avoid these brands because I find them troublesome.) Holding the film with thumb and finger of your right hand, feed the film into the open slot in the core of the reel; then turn a few inches of film onto the innermost spirals of the reel. These first turns are criti-

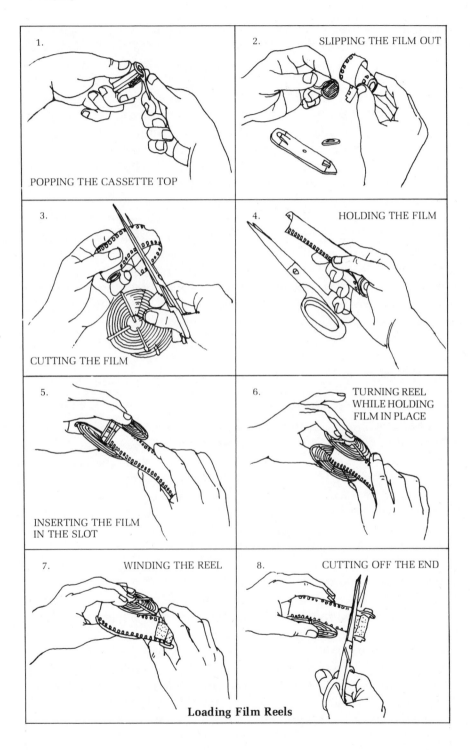

1. POPPING THE CASSETTE TOP

2. SLIPPING THE FILM OUT

3. CUTTING THE FILM

4. HOLDING THE FILM

5. INSERTING THE FILM IN THE SLOT

6. TURNING REEL WHILE HOLDING FILM IN PLACE

7. WINDING THE REEL

8. CUTTING OFF THE END

Loading Film Reels

cal; the film must be fed squarely into the reel, and a little practice will educate your fingers. Now let the rest of the roll drop so that it dangles freely from your hand. The tension of thumb and finger is important, for it causes the film to buckle and feed onto the reel properly. With your left hand turn the reel so that the film winds around it, resting on the reel's metal spirals. When you have wound the roll completely, snip off the end as close as possible to the tape that connects the film to the spool.

You can only practice loading with the same roll of film a few times before it loses its tensile strength and goes limp. When this happens, it loses the ability to buckle and thus its ability to feed onto the reel properly.

If you haven't cut the film off squarely, it might wind on incorrectly and become crimped. When you've made this sort of mistake, you'll unreel the film after developing to find irregularly shaped or half-moon marks where the free flow of chemicals has been blocked. You should be able to sense whether the film is feeding properly within the first few turns; if it's wound wrong, you'll feel the film bend off the track. If it starts to bend, you can unwind the film and start again.

Loading the reel requires a fine touch. Nikor makes an accessory, a metal bridge, which holds the film and feeds it evenly onto the reel at the correct tension. But in the long run, doing it with your hand is easier. A little practice will help you overcome the initial difficulty, and you won't have to rely on a "training bridge."

Some people prefer to leave the film in the cassette and feed it onto the reel directly; they cut off the tongue so that it is square and then pull the film through the felt lips of the cassette, which help provide the right amount of winding tension. Although this method might be easier because you don't have to worry about how to hold a dangling strip of film, it can cause scratches on the film if there is dirt or dust on the lips of the cassette. Another trick in loading is to place the reel on a flat surface while you feed the film onto it. This helps insure even winding.

Loading the Tank and Agitating

Most people use the classic developing method, which takes advantage of the light-tight capacity of Nikor tanks. With this method, you load the reels in the dark and place them into a tank full of developer; then you put the top on, turn on the lights, give the tank a sharp rap to dislodge any air bubbles clinging to the film, and complete the developing process in the light. Agitation is accomplished by lifting and turning the tank. But I don't use this method. In fact, I never put the lid on the tank. I load the reels into a tank filled with developer and agitate them by lifting and turning the stem. There are a couple of advantages to doing it this way. With the classic closed-tank method, there's the danger of *surge marks*, overdeveloped areas on the edges of the film and pronounced streaking around the sprocket holes caused when excessive agitation of the tank forces developer through the sprocket holes. This is a problem that can be seen in many negatives, but most photographers don't notice. The reason surge marks aren't more of a problem is that they blend into any dark detail on the edges of a print. They are most likely to show up in smooth areas of lighter tone—sky, for example—and if this does happen, there's no way to correct it in printing.

Another reason I use this method is that my developer has a very short developing time, and errors of a couple of seconds have a relatively large impact. It takes several seconds to load and empty developer from a closed tank, whereas pulling the reels up by the stem is quick—the timing is much more crisp.

Whichever method you use, you should place the loaded reels into the tank in one smooth motion. If there are multiple reels, ease them in, being careful not to let any of them hang up on the edge of the tank. Lift the stem no more than an inch, turn it gently a quarter-turn, drop it; then lift it again, take a quarter-turn in the opposite direction, drop it; and then once more lift the stem, turn it a quarter-turn in the original direction, and then drop it. Do this continuously for the first fifteen seconds of developing to coat the film evenly and eliminate the possibility of air bubbles sticking to it. Then repeat the agitation process during the first six seconds of every minute in the developer. Agitation has to be gentle. As with temperature, when you increase agitation, you increase the film's gamma.

Stop Bath

The developing process stops when the film is bathed in water. If you are using the open-tank method, you lift the reels out of the developer, let them drain a second, and drop them into a separate container of water. If you're using a closed tank, you simply dump out the developer and pour in the water. After fifteen seconds of agitation in the water, the film is ready for hypo.

Although an acetic acid solution is sometimes recommended as a stop bath, this is inadvisable for 35mm film because it is too harsh.

A word about the temperature of the stop bath and the remaining solutions. While film is developing, its emulsion is impregnated with fluid. This means that it is susceptible to expansion and contraction caused by changes in temperature. If you were to plunge the film into water much hotter than the developer, the emulsion would expand; if you dropped it into icy water, it would quickly contract. During this expansion or contraction, the particles of silver in the emulsion would move around and create a more pronounced grain pattern, a form of emulsion damage referred to as *reticulation*.

Kodak has made such great strides in improving film's surface stabilization that you don't have to worry very much about slight fluctuations in temperature of water, hypo, and hypo clearing agent. That doesn't mean you shouldn't pay attention to temperature control, however. Keep these solutions within five degrees either side of the developer temperature, but don't spend twenty minutes of darkroom time trying to get the water down two degrees. Just remember that consistency contributes to the overall quality of the final print.

Hypo

After fifteen seconds or so in the water, the film is immersed in *hypo*, which removes the unexposed, undeveloped silver from the image and halts development completely. If you're using the closed-tank method, you'll empty the tank of water and replace it with hypo; I dunk the rinsed reels in a separate graduate filled with hypo. After a minute, the lights can be turned on.

Follow the manufacturer's recommendation for length of time in the hypo and agitate the film to remove unaltered halides. Because I've come to enjoy short times, I use Rapid-Fix, which costs a bit more than regular hypo but only takes a few minutes.

At this point you should take the Nikor tank full of developer and pour it back into the jug, if you haven't already. Establish a routine of immediately replenishing the jug of developer, so there's no chance of forgetting. If you lose track, you might as well toss the jug.

It may not make a significant difference whether the reels are in the hypo for two or four minutes, but for the sake of consistency I do it the same every time. If you leave the reels in the fixer longer than the recommended time, it will begin to eat away at the developed film crystals. This destroys the shadow detail by corroding the tiny wisps of silver in the thin areas of the film.

Washing and Swabbing the Film

Once the hypo has done its job, the film should be rinsed in running water. Usually this is done in an open Nikor tank or a fancy, expensive container designed for this purpose. The film is washed for one minute in running water and then immersed in hypo clearing agent, usually Perma

Wash, for one minute with intermittent agitation. Then it is given a final, one-minute wash in running water. If you have an especially dirty water supply, it's a good idea to purchase a filter for the water line.

The film is then dunked in a wetting solution. Kodak Photo-Flo seems to be the most popular. It has a dilution rate of 1 to 200, or a couple of drops in a quart of water.

The wetting solution helps to guard against streaking by preventing the water from beading and drying on the film in spotlets. Kodak says to immerse the film in Photo-Flo and hang it up, and the sheeting action will dry everything smooth and clean. But it doesn't work that way. The film dries irregularly anyway, and the little beads of water remain and collect dust.

Swabbing down your film once it is hung is one of the most important things you can do to keep your negatives clean. If a little dust fleck dries onto the film and you enlarge that film, it becomes a huge dot. You

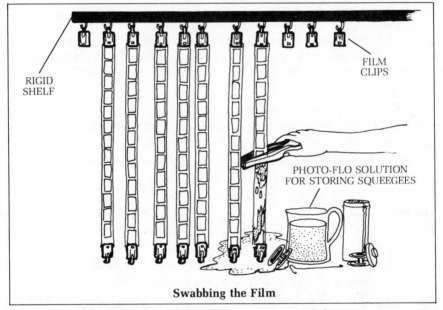

RIGID
SHELF

FILM
CLIPS

PHOTO-FLO SOLUTION
FOR STORING SQUEEGEES

Swabbing the Film

can remove these spots from the print with a special dye (see pages 212–13), but you won't want to spend all of your time spotting prints.

A special film squeegee, available at camera stores, comes in handy for wiping off water before the film dries. You can use sponges designed for this purpose, but they accumulate grime. The objection to the squeegee is that this tool might scratch the film by dragging heavy pieces of grit over it. I get around the whole problem by storing my squeegee in a Photo-Flo solution between darkroom sessions. As long as it's always wet, there's little chance for a hard, dry piece of dirt to sit on the rubber surface. So, as far as I'm concerned, the whole secret to wiping down film is keeping the squeegee wet. Of course, this is the type of thing you can do most easily if you have your own darkroom.

You can buy special film-drying clips for holding the film, and they're preferable to clothes pins. The latter don't grab the film as well, which is important when you are swabbing down a roll. If you suspend the clips or clothes pins on a wire or rope, you'll probably find that they spring off the line when you pull down the film to swab it and then release it. And if the film falls on the floor and collects dust and grit, then you've got to wash and swab it again. Also, the springing wire causes the squeegee to jump, preventing a smooth swab. A good solution is to attach the clips to the underside of a stable shelf.

Once the film is hung, place a clip or clothes pin on the bottom of the strip to help prevent the film from curling up when drying. It will also make the film easier to handle when swabbing.

To swab, run the squeegee slowly and smoothly down the film, removing all surface water from both sides. If you're not in a tremendous hurry, it's best to let the film dry for several hours at room temperature. Forced-heat drying of negatives is usually frowned upon because the emulsion side dries faster than the other side of the film, causing the film to curl. And that makes handling and contacting tricky. At a large newspaper, where they aren't so concerned with permanency or quality of image but are worried about time, they dip the film in an alcohol solution or Yankee Instant Film Dryer. Then they run a squeegee down the roll and it dries almost immediately.

Storing

Once the film is dry, it should be placed on a countertop long enough to hold the entire strip. Cut the film carefully with a scissors into strips of five or seven frames each, depending on whether you want vertical or horizontal contact sheets. Place the strips in glassine envelopes, with one roll to an envelope. (Recently, manufacturers have proposed various complicated systems for storing negatives. I've tried a few, but find that one roll to a glassine is the most trouble-free and convenient method.)

You'll want to develop a filing system to keep track of your negatives. If you're an accountant, you may enjoy working out an intricate system, but the easiest seems to be filing according to consecutive job numbers and roll numbers. I keep a ledger with a list of jobs, including date, subject description, and number of rolls shot. For each new job, I refer to the ledger and label the glassine envelope with the latest number, followed by the particular roll number. For example, an envelope might be marked 86-1, meaning job number 86, first roll shot. I also write that combination number on the back of the contact sheet and stamp the back with my name.

Your goal, a "perfect" negative, is elusive indeed. Everything in photography is variable, and you've got to steer your way down the middle of the variables as best you can. Your thermometer may be off a few degrees: your meter, developer, and shutter speed may also be incorrect. If these things vary in the same direction, your negative may be way off; on the other hand, it's possible these variations will cancel each other out.

As explained at the opening of this chapter, the best way to judge a negative is in terms of how the print looks. This requires experience and knowledge of a few guidelines. Obviously, a negative should have full shadow detail when you look at it; also, you should be able to read a newspaper through the highlight (black) areas—they should not be opaque. Consistency and care will give you a negative that prints easily and produces a vibrant photograph.

11
PRINTING

Printing can be viewed as a relatively mechanical process for transferring the image from the negative onto photographic paper or as an opportunity for creative manipulation and interpretation of the photographic image. To my way of thinking, there are three distinct approaches to printing which are best exemplified in the work of photographers Henri Cartier-Bresson, Ansel Adams, and W. Eugene Smith.

For Cartier-Bresson, a 35mm photojournalist, the real beauty of photography lies in capturing the essence of a particular instant within a frame of film. He is a purist in the extreme. Any alteration in the essence of the instant—any manipulation of the image once the film has been exposed—conflicts with his philosophy. Thus, he has a talented printer produce straightforward prints from his negatives. The only corrections the printer makes are related to limitations of the film: for instance, exposure problems which film cannot handle adequately. In these cases, he might lighten or darken areas of the print slightly to make them more lucid.

Another approach can be seen in Ansel Adams' work with the Zone System. For the most part, he photographs subjects that are immobile and thus has a great deal of time to map out exactly how he can best capture their tonal values on photographic paper. He is concerned with pre-visualization of expressive tones; he very carefully measures all the different exposure values in the scene and then plans how to expose and develop the film so that all of these values will fall properly in the print. He uses 4x5 or 5x7 negatives and soups them individually, each at a custom-selected time. Therefore his prints need few adjustments, having come from well-planned negatives. When Adams places a negative in the enlarger, he intends to make a perfect print on #2 contrast paper every time, with a minimum of manipulation.

Both of these photographers are concerned with purity—Cartier-Bresson with the purity of the instant and Adams with the purity of tones and their range on the paper.

A third approach is that of W. Eugene Smith, whose concern is the impact of the final print, regardless of how the picture was taken. In certain cases he has taken very bad negatives and made very beautiful prints through extreme manipulation in the darkroom that includes extensive dodging, burning, and bleaching. In other cases he has taken photographs that were technically adequate but unspectacular and has made them into strong visual statements by using the above techniques. This type of interpretive printing, which concentrates on the beauty and effectiveness of the final print, will be the focus of this chapter.

INTERPRETIVE PRINTING

Throughout this book, we've emphasized the beauty of silver on paper. Here we hope to show you how to take full advantage of the potential for beauty that the medium affords by means of creative printing: by heightening certain tonal areas and obscuring others, by playing with film's subtleties—in general, by painting with light. This approach conflicts somewhat with the usual textbook view that the darkest tone in the scene should be the blackest black in the print, that the brightest highlights in the scene should be the whitest white on paper, and that if this correspondence is achieved and you've chosen the correct contrast grade of paper, all the other tones which lie between the two extremes will fall into place correctly in the print.

If you want to express a particular mood or thought in a print, you might decide to alter the tones to enhance the mood. You may choose to darken a light area of the print until it is much darker, so that it blends in with the background and disappears. You might also want to alter the tones in a picture that was shot with mixed light. You may find, as I do, that some of the most interesting photographic situations are those illuminated with mixed light; and these situations, with their extremes of dark and light, do not fall easily into the nine zones we discussed in Chapter 8. To a certain extent, you can use printing techniques to make sure that all of the tonal areas which you find important are recorded lucidly, whether they were originally blasted with light or hidden in shadow.

In our discussion of printing technique, we'll only chip at the tip of the iceberg that photographic printing can be. There are many other techniques—e.g., double printing, montage, solarization, and duotone printing—which alter the original image even more drastically, submerging to an even greater extent the content of the original instant of exposure, the original negative, or the intent of the photographer at the time he took the picture.

I do want to express a certain reverence for the photographic image as it is recorded on film. It does have an integrity of its own. Among photographers there are different attitudes toward purity; one of the most prevalent is the belief that photography is a magical process which exists on its own and that once the photographic image has been recorded it should be left unencumbered as much as possible by gimmicks or afterthought. However, there are different philosophies of photography, and it's up to you to choose how much you wish to edit your photograph.

In order to gain a true appreciation of the loveliness of silver on paper, it's important that you see some really fine prints. There's a tremendous difference between an original photograph, in which light is rendered in silver, and a reproduction in a book, magazine, or newspaper, where the same image is rendered with ink on paper. There's no way you can see the full beauty of a photographic print by looking at the printed page. In fact, prints which take advantage of the full tonal range of photographic paper tend to reproduce poorly in magazines or newspapers, especially their very dark or very light tones. There's nothing like seeing the real thing to know what silver on paper can do, and so I recommend seeking out museum or gallery exhibits in order to get the full impact of beautiful, glowing prints.

Keep in mind too that most printing does not take full advantage of the medium's potential for expression. However, custom-made prints created by the photographer or prints made by a custom lab in keeping with the photographer's special vision will show best what silver can do. I feel that at least fifty percent of the impact of a print can derive from expressive printing.

LIMITATIONS OF THE 35MM FORMAT

When Ansel Adams takes pictures of Old Faithful, which goes off regularly in Yellowstone National Park, he sets up his view camera and takes exposure readings off the geyser. As with all of his pictures, he keeps a record of each reading, filling out an exposure card and noting how many footcandles each tonal area of the scene measures and exactly how he exposed it. Then he waits forty-five minutes for the geyser to go off again and takes a picture of it.

The 35mm photojournalist may take two and a half or three rolls of film in the time it takes Adams to fill out his exposure card. However, the journalistic approach allows less time for meter readings and is therefore much more vulnerable to errors in exposure. It is much more a take-them-as-you-can style, with far less opportunity for manipulating the subject, camera, and lighting to achieve proper exposure. And this means that there are times when you'll come back from a shooting session with negatives that are less than acceptable, where even your best image has lots of problems.

Take the case of the girl pictured in photo 5. She was standing in the dark shadow of a tree, wearing a bright white shawl. Behind her stood people in blazing sunlight, wearing white clothing. The proper exposure for her darkened face placed the background figures eight stops overexposed, jammed up into the shoulder of the H&D Curve, and thus blocked up. Added to this problem was the aesthetically unappealing pattern created by the background figures; there was no grace or rhythm to the way their shirts blended, and dark spots in the wrong places threw off the picture's balance. It took a lot of manipulation of the print to reduce the influence of the background and enhance the image of the girl, giving the picture an impact it wouldn't have otherwise had.

Beyond helping you to cover errors or difficulties in shooting, expressive printing can also help you overcome the gradation limitations of the small 35mm format. As mentioned before, the large format films like 4x5 and 8x10 have a much greater ability to achieve delicate separation of tones. You have to work especially hard in printing to get the same long, smooth range of tones with a 35mm negative because these qualities suffer in enlargement. Finesse in printing can help you recapture the subtleties originally contained in the tiny 35mm image.

IN THE DARKROOM

Printing is essentially a separate process from that of taking the picture. You're there in the darkroom, and it may be days or even months since you actually took and developed the picture. Your camera technique, choice of exposure, and use of the Zone System are all behind you now; once you go into the darkroom to make a print, you begin a new process. Your immediate concern is a good-looking print. But it is essential to evaluate every step which has come before, including your previsualization, or what you thought the picture would look like before you took it.

First we'll discuss printing papers, how they vary, and the chemicals needed to process them. Then we'll get into contact printing and how to proof your work on a contact sheet. Next follows a detailed discussion of the actual printing process, followed by a description of the finishing touches.

SUPPLIES

Paper

Printing paper comes in a wide variety of styles to suit your photographic purposes. It varies in surface texture and tone, weight, speed, and contrast.

SURFACE

The emulsion coating on the paper usually consists of some combination of chloride and bromide chemicals. Warm, soft portrait papers have more chloride than bromide, while the papers with cold black tones are predominantly bromide. The colder, harsher types are standard journalistic papers and tend toward bluish black, while the portrait papers tend toward brownish black tones. As far as reproduction in a magazine or book is concerned, any coloration in the print is lost when the photo is translated into printer's ink. For this reason, most reproduction is done with photos printed on cold black commercial paper.

Kodak—the biggest manufacturer of photographic paper—makes a standard neutral black paper called Kodabromide and a slightly warmer one called Medalist, among many others. Agfa's cold black paper is Brovira, and their warmer paper is Portriga Rapid, which may be difficult to get these days. Ilford makes a popular cold paper called Ilfobrome.

Paper surfaces range from heavy textures resembling tweed and burlap to those that are sleek and glossy. The heavily textured papers are not well suited to reproduction and are more often used for special purposes such as portrait photography. Most commercial prints today are printed on glossy paper and then dried with a matte finish; this means that they are not ferrotyped (see page 160), but are dried with their emulsion facing away from the chrome or stainless steel of the dryer. Although many clients ask for glossy prints, this is what they actually get. However, contact sheets are traditionally glossy, and the resin-coated papers mentioned in Chapter 9 are ideal for this purpose. Kodak's Polycontrast Rapid RC is a popular resin-coated stock.

WEIGHT

Papers usually come in single- or double-weight varieties; this refers to the thickness of the paper backing. Exhibition prints are generally done on double-weight paper, which is a little more expensive. Prints have a better feel when they are double-weight, and I use this type of paper most of the time. Contact sheets are usually single-weight, though, unless they are printed on resin-coated paper, which is middle-weight. Throw-away commercial prints—those used for reproduction—are usually single-weight.

SPEED

There's no standard rating system for speed applied to photographic paper as there is with film. However, in general, the warm-toned papers are much slower than the colder black ones; the portrait papers may require up to thirty seconds of exposure under the enlarger, while the journalistic papers take five to ten seconds. Kodak and Dupont make rapid papers which are even faster than the standard journalistic papers; these are used mostly in commercial labs where the longer the paper is under the enlarger, the higher the lab costs. For my purposes, though, longer exposure times are better, and I take extra steps to make my exposure time at least ten to fifteen seconds. This is because I make corrections in the print while it is under the enlarger, and the longer the exposure time, the more time I have to work on the image. Corrections in image lightness or darkness are made in terms of percentages of normal exposure time; if you want to increase darkness twenty percent for a picture that has a three-second exposure time, that's a pretty subtle and tricky time adjustment to make.

Neutral density filters help you to cut down paper speed; these are pieces of grey acetate which fit in the enlarger's filter drawer. They cost about $5 each, and if you have an enlarger which is bigger than the Omega B-22, you'll have to lay out more money for a larger size. Unfortunately, they are extremely fragile and easily scarred. I don't know too many people who use them, but I find that they are extremely valuable and use them all the time. Neutral density filters are labeled either .30, .60, or .90, and are called ND3s, ND6s, or ND9s. The ND3 will increase exposure by one stop, the ND6 by two stops, and the ND9 by three stops. For example, you can add an ND3 filter and compensate by doubling the time in the enlarger. If you don't use a filter, the only way to increase exposure time is to change the *f*/stop of the enlarger lens. The filter enables you to retain the enlarger's optimum *f*/stop and preserve image quality.

CONTRAST

With each brand of paper, a particular surface is usually available in several different contrast grades. Given one negative, different grades of paper can be used to produce prints with varying degrees of contrast. In

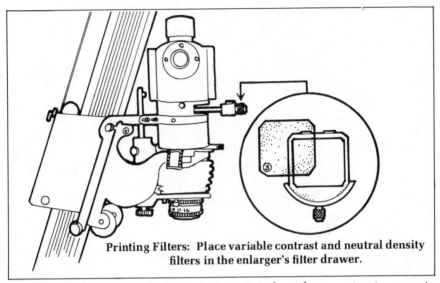

Printing Filters: Place variable contrast and neutral density filters in the enlarger's filter drawer.

general, high-contrast negatives are printed on low-contrast paper to even the contrast. Normal contrast negatives are printed on medium contrast paper. Low-contrast negatives are printed on high-contrast paper. The lower the number of the paper, the lower the contrast. If you have a normal contrast negative and print it on paper that is graded "1", you'll get a print with relatively soft contrast. If you print that same negative on paper graded "4" or "5" you'll get a very hard, contrasty print. The numbers used to indicate contrast grade do not correspond from one manufacturer to the next. For example, a number 2 grade from one manufacturer might be the equivalent of a 2½ with another manufacturer. Kodabromide comes in grades one through five; Medalist, one and two; Dupont makes graded paper in a cold black stock called Velour Black, with grades one through four; Agfa is the only company with six paper grades.

However, you can buy another type of paper, called *variable contrast paper*, which has almost the entire range of contrast grades built into it. One of its advantages is that it is less expensive because you don't have to stock a box of each contrast grade of paper. This system involves the use of colored filters representing different contrast grades which are placed in the enlarger's filter drawer. The paper has an emulsion mixture, with half the emulsion sensitive to the magenta light of high-contrast filters and the other half sensitive to the yellow of low-contrast filters. The intermediate-range filters transmit a combination of magenta and yellow. Kodak's resin-coated paper is variable contrast, as is their standard Polycontrast paper, and the filters are numbered 1, 1 1/2, 2, 2 1/2, and 3.

Dupont used to produce two kinds of variable contrast paper: Varilour, a slightly warm paper similar to Medalist, and Varigam, a cold black paper. I used Dupont Varigam for years but it was discontinued. Varilour is coded either "VR BTW" or "VR TW." The "BT" indicates a paper with a slightly pebbled surface while "T" refers to a glossy surface. "W" means the paper contains a phosphate white that responds to ultraviolet light—the same type of phosphate that is used in laundry detergents to make clothes "whiter than white." As yet, filters for variable contrast paper do not reach as high a contrast grade as the manufacturer's corresponding highest graded paper. For instance, Dupont's #4 Velour Black is about half a grade more contrasty than the Dupont variable contrast paper printed with a #4 filter.

In general, variable contrast paper, when used without a filter, is equivalent to #2 graded paper.

I feel the same way about photographic printing paper as I do about film: in the beginning, it's best to find one paper and stick with it. As you become more experienced with different type papers, you'll find that the tonal qualities of certain papers will express your ideas better than others—in effect, that silver on paper will look different with different papers. Many photographers stock a variety of papers for different types of expression. I use variable contrast paper and many of the techniques in this chapter are based on the use of variable contrast filters.

Developer

Print developers are designed to match the characteristics of photo papers. You can buy a developer suited to the warm portrait papers, for instance, or to the colder blue-black papers. The print developers of one manufacturer can be used with the papers of another; although they don't recommend it, there's really no harm in doing it. I use a relatively obscure brand of developer called Printofine with the Dupont paper.

As with film developer, print developer is available in both proprietary and public formulas. Kodak Dektol (D-72) is perhaps the most popular public formula for use with cold black papers. Another famous public formula is Beers', which is not available in stores and must be mixed at home. The formula is in Ansel Adams' book, *The Print* (see Bibliography). It calls for varying percentages of two stock solutions, depending on the contrast grade you want. Ansel Adams uses this developer to alter the contrast of his paper, but I prefer to change contrast by changing grades or filters and enhance local contrast with dodging and burning.

Print developer is usually mixed in a ratio of one to two with water.

Exact quantity of the solution is not important; it should be deep enough to cover the prints in the tray. For one print, 16 ounces of developer and 32 ounces of water is actually enough, but it's easier to handle prints in a full tray and it's more satisfying. When measuring developer, it's a good idea to always use the same container so that there's no chance of contamination. After you've poured the developer into the tray and added water, tilt the tray a little to help mix the solution.

In theory, the temperature of the developer will affect the developing time, but in practice, if the developing solution is approximately room temperature and your developing time is consistent, precise temperature won't matter much. Length of time in the soup is much more crucial to consistent printing; this influences the lightness or darkness of the print, and, with some papers, the contrast. It's best to follow the manufacturer's recommendations for developing times, which usually range from ninety seconds to three minutes. The paper must be in the developer for at least ninety seconds in order to deliver a solid black, regardless of the amount of exposure the paper has received under the enlarger. After a minute and a half, all of the tones in the print will darken with increased developing time, up to three minutes. So if your print looks dark enough after ninety seconds, you can pull it out of the tray; if it looks too light, you can leave it in for as long as three minutes. But it's my feeling that you shouldn't manipulate developing time to control the darkness or lightness of the print. Set a standard developing time in order to determine the effectiveness of the exposure time in the enlarger.

Unlike some film developers, print developer is not reusable. Once you've diluted and used it for a printing session, it has to be tossed out. Air will weaken the developer solution over time through oxidation, so you can't leave it sitting in the tray for more than a few hours or what you'd call a normal printing session. Capacity is indicated on the developer instructions; I tend to change it more often, usually when it begins to look noticeably yellow.

Stop Bath
Print developer is alkaline and therefore its action is stopped with an acid solution. So the second tray holds a solution of acetic acid and water as a stop bath. There are two ways you can buy it: glacial acetic acid, which is 99 percent acid, and a diluted solution of 28 percent acetic acid.

Glacial acetic seems to be the better alternative in terms of cost. But it is a rancid, dangerous chemical, and a glass bottle of it in your darkroom is potential for terror. When I was working for a Washington photographer whose shop was located in a large downtown office building, someone in the darkroom accidentally dropped a bottle of glacial acetic acid. They had to evacuate the entire building for a couple of days until the fumes cleared. I keep it tightly closed in a plastic bottle. It can cause burns, but if you rinse it off right away, it won't hurt you. For safety, it's always best to fill the tray with water and then add the acid; this way there's less chance of splashing acid all over.

The proportion of acid to water is not crucial. To a full tray of water I usually add about half a glug of acid. I change stop bath every time I put out fresh developer for consistency's sake. You can buy what is known as an indicator stop bath that is 28 percent acetic acid plus a pH color indicator. When developed prints have transferred too much developer into the stop bath and it is no longer acid, the solution turns purple.

Hypo

The third tray contains hypo, or fixer—the same fixer used when developing film but mixed with more water. I use Kodak, but one brand seems as good as another. Kodak Fixer is one of those chemicals with the easy-to-miss instructions, "add enough water to make one gallon." The less expensive powder forms of hypo are a hassle to mix—the powder tends to float around the darkroom and settle on things. Liquids are always easier in the darkroom. I use the liquid concentrate Rapid Fixer made by Kodak, but it's the most expensive one you can buy. It enables you to turn on the room lights quickly—within five or six seconds of immersing the prints.

As mentioned in the darkroom chapter, the sign of a permanent darkroom is a standing tray of hypo covered with a lid. However, hypo should be fresh; you wouldn't want to leave the same batch standing for more than a month or so. The instructions indicate how many 8x10's you can run through it before it gets old, but I never manage to count. You can purchase a small bottle of hypo tester if you worry about it. When the hypo begins to look a little cloudy and you notice that it is taking longer for the yellow in the prints to clear away, you know it's time to change the hypo. Even though it isn't cloudy, used hypo may be old enough that it doesn't completely fix the print; see pages 214–15 for more on print permanence.

If you do a lot of printing and are concerned about chemical costs, you can cut down your hypo bill by using a two-bath system. This means filling two trays full of hypo. Prints are placed in the first bath for a short time and then moved along to the second bath. The first bath does all of the hard work, and the second just completes the fixing process. When you've done the limit of one hundred 8x10's, or whatever the capacity of the hypo, you dump out the first hypo bath and then use the second as the new first bath. Then you mix a fresh hypo bath for use as the second bath. The two-bath method extends the life of hypo and gives added insurance that the prints have been completely fixed.

Washing Solutions
In order to remove hypo from the emulsion and paper fibers, it's necessary to wash prints in rapidly moving water of approximately room temperature. Using the Kodak Tray Siphon described in Chapter 9, you can wash the prints in a tray of water with the water replacing itself every five minutes for two hours. But there are chemicals available which radically shorten the washing time; these are *hypo clearing agents.* Kodak's is a powder called Hypo Eliminator; probably the most popular is a liquid concentrate called Perma Wash.

When using a hypo clearing agent, you first wash the prints in running water for about five minutes with the siphon, giving them intermittent agitation. Then you place the prints in a tray filled with hypo clearing agent solution for about five minutes, agitating them occasionally. After this, you wash the prints for another five minutes in water, using the siphon, and shuffling the prints every so often to make sure the water is circulating to all of them. This timing applies to double-weight paper; for single-weight it is one minute each in water, Perma Wash, and the final wash.

CONTACTING
After you've developed, dried, and cut the negatives—and before you make a print—you'll want to make a *contact sheet.* The primary function of a contact sheet is to let you view the pictures you've shot and choose the ones you want to print. On an 8"x10" piece of photo paper you can contact up to thirty-five frames of film. When contacting, the negatives are placed in direct "contact" with the paper and then exposed; thus, the resulting prints are the same size as the negatives.

Another reason for contacting is that a contact sheet helps you to judge your work. By studying these sheets you can see how well you've carried through in exposing and developing or seeking variations in a theme. In my experience, only one or two prospective clients have asked to see contact sheets when looking at my portfolio, and yet they reveal a lot about a photographer's technique. As you peruse the series of frames, it becomes evident whether you've explored the subject with an intelligent, unified plan or a scattered, unsure approach. It is often like watching a movie in stop action.

There are all sorts of devices you can buy to help you with contacting; most of these are variations of contact printing frames designed to keep the strips of film evenly aligned and smoothly contacted to the paper. Most consist of plastic or foam bases with hinged pieces of glass attached on top. The film is sandwiched between the base and the glass. However, I find that an 11″x14″ piece of quarter-inch thick plate glass used directly on the countertop can do the job adequately, and this is a lot

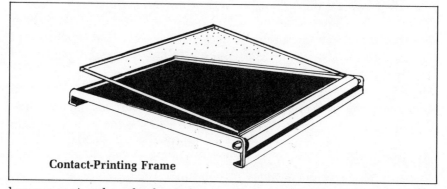

Contact-Printing Frame

less expensive than the fancy frames. Even better than placing the glass on the bare countertop is laying it on a mat of dense foam rubber to ensure that there is a smooth and secure contact between film and paper.

Traditionally, contact sheets have been printed on glossy paper. That's why the resin-coated paper is so ideal for contacting, and it seems to be gaining popularity among working photographers for this and other kinds of prints. As mentioned in Chapter 9, you don't have to dry the plastic paper in a dryer; you do use the same kind of developer, stop bath, and hypo with it as you do with other papers. Single-weight glossy paper was the popular contact paper before resin-coated came along.

The Process of Contact Printing
Mix and set out your chemicals. Before you open the box of photo paper, turn off the regular lights and switch on the safelights. If you are using resin-coated paper, use an indelible marker to write the file number on the back of each sheet; regular ink will come off in the developer and pencil lead does not adhere to this surface. With other types of paper, you can use pencil for coding.

You'll need a light touch to place the negative strips evenly on the contact sheet and this might take some practice. The seven strips of five frames should lie side by side, with sprocket holes barely touching. The strips should never overlap, not even the sprocket holes. If they do, the smooth contact between negative and paper will be marred, because the film will be lifted away from the paper in the area of overlap. Even if it's just the very edges of the film that overlap, there won't be a good contact seal.

It's important to have the strips evenly aligned if you're doing an assignment; it adds to the aura of professionalism. Some commercial contact printing frames have grooves so that you can actually insert the negatives into the glass evenly at regular intervals. But it takes so long to insert the negatives that it hardly seems worth the trouble.

Handling the negatives by their edges only, you should place them emulsion side down on the paper. The matte emulsion of the film is in contact with the glossy emulsion of the paper. A hint about getting the negatives out of the glassine sleeve—blow into the sleeve to open it up. Keep your negatives in original shooting order when you file them in glassine sleeves, and preserve this sequence when you lay the negatives down on the contact sheet. This way you can see the progression in shooting and also can find a particular frame in the sleeve when you want to print a picture.

Through experimentation I've determined that my negatives look best when contacted on #2 resin-coated paper with an exposure of about four seconds at $f/11$. With each new box of paper I re-establish this exposure time; this is because paper emulsion speed varies from batch to batch. It's good to establish a standard time for contact printing. If some of your exposures were extremely radical when you were shooting, you'll be able to discern this in standardly printed contact sheets.

Once you have the negatives laid out on the paper, lower the plate glass over them and apply pressure with both hands at the sides of the glass. Then expose for that standard amount of time, tripping off the enlarger with the foot switch or your nose. When exposing a number of sheets, hide the already exposed sheets somewhere where they can't get fogged by safelights or by scattered enlarger light. There's no need to hurry with souping the exposed paper. You can store exposed prints in a box for a day or two if you prefer to soup them at another time.

There's a special method for souping a number of prints at one time, which you'll find described on pages 207–08; the basic procedure for developing a print is described in the next section.

Once it's been processed, take a close look at the contact sheet. You'll see that there's an ultimate black that the paper can produce; this is the area of the sheet which has not had contact with the film. There is another, slightly less intense black produced from parts of the negative which were not exposed when you shot the film—for example, the areas around the sprocket holes. This lighter black is the film base plus fog.

You can expose the contact sheets longer to drive this film base plus

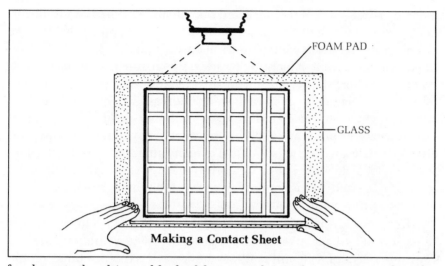

Making a Contact Sheet

fog down to the ultimate black of the paper, but in the process you lose the shadow detail in your contact sheet. In fact, one reason I choose to print my contact sheets with #2 paper is that I want to be sure that the shadows are grey enough to see all the detail possible; in the contact sheets I want to be able to see all the information the film has recorded. Later, in the individual prints, I can drive the key blacks all the way to pure black.

Because they are so tiny, the individual frames are difficult to read on the contact sheet. It's a good idea to view them with a magnifying glass; the most popular ones have a flashlight attachment that illuminates the picture.

MAKING A PRINT

Probably the most beautiful print, the one with the potential for greatest tonal beauty and finest gradation, is a contact print made from an 8"x10" negative shot with an 8x10 view camera. Because the picture is not enlarged, all of the very precise detail of the negative is retained in the print grain-for-grain.

The 35mm negative can also have perfect gradation if it has been well exposed, developed, and contacted; but as soon as you put it in the enlarger and move it farther and farther from the paper for larger and larger prints, you increasingly lose gradation, contrast, and sharpness. What we're concerned with, then, is developing the finesse in printing that enables you to compensate for the inherent limitations of the 35mm format. It is possible to achieve beautiful tones and subtle gradation with 35mm film, but it requires some work.

When you first start printing, you have to experiment a lot. You also have to learn to look at the print and see the problem areas. Most beginners, upon seeing their first print, are thrilled with it, proud that they've got an image and that it contains dark blacks and bright whites. But all too often, when you're first learning to print, you're satisfied too early. You don't realize the full potential for beauty in the silver on the paper. On the other hand, it's possible to go to the other extreme and make hundreds of prints which, when spread out over your living room floor in the light of day, appear very much alike. With some negatives you'll get a good print after a few tries, with others it will take many attempts. The point is that there is a lot of flexibility with each print—a range within which the print looks "OK"—and you learn to play within that range, looking for truly luminous prints with fine gradation.

Early in your printing career, it might be a good idea to take two or three of your best negatives and make straight sample prints with them to learn the effect of different contrast grades and exposure times on the image. Each negative should be a substantially different lighting situation—an evenly lit scene, a mixed-light or high-contrast situation, and a low-contrast situation. You might make nine or more prints of each negative, doing each one with three different contrast grades—high, medium, and low—and using three different exposure times with each contrast grade.

In discussing the printing process, we'll go through the making of a test print to establish a base exposure time, the making of a "road map," or straight print, from which to plan manipulations of darks and lights in the print, and the use of dodging, burning, and bleaching to alter the tones. We'll consider the question of contrast and the possibilities in modifying it. Also, print toning, drying, spotting, and mounting will be covered, along with the question of permanency.

Making a Test Print

To determine the correct exposure under the enlarger, you'll make a test print. By looking at the test, you can make judgments about contrast and darkness. Learning which judgments to make is an essential skill in printing.

Begin by choosing a contrast grade of paper—or a contrast filter if you are using variable contrast paper—which you think is appropriate to the contrast of the negative. If the original shooting situation was high-contrast, choose a low-contrast grade. If it was low-contrast, choose a high-contrast grade. For the purposes of this discussion, we'll assume that you're working with a medium-contrast situation and that you're using either #3 paper or variable contrast paper with a #3 filter which you place in the enlarger filter drawer before you start to print.

In practice, you'll find that ninety percent of your pictures will fall on one grade of paper. In my case, I've found that most of my pictures look best when printed with a #3 filter. So I have adjusted my negative developing time so that most of my pictures suit this filter. It seems to enhance the texture and sharpness of 35mm film. In general, if you expose and develop film consistently, the two main variables that will determine contrast in your prints will be the choice of filter or paper grade and the contrast inherent in the lighting of your subject.

When making an 8"x10" print, I usually adjust the bands of the easel to make a 6"x9" rectangle. This conforms to the 2:3 aspect ratio of the 35mm frame rather than the 4:5 ratio of the paper. Insert a piece of photo paper in the easel; you will use this sheet for cropping and focusing, and won't make a print with it. It's a good idea to mark your focusing paper in some way so that you don't confuse it with fresh sheets.

Next clean the negative with the Static Master Brush, lightly sweeping the brush across the film in one direction, holding the film obliquely under the lamp to get a look at the dust.

Insert the negative, emulsion side down, in the enlarger's negative holder. Crop the picture by moving the enlarger head up or down so that only the part of the image you want in the 6"x9" rectangle will be there. You can also move the easel around to situate the image where you want it. The more you move the enlarger head away from the easel, the bigger the enlargement that you make, and the more exposure time you'll need. This relates back to the Inverse Square Law: light falls off in an inverse geometric progression as you move the light source away from the paper.

Next set the enlarger lens to one of the two optimum f/stops: f/5.6 or f/8.

Turn the enlarger on, place the grain focuser over the focusing paper on the easel, and look through it to see the individual grains in the projected images. Turn the enlarger's focusing knob to make the individual grains as sharp as possible. Check the focus each time you expose a fresh piece of paper.

Now turn out the lights and turn on the safelights, and get ready to make a test print. Place a fresh piece of paper in the easel. Use a piece of cardboard to cover all but the top inch or so of paper. Expose this top strip of paper for 3 seconds; then move the cardboard down another inch to uncover more of the paper. Expose the paper for another 3 seconds. Continue moving the cardboard down the paper, exposing equal strips of paper for additional 3-second intervals. As with all prints, it's important that the easel not move while you are exposing; if it slides around once you have cropped the image, you'll have to recrop and start the print all over again.

After you've exposed the entire sheet, plunge it face down in the developer tray. Use rubber tongs to press the paper down completely into the solution, agitate it immediately, then flip it over and continue agitating. Often, developer instructions will tell you to slip the paper into the tray face up, in order to avoid air bubbles, but I've never had any problems from merely plopping the paper in all at once, face down. The print should remain in the developer with mild agitation for 2 minutes, counted out on the GraLab clock. Keep this time constant, as well as all other routines on the wet side of the darkroom; the dry side is where you should play with the variables.

Holding the print with tongs, let it drain a bit into the developer tray, then plop it face down into the acid bath. It should stay there for about 10 seconds. The trick is to let go of the print before it hits the acid, so your tongs won't be contaminated. Then you can agitate the print in the acid with your other tongs.

Again, let the print drain into the acid solution, and then put it into the hypo. Before you reach for the lights, check to make sure that the paper box is closed.

Once the print has cleared in the hypo, squeegee it up on the splashboard. The bands representing different exposure times provide a guide to choosing the best exposure.

This test is the fastest, most precise way of pinning down what your base exposure time should be. But if your film exposure and developing techniques are consistent and you always use the same type of paper, eventually you'll find that you can select the base exposure time under the enlarger with a fair degree of accuracy. Then you'll be able to begin your printing sessions with the next step instead of this test print.

A Straight Print

Look carefully at the print on the splashboard and pick the band that appears to have the best exposure. For the purposes of this example, we'll say that it seems to fall between the 3- and 6-second bands—maybe 5 seconds. Since I like at least 10 seconds of exposure, so that there's enough time to dodge and burn the print and enough time to make manageable percentage changes in exposure time, I decide to double the 5 seconds. This is accomplished with the addition of a neutral density filter, the ND3. The filter decreases the intensity of the light source by one stop; to retain the same exposure, I compensate by doubling the time under the enlarger to 10 seconds. Use of the filter allows me to keep the optimum *f*/stop on the enlarger. The neutral density filter is lightweight and prone to curling from the heat of the enlarging lamp. So if you're using a contrast filter, put the contrast filter above the neutral density filter in the filter drawer to protect it.

Now you check your focus, turn out the lights, and put another piece of paper in the easel. The timer is set for 10 seconds, and the paper is exposed. When the 10 seconds are up, I place a black card over the print, covering all but a 1/16" border around the image. Then I remove the negative in its carrier and turn on the enlarger again, exposing for another 5 seconds. This places a black line around the print and is a matter of style, not a standard practice. I even put the black line around initial test prints, as it is part of the composition and affects the total impression of tones.

The resulting straight print is used to judge the base exposure time and the selection of contrast grade. Does the print look grey and muddy or harsh and sooty? Is it too dark overall or too light? Until you've gained some experience, this juncture is a tricky one. It's a matter of gaining judgment. Controls for contrast and exposure time and manipulations of individual tones in the picture are interrelated.

If the print looks muddy or grey, chances are that you'll need a higher contrast grade. If it looks chalky or sooty and the gradation is quite abrupt, then you'll probably need a lower contrast grade. If the picture is generally too dark or too light, you'll have to adjust the exposure time. If the highlights look dark and the shadows are black, for example, you

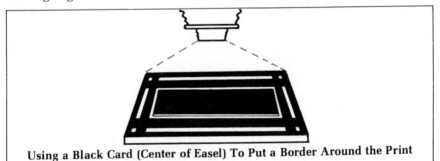

Using a Black Card (Center of Easel) To Put a Border Around the Print

would shorten your exposure time by a certain percentage. Is it 20 percent too dark or maybe 15 percent? Or does the whole image look washed out and are the tonal areas that should look black, grey instead? Then you would increase the exposure time by a certain percentage.

If you opt for a different paper or filter to change general contrast in the midst of a printing session, you'll have to make a new test print and experiment with exposure time. The various grades of paper differ in their exposure needs. That's why it's important to judge contrast correctly at the beginning; it's a hassle to start all over again with a new base exposure time once you're well into making a print. You'll notice that the high-contrast grades and low-contrast grades respond differently to changes in exposure time. The high grades have a hair-trigger response to a change of only a few seconds, while the lower grades respond much more slowly and need many more seconds of exposure to show a significant change in image darkness or lightness.

Often you'll have to make adjustments in both contrast grade and exposure time: a print may be too contrasty and too dark. On the other hand, you may not want to change either. If the center of interest in the photograph is well-articulated but the rest of the picture lacks impact, you should use the controls of dodging and burning to adjust the print, rather than changing contrast grade or exposure time.

In a sense, this straight print which you've just made is a road map. You should squeegee it to the splashboard so you can turn and refer to it while you're working. Study it to see which areas need lightening or darkening to draw emphasis to the subject, to correct imperfections in the tones, and to give the print overall brilliance and impact.

You might want to lighten a dark face and show more detail around the hairline. You might want to darken the outer edges of the picture so that attention is drawn to the center. From a graphic point of view, light areas seem to come at you, dark areas tend to recede. Also, local high contrast, such as a small white tone against a dark tone, will tend to draw your eye, as opposed to a grey against a grey. You might find imperfections in the print, faint splotches, or isolated muddy areas that result from weaknesses inherent in the photochemical process or your technique. Using this straightforward, 10-second print, you'll be able to make a plan of how to manipulate the next print.

Dodging and Burning

This is where dodging and burning come in. *Dodging* refers to using your hands or the small dodging implement described in Chapter 9 to interrupt the flow of light from the enlarger during the initial exposure. It is a technique used to lighten specific areas of the print. Shape your fingers to conform to the shape of the tonal areas which need attention; it's like making shadow figures on the wall, except you are making them on the print. It requires a light touch. The circular dodgers are especially handy for holding back small areas.

Burning refers to manipulations carried out after the initial exposure. It involves blocking out with your hands or a burning card all areas of the picture except one that you want to darken; then exposure is given to the uncovered areas. Burn in areas with your hands, but for small areas of the print use the cards with various sized holes in them.

When dodging and burning, keep your hands moving constantly in small back and forth motions. This helps blend or feather the burnt-in or held-back areas with the adjacent parts of the print. The idea is to make your manipulations invisible. If you're using the dodger or the burning cards, also keep those moving. The movement is important; in effect, you are painting very subtly with light.

While dodging needs a quick, light touch, burning can often take much longer. You may find extreme highlights that need up to three or four times the initial exposure time. For example, you might burn in a section of a print for 30 or 40 seconds while the initial exposure was only 10 seconds. Dodging on the same print may take only 3 or 4 seconds per area.

When dodging and burning, you needn't worry very much about following the precise borders of large or general tonal areas; you'll have to be more exact, though, to control small tonal detail. For both dodging and burning, you'll notice that holding your hands close to the enlarger lamp will create more feathered edges around the manipulated areas, while holding them closer to the paper will create a firmer outline, appropriate

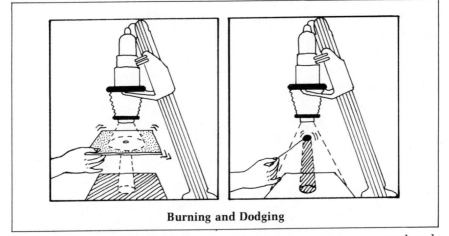

Burning and Dodging

for more clearly defined tonal areas. It's important to move your hands confidently; this will be tricky at first. You'll have to try it and then do the print again and again until it comes out right. What was said about shooting a lot of pictures goes double for making a lot of prints—especially when you're just starting out. It's in printing that your sense of perfection really comes through; you have to be committed to doing it over and over again until you get it right.

Carrying Out a Plan

Let's say that you look at the 10-second print and decide that it looks a little dark. Since you plan to burn down the edges somewhat, the picture will look even darker. So you decide to decrease the total exposure by 10 percent in order to lighten up the picture; the new exposure time is 9 seconds.

In studying the straight print or "road map" you notice that the top half of the picture is lighter than the bottom half and that this draws attention away from the more important faces in the middle. You decide to burn in the top for a few seconds and hold back the bottom for 4 or 5. Also, one of the faces looks dark, and you'll hold that back for a couple of seconds too. Burning in the highlights always takes longer than holding back the dark areas. You develop a sense of exactly how long to allow for these things as you get to know your paper and get a feel for printing. Sometimes you'll need a light touch; sometimes you'll need to be very strong.

Refocus, place a fresh piece of paper in the easel, and set the timer at 9 seconds. During this exposure interval move the dodger over the dark face for a few seconds, then use your hands for another few seconds to hold back the bottom, lighter half of the print. Once the 9 seconds are up, spend another 7 or 8 burning in the edges of the picture; be careful not to spill over the rest of the print. Then take another 5 seconds or so to burn in the lighter top half of the picture. Develop the print, squeegee it, and take a look.

You may find that this new print is just what you want. Or you may find that you lightened the picture too much and should go back to the 10-second exposure time. Perhaps the burning was uneven and as a result there is a splotchy area in the bottom half of the print; you'll have to do the whole thing over again, moving your hands more smoothly.

Even if the picture seems dark enough and was burned in evenly, there's another important question to ask—and that concerns total brilliance and luminosity. Do the greys wash out, are the tones muddy and dull? You're aiming for overall brilliance, for an exciting transition of tones, and most often you achieve it through perseverance. In dodging and burning, a difference of a fraction of a second might be crucial—you just have to persevere until you get a print that sings.

This is a good time to point out that you shouldn't try to judge a picture while it is in the developer under safelights. This can be very misleading. Sometimes a print coming up in the developer will look rather uneven in certain areas as a result of dodging and burning; this is because you are sensitive to these areas and are looking for problems. But these difficulties often disappear in the light of day. This is not to say that you shouldn't soup a print a little longer if you have dodged and burned it and it comes up in the developer looking a little light but otherwise acceptable. Also, prints look most brilliant when they are wet and lose luster when they've dried. This varies with the type of paper you are using. Glossy papers are less prone to this effect, whereas matte-textured papers are more so. You'll have to learn to discount your judgment of a wet print, depending on the type of paper you're using.

Multiple Filters
Standard printing manuals tend to emphasize the importance of selecting the right contrast grade and length of exposure under the enlarger. Most manuals say that if the total print doesn't look dazzling you should use the controls of contrast grade or base exposure time to effect a change in the whole print. But often you'll find that a portion of a particular print looks best with one contrast grade and exposure, while the contrast in another part of the picture looks too weak or too strong. Given a good-looking center of interest, corrections can often be made in the supporting tones using variable contrast paper and changing filters while printing.

The trick in printing is learning to get the best of all worlds. To most printers, using different contrast filters to print a single image is an obscure and seldom-used technique. But I find this method invaluable, especially when dealing with mixed-light situations. I feel that using multiple filters is an excellent tool to recapture inherent gradation lost in enlarging the 35mm negative.

It's better to print shadows through high-contrast filters and highlights through low-contrast filters. The high-contrast filter will enable you to retain the strong darks of the shadows, and you can dodge any areas within the shadows that you want printed lighter. The low-contrast filter will retain the light quality of the highlights, and you can burn in any areas within the highlights that should be darker.

You should select a base exposure time and contrast grade to take care of the large areas of your print; later you can dodge or burn the smaller areas using different filters. For example, in a picture initially exposed with a high-contrast filter, you may lose detail in the highlights because they have become blocked up. After initial exposure, you can burn in the highlights with a low-contrast filter, retaining the delicate texture as well as tonal information. If you want to deliver an overall impression of soft contrast in the print, you can give it an initial exposure with a low-contrast filter. This may give you unsupported blacks—dark tones that should be pure black but instead look greyish—in certain areas, but you can regain the full, pure blacks by burning them in through a high-contrast filter.

The Dupont filters are all matched in exposure time required to produce Zone 8 tones. This means that if you change filters, you have to increase or decrease the exposure time to maintain the same intensity of dark and middle-range tones. This applies to all the filters except the #4, which needs double the amount to produce the same highlight. This is because it's twice as dense as the others. It's as if the #4 had a built-in neutral density filter; if you were using a #3 filter with an ND3 and wanted to increase contrast by using a #4, then you'd use a comparable exposure time and remove the ND3.

Let's consider those special cases where you might want to use more than one contrast filter for the same picture. In these instances the picture has two or more distinct lighting situations, each with its own particular texture. Each part of the picture must be treated as a different exposure problem, and a different contrast filter is used for each. This type of picture will tend to come along often if you like to shoot in mixed-light situations. As mentioned before, pictures shot in mixed light tend to be the most vibrant ones, but they are problematic in terms of exposure and printing because some areas of the photo are lit quite differently than others. Shooting in mixed light is like walking into trouble, but if you can pull it off, the resulting pictures will be especially interesting and beautiful.

Again we can refer to the case of the person seated in front of the well-lit window; photo 2 provides a useful example. The upper half of the picture, which is filled with the sun-drenched window, is an exposure problem in itself; the bottom, much darker half of the picture is another situation entirely. If there had been a dark grey wall behind the woman instead of the window, then the picture would have had the same contrast throughout. The woman would have been lit by the delicate light flowing from the side of the scene, the lighting would have been even, and the whole picture would have been printed with the same filter. But with the window, you need to consider the detail in the curtain and the extreme brightness of the light, which in reality is beyond the ten zones possible in the negative.

When shooting this kind of picture, you have to split the difference in exposure between the two disparate areas. You compromise and try to save the most important parts. Because the shadows are the most important parts in black and white photography, you compromise in their favor; if you lose detail in the shadows, you can't regain it later in printing. If some of the highlights are lost in the shoulder of the H&D Curve, they can usually be burned back into the picture to a certain extent. So in this picture I underexposed the bottom half of the scene, but not enough to lose all of the detail, and then tried to rebuild the separation of tones in the shadows by printing and dodging through a high-contrast filter. The highlights were quite a bit overexposed.

The upper half of the picture, with it's delicate detail, was suited to a low-contrast filter. I had to do a lot of burning in to get this detail because of the problem with the highlights. The #1 filter was particularly good for this purpose, as it made my hand movements less noticeable. Remember that the higher grade filters, with their hard, gutsy textures, make dodging and burning more noticeable, and if I had used a #4 filter for the window area, you would have seen an unnaturally dark edge around the area where I did a lot of burning. It's important that dodging and burning blend into the overall tonality of the picture. Subtlety in dodging and burning depends, too, on your finesse with your hands and the amount of time the print is exposed.

After formulating a plan, I began by exposing the whole picture for 12 seconds with the #4 filter, dodging a muddy spot in the curtain and the highlight side of the woman's face. The fern and wall in the bottom left and the area in the bottom right had to be burned down, so I gave them an additional 4 and 6 seconds with the #4 filter to preserve separation in the slightly underexposed blacks. Then I switched filters and put in the #1 with an ND3. The curtain was burned in for 5 or 6 seconds, and then a hot area in the upper left for another 4 seconds. To burn down the small bright areas on either side of the woman's head—between her and the parrot and her and the fern—I used a card with a small hole in the middle. These areas were too small to burn in with my hands.

Multiple Prints from One Negative

There will be occasions when you'll want to make several identical prints from one negative. It's necessary to first work out a single good print from that negative. This means making a test print, figuring out the proper exposure, and deciding how you should dodge and burn. As you work it out, you should be sure to keep all this information firmly fixed in your mind—or if it's complex, write it down—so that you can repeat it consistently for each copy of the print that you make. The routine is repeated for each print; the prints are stacked away from enlarger and safelights and then souped at the same time.

The following is a good technique for souping several sheets of paper at one time. To begin with, you should fan out the exposed sheets on the dry side of the room so that you can grab each by the corner without dripping chemicals on them with your wet hands. The sheets should be placed face-down in the developer one at a time, at consistent three- or four-second intervals. On the GraLab clock, note the time at which you dunked the first print. After all the prints are in the tray, use your hands to flip each one over, maintaining the same order in which they entered the tray. Agitate the sheets by tilting the tray, until the first print has been in the solution for one and a half minutes. Remove that first print and then the others at the same several-second intervals and in the same order, so that each sheet gets identical treatment. It's mostly a matter of rhythm here. When removing the prints from the developer, stand closer to the acid tray so that you sway back and forth from the developer tray as you make the transfer. This may require some practice.

If you are souping one sheet at a time, you can use the tongs and avoid getting your hands in the chemicals. With more than two prints, it's easier to manipulate the prints with your hands.

As you lift each sheet, allow it to drain over the developer tray before putting it into the acid stop bath. Be careful with your hands and what they touch. Use one to agitate the prints in the acid; once you've used this hand in the acid, don't let it touch the developer again. Feed the prints from the developer to the acid tray with your other hand. Leave them in the acid for at least ten seconds; the exact time is not crucial. If you want, you can let them accumulate there until they're all ready for the hypo. Finish the process by fixing and washing the prints.

With skill, you can do as many as twenty-five prints at once in a full developer tray.

Sometimes it will be extremely difficult to recapture a certain effect from the original print. For example, the picture of the girl (photo 5): I've worked with that negative for years, and it wasn't until the fourth year that I really began to see the full potential of the photograph. And once I found it, it was extremely difficult to achieve the vibrancy of the best print in successive prints. I have ten prints of that negative which were produced with hand movements almost identical to those for the best version, but they just don't make it. Differences in fractions of seconds and slight variations in dodging and burning movements make a real difference in a print like that. But then there are other pictures that almost fall out of the enlarger and require very little manipulation; these are quite easy to produce again and again. A good example is the little boy flying down the slide (photo 8): the lighting was right to begin with, so I didn't have to play very much with lights and darks in the print. A print like this is easily repeatable.

Bleaching

One manipulation that you can perform to further enhance gradation and brilliance in your print is *bleaching*, or the use of potassium ferricyanide to clear some of the silver from the paper. This bleach removes any unnecessary tones from the white areas of the print; it cleans them up, so to speak. For example, I like to use ferricyanide to clear the whites in eyes and make them glow. Bleach is also good for increasing separation in areas where there doesn't seem to be enough, as when a person's hair blends into a dark background. Additionally, it can heighten textures in the print because it works more quickly on highlights than on shadows. It can make white whiskers brilliant or a striped shirt more

Potassium Ferricyanide Equipment

luminous. Basically, it has the ability to snap out areas of the print and make them glow, and is especially handy for areas that are too small to be dodged. It is, in effect, dodging with chemistry, and can be used in shadow as well as highlight areas.

From the standpoint of long hours spent for small, subtle returns, ferricyanide is perhaps the loser of them all. For this reason, commercial printers don't bother with it. I use it most of the time.

Kodak makes ferricyanide, as do a few other manufacturers, but they are relatively obscure. My one-pound bottle of ferricyanide was purchased eleven years ago, and even though I bleach all the time, I've only used half of the bottle in all those years.

There's no set formula for mixing a solution of ferricyanide; you just sprinkle some of the crystals into a small cup or shot glass full of water and mix to a pale yellow. You may find it handy to have two different solutions on hand, one weak and one strong. A plastic salt shaker is ideal for adding the crystals to the water, but be careful not to use one with a metal cap, as this will produce rust. Rust can combine with the bleach, producing blue stains on your prints. A drop of Photo-Flo should be mixed with the bleach solution to break the liquid's surface tension; this prevents bleach from beading on the print. Be careful not to allow any ferricyanide crystals to fall on nearby prints or negatives because it will eat right through the image.

Ferricyanide is applied once the print has been fixed with hypo and the lights have been turned back on. The print must be wet; you can bleach washed and dried prints, but must soak them first in water.

Ferricyanide is used in conjunction with hypo because the latter completes the action of the bleach and then stops it. The bleach is applied with a small brush or Q-tip and then the area is swabbed down with an artist's sponge doused in hypo. I used to spread the hypo on the print with paper towels but found that they shred in the hypo tray, leaving it full of paper fibers. The Japanese calligraphy brushes seem to be the most efficient means of applying ferricyanide; unlike other brushes, they don't have metal parts which can rust. I have a number of sizes for working different areas. Once the print has been swabbed with hypo, the liquid is squeegeed away to prepare the surface for the next application. The aluminum squeegee with a rubber blade is best for this since it doesn't have any rustable parts.

You need a perfectly flat working surface on which to perform the bleaching. I use the piece of formica that usually serves as a lid to my hypo tray; a 14"x17" piece of plexiglass would work as well. The board is placed over the stop-bath tray so that I can work in the sink next to the uncovered hypo tray.

Usually I let a number of prints build up in the holding tray and wait until the end of a printing session to use the ferricyanide. I begin by taking a print from the tray and squeegeeing it face up on the formica. Then I dip the brush in the ferricyanide solution, wipe it on a paper towel, and apply it to the surface that I want to lighten. I immediately wipe over it with the hypo-dampened sponge, then squeegee the whole print again. Only the areas touched by the brush will be bleached; the sponge action does not spread the bleach. After bleaching is completed, the prints are washed in the normal fashion with the Kodak siphon and Perma Wash.

The trick in using ferricyanide is to work very gradually. It should be a subtle process, with repeated applications of a mild solution. If too strong a solution is applied, it will leave a yellow stain. White areas of the print will bleach more quickly because they contain less silver to be dissolved away. A lot of silver must be removed from the black tones in order to make them noticeably lighter. This is why ferricyanide is ideal for bringing out stripes and other patterns; with a little bleaching, the whites are cleared first and thus brightened, and the blacks are left where they were.

It's not necessary to use the brush with extreme precision when following the outline of a large tonal area. This is especially true if the neighboring areas are much darker than the one being bleached; it will take a lot more ferricyanide to affect these darker areas, and if your brush overlaps them, there's no harm done. However, if you're bleaching a tiny detail, you'll have to be more exact.

Some photographers make up an entire tray of ferricyanide in very mild solution and then slip prints into it for a few seconds to clear the whites. But I don't do this for a few reasons. One of the major values of ferricyanide is that it allows you to lighten very small areas that are too difficult to dodge in the enlarger. Also, there may be whites in the print which you don't want brightened; you may want them slightly grey so that attention is drawn to other, more important parts of the print.

Often I use ferricyanide to emphasize certain lines in a picture, like the rim of a table or the swirl of an electrical wire. The bleach allows me to increase the impact of lines which I feel add to the composition of the picture.

Toners

Slight coloration of prints to enhance the tones can be achieved with the use of special *toners* which alter the composition of the silver in the emulsion. In addition to enriching tones, these chemicals increase the permanency of the image. They are even more subtle than ferricyanide and are usually used for exhibition prints.

There are two basic types of toners: sepia and rapid selenium. The sepia enriches the golden, warm tones of warmer papers like Medalist, while the bluish selenium deepens the cold black tones of journalistic papers. Be careful not to leave the print in the selenium toner too long or it will tend toward purple.

Toning is carried out after prints have been fixed and is part of an extended washing process. It is necessary to fix with fresh hypo if you're planning to tone prints, and you must be very thorough in the washing process. Toner is a liquid and is mixed with water to fill a darkroom tray. The toner instructions are quite specific and should be followed closely. The method of applying sepia is a bit more complicated than that for selenium and involves the use of ferricyanide.

Toning has absolutely no bearing on the appearance of a print which has been reproduced in a book or magazine. The richness of tone resulting from the blue or sepia toner will not translate into printer's ink.

Drying

After washing prints, as described on page 194, you should squeegee them on the splashboard and then dry them. The most common drying tool is the small, flipflop dryer. Prints are placed on the dryer with their emulsion away from the flat heating surface. Canvas is then pulled over the prints. They dry in approximately fifteen minutes if they are double-weight paper and a few minutes less if single-weight. Prints should not be allowed to overlap during drying, as they will stick together.

If you want to ferrotype, you should be forewarned about a few of the problems. Good glossies are difficult to make on the small flipflop dryers; they're easiest to achieve on the $800 commercial models. In addition, if little pieces of grit or dust get between the paper and the chrome, the emulsion won't ferrotype in those places and the surface will be speckled. If you haven't fixed the print in fresh hypo or haven't washed it thoroughly, the emulsion won't seal properly and you won't get a smooth surface. Also, sometimes the surface of the print will crack as it is peeled off the chrome. It's much easier to use the resin-coated papers if you want glossy prints.

Spotting

The final touch in printing is the application of Spotone, a dye that soaks into the emulsion to eliminate white spots left by dust and other imperfections. Spotting means cleaning up your act, so to speak, and has to be carried out when the print is dry.

There's no reason to show anyone a print that has spots on it, and I once heard someone say that he didn't know which was more important in a print, the subject matter or whether it had been spotted. I think he had a good point.

Of course, the first line of defense against dust and spots is clean negative processing and the use of the Static Master Brush. It takes a lot more time to spot than it does to clean the negative initially. Especially with 35mm film, where imperfections are enlarged along with the image, it's hard to avoid having at least some bits of dust show up in the print.

Spotone is available in three tones: blue-black, neutral black, and a slightly warm black. The instruction sheets tell you how to mix the dyes in the correct proportions to match your particular photo paper. However, for light spotting you can often use only the neutral black tone and not bother with mixing.

You'll need a high-quality artist's brush for spotting because it's important to have a fine point. The 00 or 000 Windsor-Newton is the best brush you can get.

You should pour out a little splash of Spotone and let it dry on a piece of glass or Petri dish, or let a small bit dry in the cap of the Spotone bottle.

Wet the brush with your tongue and pick up some dried Spotone. Then, before touching it to the spot, try it out on a piece of scratch paper. The tip of the brush should touch the spot in a stippling effect; the dye sinks into the emulsion very quickly and is difficult to remove once applied. If you're quick, though, you can try wiping it off with your finger.

It's best to spot darker areas of the print first, while you have more Spotone on your brush. As you move to lighter areas, you can dilute the dye with your saliva. Work gradually, applying the light dots again and again. Hard-edged scratches on the print will be difficult to blend in with Spotone, and you'll have to work very slowly, using light stippling. If the Spotone is applied too darkly or overlaps a sharp edge, it may emphasize the edges of the scratch. For larger spots, it's a good idea to stipple in from the edges to the center.

Depending on your sense of purity, you may want to use Spotone to remedy slight imperfections in printing or light. Sometimes I'll darken the pupil of a subject's eyes or other detail in shadow areas of the print.

Mounting

There may be times when you'll want to mount prints, and although a dry-mounting press retails for several hundred dollars, you can rent one from a rental darkroom or perhaps borrow one from a lucky friend. I've tried mounting prints with a household iron, but that's never been satisfactory.

Prints are usually mounted onto boards—illustrator's board, Bristol board, dry-mounting board—or back-to-back with double-weight paper.

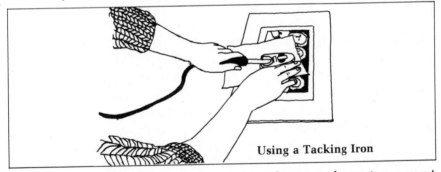

Using a Tacking Iron

With the boards, the picture is mounted inside a *complementary mount* or is fixed to the board as a *bleed mount*. If you use double-weight photo paper as a backing, you must develop, fix, and wash it so that it is permanently white; if you merely took a fresh piece of photo paper and used it for mounting, it would yellow very quickly.

You'll need a *tacking iron* and *dry-mounting tissue*, which is a heat-activated, adhesive paper. When you touch the tissue with the iron, the tissue melts and forms an adhesive bond.

First take the tissue and press it to the center of the back of the print with the hot tacking iron, moving the iron in a little circle. Then trim the tissue to fit the edges of the print; it's best to trim the print slightly with the tissue so that they match exactly. Place the print with tissue onto the

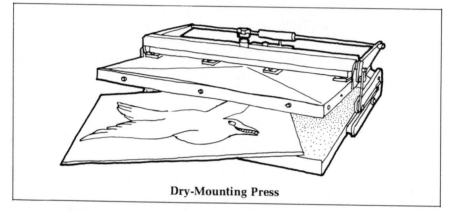

Dry-Mounting Press

mount, positioning the photograph so that it is seated the way you want it. Then lift up each corner of the print and tack the tissue to the mount with the iron. Place a cover sheet of smooth mounting board over the whole sandwich, put it into the dry-mounting press, and follow the instructions which accompany the press. The prints and mount should not be damp when placed in the press. If they are, put them in the press individually beforehand so that they can dry.

Permanency

A print is never totally permanent, but there are a number of precautions you can take to increase its life span and help preserve the tones.

If left in the sunlight, a print tends to fade. And oxides in the air will ruin even the finest prints if they are left unprotected in the open air. Museum-quality prints are stored in hermetically-sealed vaults to guard against this slow deterioration.

One measure that is more within the realm of possibility for the working photographer is to carefully fix and wash prints. Prints will yellow after a period of time if the fixing bath was not fresh enough or the washing not thorough enough to remove all traces of hypo from the emulsion and paper fibers. This doesn't mean that you have to have a fresh batch of hypo every time you print, but you should keep an eye on it to make sure that it hasn't gotten old. Using the two-bath system helps insure thorough fixing. You should be careful to give the prints the proper amount of agitation while they are in the hypo so that they are all fixed evenly—follow the manufacturer's recommendation. Also, don't leave the prints lying in hypo too long, especially in the stronger Rapid Fix, as it will begin to eat away the silver.

The importance of permanence is relative to the use of the print. If you've made prints for an exhibit, you'll want to go to extra innings to insure their permanency, perhaps by using toner and printing with fresh hypo. The East-West Gallery in Iowa has thoroughly researched the question of permanency and has published a pamphlet which explains how to achieve it (see the Bibliography). If you are especially concerned about prolonging the life of your print, you may want to send for a copy.

A Few Tips
If you are making prints for reproduction in a newspaper or magazine, you should print them a little on the light and soft side, as they tend to darken during reproduction.

It's important to judge prints under a standard viewing light in the darkroom, at a standard distance. If your prints consistently look too dark when they are dried and seen in the sunlight, then your lamp bulb is too bright or you are holding the prints too close to the lamp when judging them.

Watch for unsupported blacks in your prints. Either expose the print longer to get rid of the grey or burn the greyish blacks down. To help you judge key blacks and whites, you can make a sample sheet for reference. Take a piece of photo paper and place a black card over half of it. Without any negative in the enlarger, expose the sheet for a couple of seconds and then develop it. The result is a piece of paper with the purest white and purest black that the paper can produce. You can leave it lying in the water in your holding tray and make comparisons with it while printing.

Be careful not to overmanipulate the print by dodging and burning too much. For instance, you may dodge a face in shadow so much that it looks unnaturally light. Watch out for illogical transitions of tone.

Printing is, to a certain extent, "capturing the lucky accident"—but much less so than shooting film. With printing it's much more a question of beginners having those happy accidents and of more experienced printers gaining the confidence to repeat their successes in printing. By developing consistency and confidence in timing and controls, you give yourself an intelligent base from which to play and create. And with perseverance and experimentation, you'll learn to achieve the special luminosity that makes a really beautiful print.

12
PROFESSIONAL CONSIDERATIONS

Photography is an expensive hobby for the amateur and more often than not a thin living for the professional. We've all heard of the Richard Avedons who own large brownstones in Manhattan and make hundreds of thousands of dollars each year. But for every Richard Avedon there are hundreds of young would-be professionals living on the bare edge.

Freelance photography is more than just a job, it's a way of life. If you're going to make a go of it, it's got to be more important than anything—in a sense, it has to be your first love. You have to be prepared to spend years developing competency and learning the business and then take considerable time building a network of clients. You have to be on call at all hours. If you have a mate, he or she has to be willing to deal with the uncertainties and uneven hours, and can't be jealous of your assignments—whether it's a six-week trip to India or a 6 A.M. assignment to shoot nudes.

Somewhere between the extremes of spending all your money on photography and earning all your money in photography is the possibility of combining photo work with some of your other interests so that it will partially pay for itself. You might be able to pick up some money doing portraits, models' portfolios, children's pictures, and if you're so inclined, wedding pictures. Occasionally you might be able to sell a photo to a magazine or supply art for a commercial brochure. Then again you might be the next Richard Avedon.

This chapter, then, will give you some information about professional markets and business practices. It also discusses trends in photography, art direction, and methods of reproduction.

MARKETS

It's a buyer's market today: there are more photographers than there are jobs to fill. This means that if you are a free-lancer, you have to be competitive. In seeking work, there are a number of markets which you can explore.

Probably the most accessible market is the private party seeking personal photos. As mentioned earlier, this includes weddings, children's portraits, and portfolio pictures, and getting business depends mostly on word-of-mouth. Wedding photography is a mainstay of many photographers and a large portion of the money made in photography is earned by wedding photographers. However, many find this type of work a hassle and somewhat demeaning, for it involves acting as a social director, handling family, in-laws, and all the tensions of a wedding scene. There are three basic problems with wedding work: the clients usually want clichéd scenes—for example, the bride cutting the cake and throwing the bouquet, and all the friends and relatives grouped together; if you blow the job, there isn't going to be a repeat of the wedding reception (I even blew my own sister's wedding); and the clients are difficult to please and often disappointed. The children's market is relatively large and lucrative and usually involves taking the kids to a zoo or the countryside and coming back with a dozen or so candid shots. The primary consideration here is whether you like kids. As with weddings, the presentation of the final product is an important part of the package delivered to the client. But with children you have the possibility for more creativity in your presentation; for instance, you can dry-mount the photos back-to-back and have them spiralbound into a book. More often than not, marrying types want wedding photos in a traditional wedding album.

A second market is the commercial field. Commercial work can range from taking a few pictures for a real estate agent to doing the annual report for General Motors. This is the whole ball of wax as far as big money is concerned. Basically, reaching this market means becoming a business person—assembling a stunning portfolio and hustling. Commercial photography includes work for advertising agencies, but in general, all commercial work is some form of advertising. You are hired to make the client's service or product look good. Your photographs might appear in brochures, newsletters, annual reports, television graphics, trade and textbooks, and audio/visual aids; and as billboards, record jackets, display posters, and movie stills.

Another market is the editorial world, probably the most romantic kind of work the photographer can pursue. This is photojournalism— photography for magazines, newspapers, and books—it means telling stories about people through pictures. Editorial photography is less lucrative than commercial work because it does not sell a product. However, the compensation is the excitement of possibly traveling halfway around the world or having the latitude to express the story from your own point of view. Like commercial work, it involves a great deal of hustling and is dependent upon developing contacts. Many working photographers try to make a living doing a combination of editorial and commercial work.

Commercial and editorial photographs are usually reproduced in another medium. This brings us to the point of changing patterns in media: the printed page versus film and television. In the minds of many photographers, the death of general interest magazines such as *Life* and *Look* was tantamount to the death of photojournalism. More recently, rising prices of postage and paper have financially threatened the printed media. Yet, despite all of this, today there are more pictures being printed in more magazines than ever before. This is explained mostly by the growth of special interest magazines. A good example of special interest publications are the photography magazines designed for a particular, well-heeled audience. They are printed on fine paper and filled to the gills with expensively produced photo-advertisements. You see more and more of these magazines all the time. This still doesn't mean you'll have an easy time placing a sensitive essay on the plight of the aged in America, but it's possible that you'll find an outlet. It will require ingenuity on your part to research and find a suitable publication.

Another area you might want to research is grants. Thousands of dollars are given to photographers by foundations to pursue worthwhile visual studies.

As this book is being written, there's a rising trend in the marketing of photographic prints as fine art. Increasing numbers of galleries and museums are interested in displaying fine photographs, and the public is responding. You may want to look into this market, but I don't think you'll find it the avenue to owning a brownstone in Manhattan. In fact, you'll be lucky if you get lunch.

BUSINESS PRACTICES

If you're going to get money for your work, you should know how pictures are paid for and who owns what rights. Remember, it's a buyer's market, and for the most part you get what you can. However, there are standard practices which provide the photographer with a basic guide to rates and rights. Generally, these apply to commercial and editorial work.

The basic concept in charging for work should be "day rate plus expenses." This means that the client agrees to pay you a set fee for your time and will reimburse you for any expenses incurred in the process of carrying out the assignment. These expenses include the cost of film, processing, and printing, as well as transportation, props, model fees, and any other miscellaneous costs you incur.

Day rates for professional photographers range from $200 a day to more than $2000. Shorter assignments are charged on the basis of a half-day. Unless you're on the top of the heap and command your own prices, the client will usually suggest the fee, on the basis of his or her budget. The rate is partially determined by the use of the picture. For example, a photograph used in a national advertisement will bring more money than one included in a small company newsletter, regardless of the amount of time it took to take the picture. If rates of $200 to $2000 a day sound outrageously high, keep in mind that work is not steady, your equipment costs are substantial, and the client is paying for years of experience, reliability, and creativity (mere competence is assumed). Day rates vary considerably from one industry to another and in different parts of the country and the world. New York is the big apple.

Most people in photography are in it because they love it, not because of the money. Knowing this, some business people take advantage when establishing the fee for an assignment. They will try to get you down as low as they can, figuring that your "artistic integrity" will provide sufficient incentive to do the job. Be forewarned. The experienced businessman knows he gets what he pays for.

The next question is ownership of the picture. Usually the photographer owns the pictures and sells to the client the right to use them for specific purposes. The photographer retains the right to sell the pictures to other clients for purposes not in direct conflict with the original client. If you take a picture of a particular product, chances are you won't be able to find another market for it. But you may find that certain photographs, especially editorial ones, can be reused in a number of situations; for example, if I photograph a rock star for *Rolling Stone*, I can resell the photographs through a stock photo house to another magazine or client. (The stock photo companies are clearing houses where picture-buyers can look over the photo files of numerous photographers. The house takes pictures on consignment and retains up to fifty percent of the resale price.) However, if one of my photos is used on the *Rolling Stone* cover, it would be unethical and bad business for me to sell the same photo for cover use in another magazine. The idea is not to sell the photo for competing purposes. This business of rights is a quagmire, and each situation is different. It's best to establish at the outset of an assignment, in writing, who owns what.

Sometimes you'll find yourself dealing with business people who are not experienced picture-buyers. They may be more accustomed to buying plumbing fixtures or hospital equipment and may quake at the prospect of agreeing to pay for pictures which they haven't yet seen. They may also insist on owning the picture. You'll just have to educate them as to standard practice.

Another standard business practice important for your own protection is the use of model releases. These are legal statements giving permission for use of the subject's picture; you can buy a pad of standard release forms at a camera store. For the most part, releases concern the use of the picture, and not the *taking* of it. If you are shooting on public property or if the subject is in public view and you use the pictures for editorial purposes, you don't have to get a release. But the pictures must be used in the proper context; their use must be consistent with the reality of the situation. If the caption is not correct or the context on the printed page is misleading, you can be sued for libel. Truth is the best defense against libel.

The other area of the law brought into play here concerns invasion of privacy. If you use the photos for advertising or commercial uses of any sort, if the use of the picture implies the subject's endorsement of a product, then you must get a signed release. Otherwise it can be considered an invasion of privacy. Also, when you are photographing on someone else's private property without the owner's permission, you are vulnerable to trespassing laws as well as the invasion of privacy statutes. The invasion of privacy statutes protect people from having their personal lives exposed to public view, but these statutes are somewhat hazy because they are modified by the person's newsworthiness. If people are public figures, or are in the public eye, then they have sacrificed their privacy to a certain extent. However, the law is rather circular, because the act of publishing a person's picture may make him or her newsworthy. Ask a judge.

This whole matter of releases is a sticky one because the law varies from state to state and court to court. Many times it won't be feasible to get a release, but if you think that the picture has commercial value, you should do your best to get one.

Another important business consideration is copyrighting. If a picture is published without any copyright indicated, the picture becomes part of the public domain and anyone can use it without paying for it. This is another difficult law to get straight, and it's best if you send for the free copyright pamphlet available through the U.S. Department of Commerce.

If at least a portion of your income derives from photography, you must report your earnings to the Internal Revenue Service using Form C: Profit or Loss From a Business or Profession. In reporting this income, you can take deductions for the cost of photographic materials and equipment depreciation. However, you can't deduct from your total taxable income more than the amount which you actually earned in photography.

One more point: if you are planning to sell your work commercially, you should have a rubber stamp made with your name, mailing address, and phone number on it, and stamp the back of each contact sheet and print that you hand clients. This helps to protect your ownership of the photographs and lets them know who to call if they like the pictures.

PROFESSIONALISM

When clients buy your services they buy more than your picture-taking ability. First of all, they buy your ability to deliver, and this means that you won't be able to come back and tell them that there weren't any "happy accidents." The comment about batting averages in Chapter 5 must be modified here; you've got to come back with pictures. You're a problem-solver; to a certain extent, you're paid to make happy accidents happen. If you're going to succeed at this, you've got to make certain preparations: scout out the territory or the subjects beforehand, if you can; find out as much as you can about how the pictures will be used; obtain as much information as possible about the subject. Also, you've got to plan for contingencies—a change in the weather, camera failure, damaged props, or hostile subjects.

In some cases, you'll be hired to carry out someone else's ideas; in others, you'll be paid to express your own special vision or hired for your expertise in a particular field.

Whatever the case, when the client hires you, he hopes that you'll make his judgment look good in the eyes of his boss, his boss look good in the eyes of the company, and the company look good in the eyes of the public. He pays for more than your ability to deliver an adequate photograph; he pays for an aura of professionalism, which hopefully you'll back up with thoroughness, consistency, dependability, and results.

ART DIRECTION

In almost every situation where your pictures will be reproduced, you'll be working with an art director to some extent. In many cases the art director will hire you, and you'll deal solely with him or her. It is the art director's job to oversee the design and production of the published piece. This includes placing the photographs in harmonious relationship with other design elements: body type, display (headline) type, and illustrations.

Some art directors are more sensitive to photographs than others. Often photographers feel differently about their photographs than the art director does. For instance, an art director may feel the need to crop your pictures and may cut them in such a way that you feel they have been destroyed. You have to be prepared for something like this; try to talk to the art director and establish a rapport. Express your feelings about cropping and let him or her know how you feel the pictures should be used, even though you may be ignored. The best time to discuss matters of this sort is before you take the pictures: determine exactly what the art director wants and the context in which the pictures will be used.

Photographers vary in their approach to editing. Some bring to the art director all the pictures they have shot and say, "Here they are—do what you want with them." Others carefully select a few pictures and present only these to the art director. But it's important to keep in mind that the art director has a job to do and needs as much material as possible in order to carry out his or her work. You should try to provide both horizontals and verticals of each shot so that he or she has an easier time fitting them into the page layout. Also, in situations where it seems that cropping is probable, try to leave cropping room when you shoot.

REPRODUCTION OF THE PHOTOGRAPHIC IMAGE

Photographic images are applied to paper using one of three printing methods: letterpress, gravure, or offset lithography. Of these three, lithography is the most widely used and has seen significant technological development over the last few decades. Gravure is considered the finest method for reproducing photographs, but it is more expensive

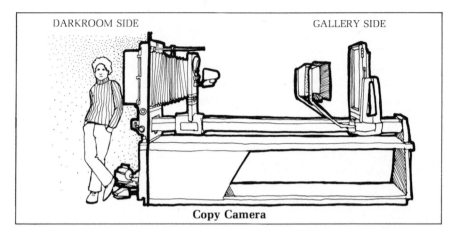

DARKROOM SIDE   GALLERY SIDE

Copy Camera

than lithography and most appropriate for large quantities. Letterpress, the grandfather of printing methods, is used mostly by giant city newspapers which have not yet converted to lithography. If you'd like to know more about printing processes, you'll find suggestions for further reading in the Bibliography.

Lithography is based on the principle that greasy ink and water don't mix. The image is applied to the paper through the use of a specially treated plate which accepts greasy ink in areas where ink is needed and rejects ink where it is not needed. The plate can only apply a full value of ink and not a grey tone, so in a black and white reproduction there can only be black ink and white paper. This is no problem when solid black images such as type or line drawings are reproduced, but when reproducing photographs the image must be applied with a regimented pattern of black dots of varying size in order to simulate various shades of grey. Dark grey areas in the photographic image are made up of large, overlapping black dots with little white paper showing through. Light areas in the photo are represented by small black dots spaced widely on the paper. This dot pattern is easy to see in any publication if you look at the picture through a magnifying glass. A continuous-tone image like a photograph, when reproduced in dots, is called a *halftone*.

The lithographic plate is a positive image of a special negative made by the lithographer. The film used to make the negative is like High Contrast Copy; it reduces all tones to either black or white. A picture is rephotographed on this film through a screen which translates the grey tones into patterns of appropriate-sized dots. The screen is held in contact with the film. During this step the photo is either reduced or enlarged to the exact size it will appear on the printed page. The lithographer does all of this using a special *copy camera*, sometimes called a *process camera.* This camera is often so huge that it is horizontally mounted on rails on the floor. The back of the camera, or film plane, opens out into the lithographer's darkroom.

The quality of gradation of halftones depends on the number of dots per square inch on the screen. Coarse screens have between 65 and 85 lines of dots per square inch while fine screens have up to 300 lines. Halftones printed on porous paper such as newsprint need coarse screens, while the tiny dots of a 300-line screen require high-quality, coated paper stock. The dots of ink spread more widely through porous paper; if the dots are too close together, they spread into each other, leaving a splotch of ink on the paper.

Beyond paper quality and dot size, the overall quality of the halftone is affected by several factors. One is the expertise and diligence of the lithographer and the printer. Also, lithographers sometimes use a short-cut in preparing a full page for reproduction: they make a contact print, or *velox,* of the halftone negative and place it on the page before it is shot by the lithographer instead of stripping the halftone negative into the negative of the entire page, or *flat.* This, in effect, means rephotographing the picture a second time, and while it is a cheaper technique, it means a loss in quality. The shape of the dot also affects halftone quality. Recently it was discovered that elliptical dots produce a smoother gradation in the middle tones of the photograph than the traditional square dots. However, the elliptical dot has not yet come into widespread use.

Color photographs are reproduced in a *four-color process.* The paper is printed with four different overlapping layers of ink—yellow, magenta (red), cyan (blue), black—which must be in perfect register. *Duotones* are black and white photographs which have been run through the press a second time (inked with black or a second color) to deepen the blacks in the shadow areas. A 300-line duotone, carefully printed on fine paper, probably comes closest to capturing the brilliance of the original black and white photograph.

Photography as a vocation may seem quite distant to you now. But I think you'll find that these first experiences with photography will be the door to a life-long friendship. There's something about the craft that inspires devotion.

BIBLIOGRAPHY

As mentioned in the first chapter, this book is intended to be only one of many you read if you're serious about photography. The following are publications and particular authors you may want to consult.

BOOKS

Adams, Ansel. *The Negative, Exposure and Development: Basic Photo 2.* New York: Morgan & Morgan, Inc., 1959.

_____. *The Print, Contact Printing and Enlarging: Basic Photo 3.* New York: Morgan & Morgan, Inc., 1950.

_____. *Natural-Light Photography: Basic Photo 4.* New York: Morgan & Morgan, Inc., 1952.

_____. *Artificial-Light Photography: Basic Photo 5.* New York: Morgan & Morgan, Inc., 1968.

Aperture Monograph series (for example, on the work of W. Eugene Smith and Robert Frank). New York: Aperture, Inc.

The Camera. New York: Time–Life Books, 1970.

Cogoli, John E. *Photo Offset Fundamentals.* 2nd. ed. Bloomington, Illinois: McKnight & McKnight, 1967.

Color. New York: Time–Life Books, 1970.

A Comparative Pricing Guide to Buying Photographic and Hi-Fi Stereo Equipment in Hong Kong, Japan and Singapore. ($1.75, including air mail delivery) Hong Kong Media Corporation, Ltd., Kowloon City, P.O. Box 9232, Hong Kong, British Crown Colony.

Gernsheim, Helmut and Alison, eds. *The History of Photography.* New York: Aperture, Inc., 1973.

Horder, Alan, ed. *The Manual of Photography*. New York: Amphoto, 1971.

Morgan, Douglas O.; Vestal, David; and Broecker, William L., eds. *Leica Manual*. 15th ed. New York: Morgan & Morgan, Inc., 1973.

Pittaro, Ernest M., ed. *Photo-Lab-Index*. New York: Morgan & Morgan, Inc. (constantly updated).

Procedures for Processing and Storing Black and White Photographs for Maximum Possible Permanence. Grinnell, Iowa: East-West Gallery, 1970.

Rodewald, Fred C. and Gottschall, Edward M. *Commercial Art as a Business*. 2nd. rev. ed. New York: Viking Press, 1971.

MAGAZINES

Camera. C. J. Bucher Ltd., CH-6002, Lucerne, Switzerland. Has beautifully reproduced photographs.

Camera 35. 61 W. 51st Street, New York, N.Y. 10019.

Modern Photography. 1 Astor Plaza, New York, N.Y. 10036.

Popular Photography. 1 Park Avenue, New York, N.Y. 10016.

AUTHORS

The following write for various publications, and I always look for their bylines.

Cora Wright Kennedy

Arthur Kramer (writes mainly on view cameras)

Bill Pierce

David Vestal

INDEX

A

accessories, purchase of, 60–66
acid bath. *See* stop bath, print
Adams, Ansel, 2, 4, 77, 126; and printing,
    184–85; and technique, 186–87; and Zone
    System, 128, 131–33, 143
advertising industry, 27, 218
agitation. *See* developer; hypo; stop bath
angle of acceptance: of exposure meter, 59; of
    light reflection, 114–15
anti-reflection coating, 40, 56
aperture (lens), 37. *See also* f/stops
aperture control ring, 41, 70; numbers on,
    37–38, 41, 69
architectural photography, 48, 55, 119
art direction, 222
ASA, 69; pushing, 141. *See also* film speed
aspect ratio, 92–93, 153, 199
automatic exposure system, 50, 123
Avedon, Richard, 126, 216

B

backlighting, 113, 119, 120, 121
bank lights, 125
bare tube (strobe), 123
barn doors (lighting), 123
Barnack, Oscar, 26
barrel distortion, 54
bayonet mount (lens), 41
Beers' Formula (developer), 191
bellows, 64–65

Berek, Max, 26
bleaching, 209–11
bleed mount, 213
bleed print, 154
blocked up highlights. *See* highlights
bracketing (stop intervals), 129
Brady, Matthew, 25
British Journal of Photography, 174
brushes: bleaching, 210; cleaning, 66, 154, 199,
    212; spotting, 212
bulk-film loader, 105–8
burners, 158–59, 202
burning, 168, 202–3, 205, 207, 215
business practices, photographers', 219–21
buying equipment, 45–67, 145–61. *See also*
    specific equipment entries

C

cable release, 89
camera, evolution of, 25–27
camera body, 32, 41–44; color of, 52–53;
    purchase of, 46–53
camera (film) formats:
——2¼x2¼. *See* roll-film cameras
——4x5, 26; detail of, 94; developing, 171, 185;
    enlargers for, 151; gradation, 102–3, 133,
    185, 187; shutter, 42
——5x7, 185
——6x7, 27
——8x10, 77, 187, 197
——35mm, 2–3, 25–53; evolution of, 26–27;

limitations of, 94, 102–3, 186–87, 197, 205; modular design, 32. See also camera body; lens; rangefinder cameras; single-lens-reflex cameras
camera maintenance, 52, 66–67
camera shake, 72; and shutter speed, 73, 76–78; and shooting technique, 84–90
camera technique. See exposure; focusing; previsualization; shooting technique
Cappa, Robert, 27, 172
Cartier-Bresson, Henri, 27, 184
cassettes, 26, 43–44; loading, 105–8; unloading, 176, 178
catadioptic lenses, 55
catchlights, 90, 125
chromatic aberrations, 39–40
circles of confusion, 35–39, 75
color film. See developing; film; light sources; transparencies
color temperature, 103, 124
commercial photography, 217–18, 219
complementary mount, 213
composition through viewfinder, 74, 90–93. See also previsualization
Compur shutter, 42
contact sheet, 188, 189, 194–97
contacting, 194–97
containers, 147, 150. See also tanks; trays
contamination, chemical, 147, 158, 169, 171, 192, 200
contrast: and developing time, 99, 140–41, 170–71; and lighting situations, 110–14, 115–20, 199; and optimum f/stop, 75; and printing paper, 189–91; and printing techniques, 197, 198–9, 202–3, 205–7, 209–11. See also exposure; filters (enlarger); gradation; printing paper; Zone System
contrast filters. See filters (enlarger)
copy camera, 223–24
copyrighting photos, 221
cropping, 93, 199, 222

D

darkroom, 7, 144–69; construction, 163–69; equipment and supplies, 146–61, 167–69, 173–74, 188–94
Davidson, Bruce, 126
daylight color film, 103
defraction, 75
Degas, Edgar, 126
degrees Kelvin. See color temperature
depth of field, 6, 35–39, 55, 72–80
depth-of-field preview button, 44, 70, 74, 91
depth of focus, 41
developer (negative), 6, 95, 102, 173–76; agitation, 170, 178–79; containers, 147, 150; replenishable, 150, 173–74, 180; rinsing off, 179; temperature, 170, 178–79
developer (print), 7, 191–92
developing (negatives), 6–7, 95–99, 170–83; closed-tank method, 178–79; color, 100–101, 104–5, 144–45; open-tank method, 146, 147, 168, 178–79; supplies, 146–50, 172

developing (prints), 7–8, 191–92, 200, 207–8
developing time (negative), 170–71, 173; and density of silver, 97–99; and enlarger filters, 199; and exposure, 140
diaphragm (lens), 5–6, 40–41, 56. See also f/stops
diffused light, 112
diopter correction lens, 86
distance: and depth of field, 38–39, 73; and distortion, 92; and focal length, 73
distance scale, 74–75
dodgers, 158, 202
dodging, 168, 202–3, 205, 207, 215
double printing, 186
dryers (print), 159–61, 211–12
dry-mounting press, 213–14
dry-mounting tissue, 213–14
duckboard, 165
duotone printing, 186, 188, 224

E

easel, 152, 153–54, 169, 199–200
East-West Gallery (Iowa), 215
editorial photography, 218, 219
elements, lens. See lens
emulsion: of film, 6, 95, 100–1; of printing paper, 188, 190
enlarger, 7, 150–53; focusing, 199; lenses, 7, 151, 152–53, 199; time under, 7, 196, 198–202, 204, 205–7. See also f/stops; filters; timers
equipment, buying. See buying equipment
exhibits, 186, 218–19; prints for, 188–89, 211, 215
exposure (film), 5, 68–80, 127–43; automatic, 50, 123; and bellows, 65; and Law of Reciprocity, 69; and lens filters, 63, 103; and strobes, 123. See also exposure meters; f/stops; film speed; H&D Curve; shutter speed; Zone System
exposure (print). See enlarger; printing
exposure meters:
——built-in: advantages of, 57, 63, 65, 129–30; angle of acceptance, 59; match-needle system, 44, 127; TTL, 44; and Zone System, 136, 137–38
——flash meter, 123
——hand-held: advantages of, 59–60, 70; difficulties with, 57, 129–30; and Zone System, 60, 134–36, 137, 139, 140, 142–43
——incident light, 58
——reflected light, 57–58
extension tubes, 64–65

F

f/number (lens speed), 55
f/stops (enlarger), 133, 189, 199, 201
f/stops (lens), 5–6, 37–38, 40–41, 68–80; choice of, 72–78; and depth of field, 37, 72–75; and film speed, 69–71; indicated in viewfinder, 44, 57; latitude of, 128; optimum, 75; and shutter speed, 69–71
fashion photography, 123, 124–25
ferrotype prints, 160, 188, 212
fill light, 112, 118

film, 5, 26–27, 94–108; black and white, 94–99, 101–3, 128; bulk buying, 105–8; color, 99–101, 103–5; effective threshold, 98; limitations of, 110–11, 131; for offset lithography, 223; panchromatic, 102; storage, 108; threshold, 98. *See also* camera format; developing; film speed; H&D Curve; negatives
film advance mechanism, 32, 43
film base plus fog, 97–98, 131, 196
film bath. *See* developer; hypo
film-drying clips, 150, 182
film formats. *See* camera formats
film holders, 26
film speed (ASA), related to *f*/stop and shutter speed, 69–71, 72; and silver halide ratios, 95–96; for types of film, 101–5
filters (enlarger): contrast, 151, 190–91, 198–99, 201, 205–7; multiple use of, 205–7; neutral density, 153, 189, 200–1
filters (lens), 41, 62–63; conversion, 103; fluorescent, 103–4; skylight (1A), 63, 67
fish-eye lenses, 54–55
fixative. *See* hypo
flares, 56, 75, 113. *See also* halation
flash meter, 123
flashbulbs, 43, 112–13, 123
flashes, electronic. *See* strobes
flats (lighting), 123
flats (offset lithography), 224
fluorescent light, 103–4
focal length, 33–35, 53; and depth of field, 36–37, 73
focal plane, 32–33, 41
focal plane shutter, 42
focal point, 32
focusing: apparatus, 6, 28–30, 32, 43; control ring, 41; mount (lens), 56; screens, 65–66; technique, 28–30, 55, 90
focusing spotlights, 120–21, 124
foot switches, 155, 196
Fresnel rings, 66
frontal light, 112–13

G

gamma, 99, 179. *See also* contrast
glassine envelopes, 182, 196
glossy prints, 160, 188, 212. *See also* printing paper, resin-coated
gradation, 96; and enlargement, 102–3, 186–87, 197, 205; of halftones, 224; and printing, 187, 197, 205–7; and proper exposure, 128–29. *See also* bleaching; burning; contrast; filters; grain; printing paper
graduates, 150
grain (film), 95–96, 102; and developer, 96, 174–75; and developing time, 99
grain focuser, 154–55, 199
grants to photographers, financial, 218
gravure reproduction, 222–23
ground-glass viewing, 28, 30–31, 43. *See also* focusing screens

H

H&D Curve, 96–99, 110; and Zone System, 128, 131–33, 140–41

halation, 94–95. *See also* flares
halftones, 223–24
Harper's Bazaar, 124
highlights, 111–17; blocked up, 133, 141, 205; and developing time, 98–99, 140–41; focusing on, 90; and multiple contrast filters, 205–7; and source size, 115–17; specular, 114; and Zone System, 133, 138, 139. *See also* bleaching; contrast; dodging; lighting situations
hyperfocal distance, 75
hypo: and bleaching print, 210; containers for, 147; negative bath, 6, 96, 180; print bath, 7–8, 193–94, 200, 208, 214–15; rinsing off negative, 6, 180–81; rinsing off print, 194, 208, 214–15. *See also* developing; printing
hypo clearing agents, 150, 180–81, 194, 210

I

images on film. *See* contrast; gradation; previsualization; print; sharpness; tones
indicator stop bath, 193
Inverse Square Law (light), 37, 117–18, 199

J

journalistic style. *See* photojournalism

K

key black, 132–33, 196–7, 215
key white, 133, 215

L

latent image, 6, 95; conversion to visible silver, 7, 96. *See also* developing
leaf shutter, 42
lens (camera), 5, 32–41, 53–57, 75; aberrations of, 39–40, 75; and camera shake, 72; cap, 67; cleaning, 66–67; coating, 40, 56; distortions of, 53, 54–55; elements, 39–41; hoods, 41, 46, 63–64, 67; interchangeable, 26–27, 29, 32, 53; mounts, 41; purchase, 53–57; speed, 55; testing, 56–57. *See also* *f*/stops; normal lenses; telephoto lenses; wide-angle lenses
lens (enlarger), 7, 151, 152, 199
letterpress reproduction, 222–23
Life, 27, 62, 218
light: defraction, 75; intensity, 37, 117–18, 199; reflection, 111–15; refraction, 32–33
light sources: artificial, 111–14, 120–26; and color film, 103–4, 118; size related to highlights, 115–17. *See also* strobes
lighting situations, 109–26, 206–7; schools of, 124–5. *See also* exposure; *f*/stops; highlights; shadows; Zone System
Limb Effect, 115
lithography, offset. 222–24. *See also* reproduction
Look, 27, 218

M

magazine industry, 27, 62, 124, 218
main light, 112
markets, for photographs, 217–19
matte center spot screens, 65–66, 90. *See also* focusing

matte finish, 160, 188
meters, light. See exposure meters
microprism screens, 65, 90. See also focusing
mirror telephoto lenses, 55
mixed light, 119, 206
modeling light, 122
Modulation-Transfer (M-T) curves, 57
montage, 186
motion pictures, 26, 121, 125
motor drive, 43, 52, 87; and camera shake, 89–90
mounting prints, 213–14
multiple prints, 207–8

N
National Geographic, 27, 62
neck strap, 46, 67
negative film, color, 99–101, 103, 104
negative holder, 151–52, 154, 199
negatives, 6–7, 95–99, 170–83; cleaners, 154, 199, 212; cutting, 182; drying, 6, 181–82; scratches on, 154, 181; storage, 182–83, 196. See also developing; film; printing
neutral density filters. See filters (enlarger)
nodal point, 33
normal lenses, 26, 33, 35, 53–54, 76–77. See also lens

O
"open shade" light, 112
"open up" stops, 70; and image texture, 73. See also f/stops
optimum f/stop. See f/stops (enlarger); f/stops (lens), optimum.
outdoor light, 112, 115–16, 118, 119
overshooting, 83–84

P
panchromatic film, 102
parallax correction, 30
Perma Wash. See hypo clearing agents
perspective, 34–35
Photo-Flo. See wetting solution
photoflood lamps, 120, 124
photographic process, summary, 5–8
photographic technique. See developing; printing; shooting technique
photography: approaches, 184–87; architectural, 48, 55, 119; business practices, 219–21; fashion, 123, 124–25; markets, 217–19; professional considerations, 216–24; reproduction, 222–24; studio, 58, 102, 116–17, 120–26
photojournalism, 2–3, 27, 184, 187, 218
Photo-Lab-Index, 169, 174
plane of focus, 35, 91
portrait lens, 26
positive film, color, 100–101, 103–5
potassium ferricyanide, 209–11
pressure plate, camera, 41
previsualization, 4–5, 128, 135, 139–40, 143
Print, The (Adams), 191
printing, 7–8, 184–215; agitation during, 200, 208, 214–15; base exposure time, 189, 198–202, 205; bleaching, 209–211; burning, 168, 202–3, 205, 207; color, 153;

contacting, 194–97; corrections during, 118, 189; cropping, 93, 199, 222; dodging, 168, 202–3, 205, 207, 215; drying, 211–12; electrical current variation, 167, 174; interpretive, 184–86; mounting, 213–14; multiple, 207–8; rinsing, 8, 160, 166–67, 194, 208, 210, 211; spotting, 212–13; supplies and equipment, 150–61, 188–95; test print, 198–200, 201, 207; toning, 212
printing paper, 7, 188–91, 195; as backing for mounts, 213; contrast grades, 141, 189–91, 198, 201–2, 205; placement on easel, 153, 199; resin-coated, 160, 188, 189, 190, 195, 212; and safelights, 156; speed, 189, 200–201; surface, 188; weight, 188–89
prints: aspect ratios, 92–93, 153, 199; border, 154, 201; copyrights, 221; importance of darkroom, 144, 186; judging wet prints, 204–5; ownership, 219–20; permanency, 211, 214–15; as separate reality, 3–4; size influencing depth of field, 38–39. See also printing
process camera, 223–24
pushing ASA, 141

Q
quartz iodide lamps, 121, 124

R
racking, 90
rangefinder cameras, 27–31, 40–41, 43, 74
rates, photographers', 219
Reciprocity, Law of, 69
reels, developing tank, 146–47, 171, 176–78
reflectivity, 113–14. See also light
reflector floods, 120, 124
refraction, 32. See also light
releases, model, 220–21
Rembrandt, 126
repairmen, 52
replenisher, 173–74; containers for, 150. See also developer (negative)
reproduction of photographs, 222–24; limitations of, 186; and paper, 186, 189; and printing technique, 215; and toners, 211
reticulation, 180
rewind knob, 43–44
rights, photographers', 219–20
rim kickers (lighting), 121
rings, stepping, 63
roll-film (2½x2¼) format, 26–27, 42, 104, 151

S
safelights, 7, 156
screw mount (lens), 41
scrims, 123
self-timer, camera, 44, 89
shadows, 111–17; and burning, 202–3; exposure oriented to, 99, 206–7; and light source size, 115–17; and negative, 97–99, 140–41; and multiple filters, 205–7; and Zone System, 133, 139. See also burning; contrast; lighting situations; Zone System
sharpness, 35–39, 72–80, 90; testing for, 56–57, 79–80. See also camera shake; contrast; focusing

shooting technique, 81–93; composition, 91–92; hand-held, 84–88; supported, 88–90

shutter, 5–6, 32, 41–43; and strobe use, 122–23

shutter release, 5, 41, 64, 84–85, 89

shutter speed, 42–43, 68–80; choosing, 71–72; indicated in viewfinder, 44, 57; relation to *f*/stop and ASA, 69–71, 72; and strobe use, 122–23; variation from setting, 130; and Zone System, 128, 134–39, 141

shutter speed dial, 42–43, 69

side arm, tripod, 61

side lighting, 113

silver halides, 6, 95–99; alteration to metallic silver, 6, 81, 96–99; and color film, 100 –101. *See also* developing; film

single-lens-reflex (SLR) cameras, 3, 27–31

sinks, 164–66

skylight (1A), 112

skylight filter, 63, 67

slides. *See* transparencies

Smith, W. Eugene, 27, 126, 185

snap connectors, 166, 167

snapshots, flash, 43, 112–13, 123

snoots, 123

soft-touch shutter release, 64

solarization, 186

"souping" negatives, 170. *See also* developing

specular highlights, 114

splashboard, 167, 200, 212

split-image screens, 65, 90

spot meters, 59–60, 139, 142–43. *See also* exposure meters

spotting, 181, 212–13

squeegees, 149–50, 167, 181–82, 200, 210, 211–12

stabilization processor, 160–61

stack caps, 63

Static Master Brush, 154, 199, 212. *See also* brushes, cleaning

stems, 147, 178–79

step-down rings, 63

step-up rings, 63

stirrers, 150

stop, 70; fractions of, 76. *See also* f/stops

stop bath, negative, 6, 172, 179–80; print, 192–93, 200, 208

stopping down, 40–41, 70, 73

strobes, 43, 72, 79, 121–23, 124; guide numbers for exposure, 123

studio photography, 58, 102, 116–17, 120–26

surge marks, 179

swabbing, 181–82. *See also* squeegees

synchronizing mechanism, camera, 43

T

tacking iron, 213–14

tanks, 146–47, 176, 178–79, 180

technique. *See* developing; printing; shooting technique

telephoto lenses, 26, 33–35; catadioptic, 55; and depth of field, 35–37, 39, 75, 76–77; impact on image, 53–54; and shooting technique, 86; and SLR viewing, 29, 31; and Zone System, 138. *See also* lens

thermometers, 147–48

timers, 7, 148–49, 155–56, 200, 208; self-timer on camera, 44, 89

toners, 211

tones: enhancing with toners, 211; purity, 184–85; separation, 114. *See also* bleaching; burning; contrast; dodging; gradation

tongs, 157–58, 200, 208

top lighting, 113

transparencies, color, 100–101, 103–5, 144–45; and proper exposure, 129; and shooting technique, 91

trays, 156–57, 166–67; circulation in, 166, 194, 210

tripods, 60–62, 72, 88–89, 102

tungsten light, 103

U

umbrella lighting, 123, 124–25

universal mount lenses, 56

V

variable contrast paper, 190–91, 198, 205–7. *See also* printing paper

velox, 224

Vermeer, Jan, 126

viewfinder, 6, 27–31, 43; and built-in exposure meter, 44, 57; and composition, 90–93

Vogue, 124

W

Weston, Edward, 77

wetting solution, 181, 209

wide-angle lenses, 26, 31, 33–35, 53–55; and depth of field, 35–37, 39, 75, 76–77. *See also* lens

window lighting, 110–11, 118, 206–7

Z

Zone System, 128, 131–43, 184, 185; averaging method, 137–39; placement method, 60, 134–36, 138–39

zoom lenses, 55